Letts

GCSE Success

Complete Revision & Practice

AQA

Chemistry

Dan Evans

Revision Guide

Contents

Atoms and the periodic table

Atoms and elements

- All substances are made of **atoms**.
- An atom is the smallest part of an **element** that can exist.
- There are approximately 100 different elements, all of which are shown in the **periodic table**.

On the right is part of the periodic table, showing the names and symbols of the first 20 elements.

Atoms of each element are represented by a chemical symbol in the periodic table.

Some elements have more than one letter in their symbol. The first letter is always a capital and the other letter is lower case.

1 hydrogen **H**							2 helium **He**
3 lithium **Li**	4 beryllium **Be**	5 boron **B**	6 carbon **C**	7 nitrogen **N**	8 oxygen **O**	9 fluorine **F**	10 neon **Ne**
11 sodium **Na**	12 magnesium **Mg**	13 aluminium **Al**	14 silicon **Si**	15 phosphorus **P**	16 sulfur **S**	17 chlorine **Cl**	18 argon **Ar**
19 potassium **K**	20 calcium **Ca**						

The symbol for magnesium is **Mg**

The symbol for the element oxygen is **O**

Elements, compounds and mixtures

Elements contain only one type of atom and consist of single atoms or atoms bonded together

Compounds contain two (or more) elements that are chemically combined in fixed proportions

Mixtures contain two or more elements (or compounds) that are together but not chemically combined

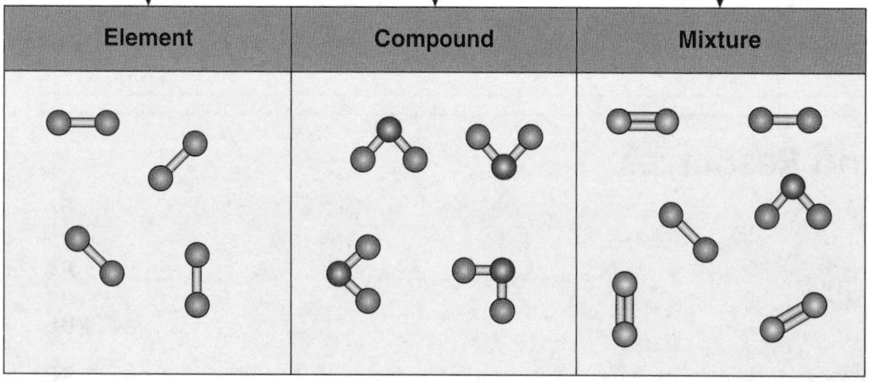

Chemical equations

We can use word or symbol equations to represent chemical reactions.

Word equation: **sodium + oxygen → sodium oxide**

Symbol equation: $4Na + O_2 \rightarrow 2Na_2O$

Write the name of each method of separating a mixture on some cards. Use a new card for each method. Write on other cards a description of each method of separation, again using a new card for each description. Shuffle the cards. Now try to match the names and descriptions.

Keywords

Atom ➤ The smallest part of an element that can enter into a chemical reaction

Element ➤ A substance that consists of only one type of atom

Compound ➤ A substance consisting of two or more different elements chemically combined together

Mixture ➤ Two or more elements or compounds that are not chemically combined

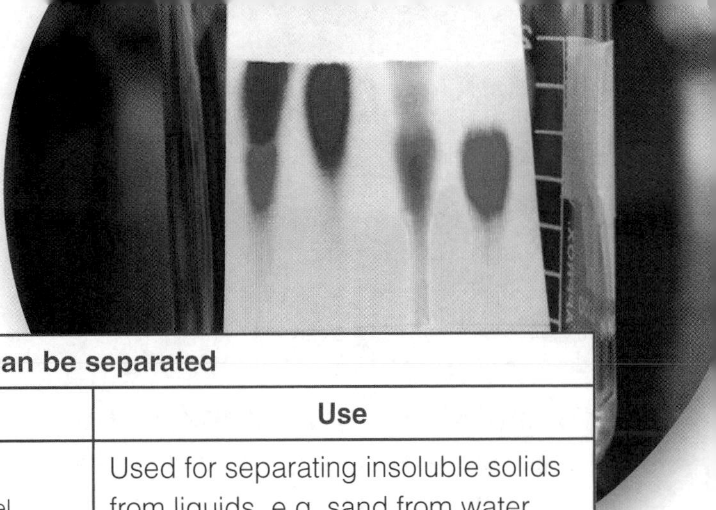

Separating mixtures

Compounds can only be separated by chemical reactions but **mixtures** can be separated by physical processes (not involving chemical reactions) such as filtration, crystallisation, simple (and fractional) distillation and chromatography.

How different mixtures can be separated		
Method of separation	**Diagram**	**Use**
Filtration	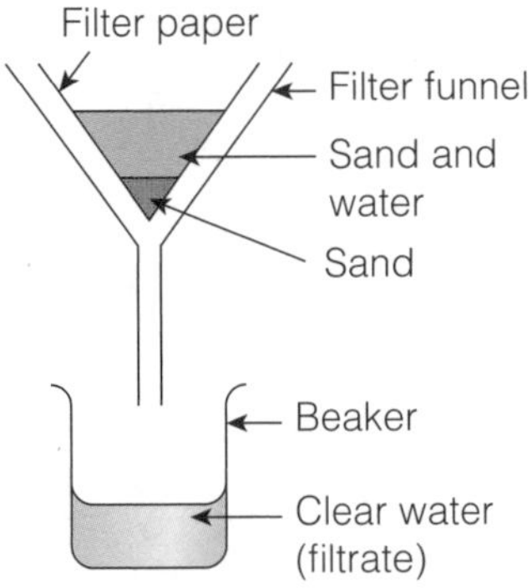Filter paper Filter funnel Sand and water Sand Beaker Clear water (filtrate)	Used for separating insoluble solids from liquids, e.g. sand from water
Crystallisation	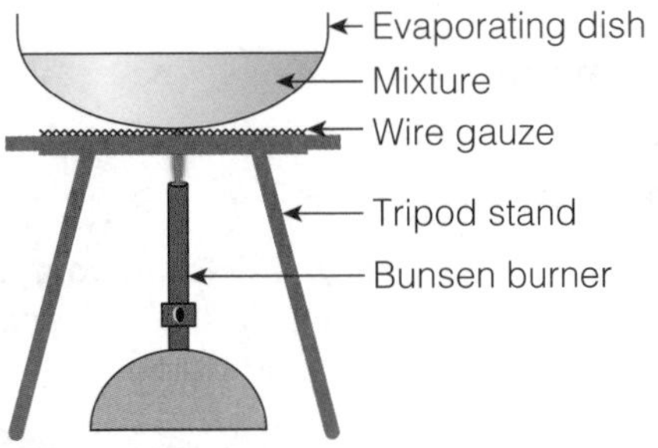Evaporating dish Mixture Wire gauze Tripod stand Bunsen burner	Used to separate solids from solutions, e.g. obtaining salt from salty water
Simple distillation	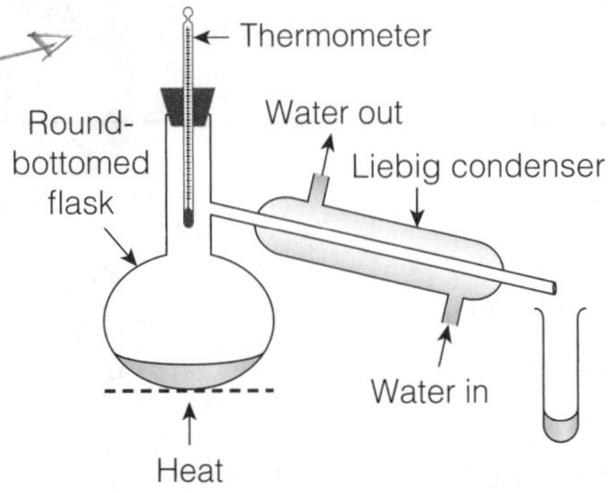Thermometer Round-bottomed flask Water out Liebig condenser Water in Heat	Simple distillation is used to separate a liquid from a solution, e.g. water from salty water
Fractional distillation (diagram is slightly different for this)		Fractional distillation is used to separate liquids that have different boiling points, e.g. ethanol and water
Chromatography	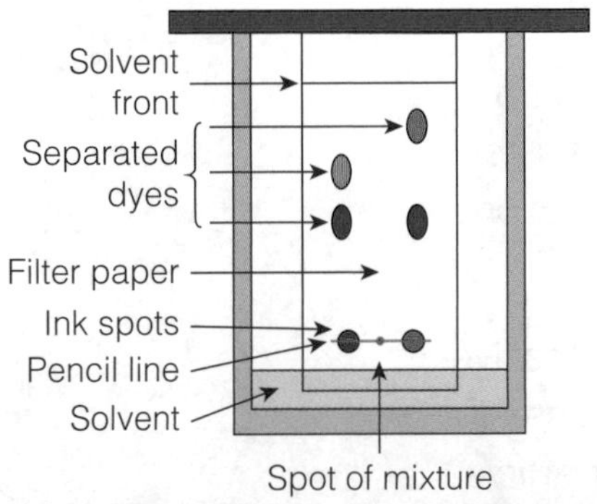Solvent front Separated dyes Filter paper Ink spots Pencil line Solvent Spot of mixture	Used to separate dyes, e.g. the different components of ink

1. What name is given to a substance that contains atoms of different elements chemically joined together?
2. Which method of separation would you use to obtain water from a solution of copper(II) sulfate?

Atomic structure

2

Scientific models of the atom

Scientists had originally thought that atoms were tiny spheres that could not be divided.

John Dalton conducted experiments in the early 19th century and concluded that…

- all matter is made of indestructible atoms
- atoms of a particular element are identical
- atoms are rearranged during chemical reactions
- compounds are formed when two or more different types of atom join together.

Upon discovery of the electron by **J. J. Thomson** in 1897, the 'plum pudding' model suggested that the atom was a ball of positive charge with negative electrons embedded throughout.

The results from **Rutherford**, **Geiger** and **Marsden's** alpha scattering experiments (1911–1913) led to the plum pudding model being replaced by the nuclear model.

In this experiment, alpha particles (which are positive) are fired at a thin piece of gold. A few of the alpha particles do not pass through the gold and are deflected. Most went straight through the thin piece of gold. This led Rutherford, Geiger and Marsden to suggest that this is because the positive charge of the atom is confined in a small volume (now called the nucleus).

Niels Bohr adapted the nuclear model in 1913, by suggesting that electrons orbit the nucleus at specific distances. Bohr's theoretical calculations were backed up by experimental results.

Later experiments led to the idea that the positive charge of the nucleus was subdivided into smaller particles (now called protons), with each particle having the same amount of positive charge.

The work of **James Chadwick** suggested in 1932 that the nucleus also contained neutral particles that we now call neutrons.

The plum pudding model

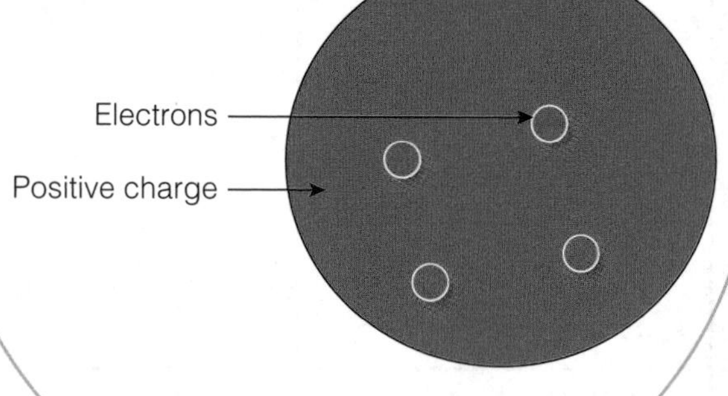

Electrons
Positive charge

Rutherford, Geiger and Marsden's alpha scattering experiment

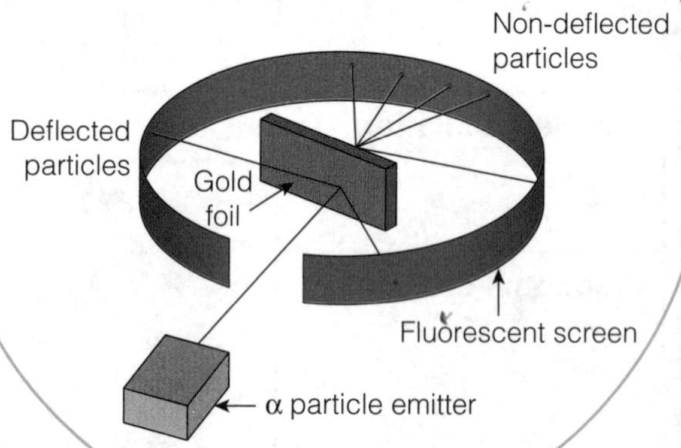

Non-deflected particles
Deflected particles
Gold foil
Fluorescent screen
α particle emitter

The Bohr model

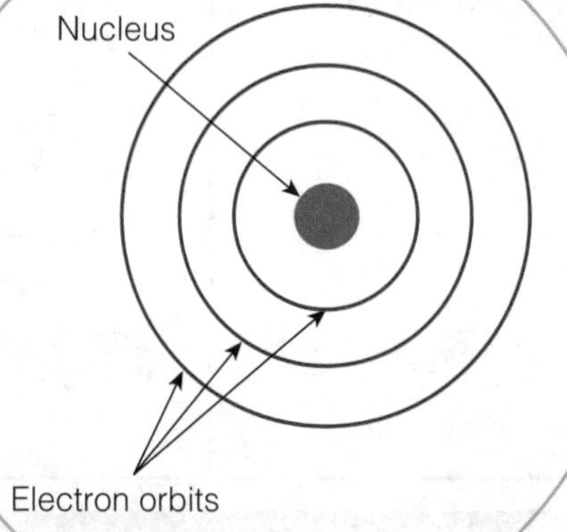

Nucleus
Electron orbits

Properties of atoms

Particle	Relative charge	Relative mass
Proton	+1	1
Neutron	0	1
Electron	–1	very small

- Atoms are neutral. This is because the number of protons is equal to the number of electrons.
- Atoms of different elements have different numbers of protons. This number is called the atomic number.
- Atoms are very small, having a radius of approximately 0.1 nm (1×10^{-10} m).
- The radius of the nucleus is approximately $\frac{1}{10000}$ of the size of the atom.

Keywords

Mass number ➤ The total number of protons and neutrons in an atom

Atomic number ➤ The number of protons in the nucleus of an atom

Isotopes ➤ Atoms of the same element that have the same number of protons but different numbers of neutrons

The **mass number** tells you the total number of protons and neutrons in an atom

$$^{23}_{11}Na$$

The **atomic number** tells you the number of protons in an atom

mass number – atomic number = number of neutrons

Some atoms can have different numbers of neutrons. These atoms are called **isotopes**. The existence of isotopes results in the relative atomic mass of some elements, e.g. chlorine, not being whole numbers.

Chlorine exists as two isotopes. Chlorine-35 makes up 75% of all chlorine atoms. Chlorine-37 makes up the other 25%. We say that the abundance of chlorine-35 is 75%.

The relative atomic mass of chlorine can be calculated as follows:

$$\frac{(\text{mass of isotope 1} \times \text{abundance}) + (\text{mass of isotope 2} \times \text{abundance})}{100}$$

$$= \frac{(35 \times 75) + (37 \times 25)}{100} = 35.5$$

Make models of atoms using different coloured paper to represent the protons, neutrons and electrons.

1. What is the difference between the plum pudding model of the atom and the nuclear model of the atom?
2. Why did Rutherford, Geiger and Marsden's alpha scattering experiment lead them to suggest that the positive charge in an atom was contained within a small volume?
3. How many protons, neutrons and electrons are present in the following atom?

$$^{13}_{6}C$$

4. What name is given to atoms of the same element which have the same number of protons but different numbers of neutrons?

Electronic structure & the periodic table

Keywords

Energy level ➤ A region in an atom where electrons are found

Shell ➤ Another word for an energy level

3

Electronic structures

Electrons in an atom occupy the lowest available **energy level (shell)**. The first energy level (closest to the nucleus) can hold up to two electrons. The second and third energy levels can hold up to eight electrons.

For example, silicon has the atomic number 14. This means that there are 14 protons in the nucleus of a silicon atom and therefore there must be 14 electrons (so that the atom is neutral).

The electronic structure of silicon can be written as 2, 8, 4 or shown in a diagram like the one on the right.

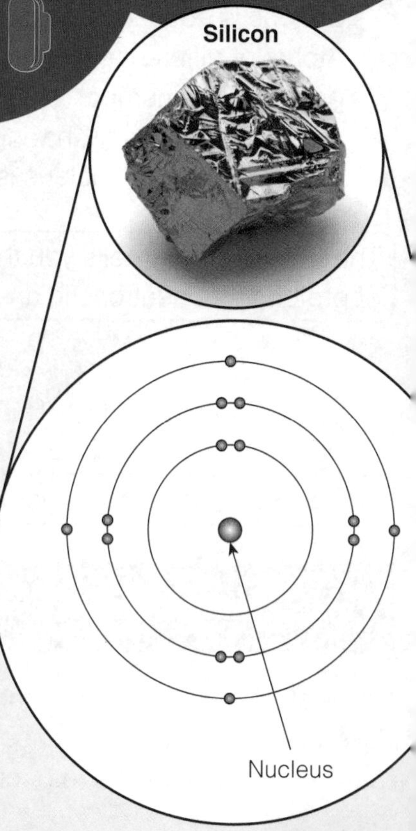

Silicon
Nucleus

Silicon is in group 4 of the periodic table. This is because it has four electrons in its outer shell. The chemical properties (reactions) of an element are related to the number of electrons in the outer shell of the atom.

The electronic structure of the first 20 elements are shown here.

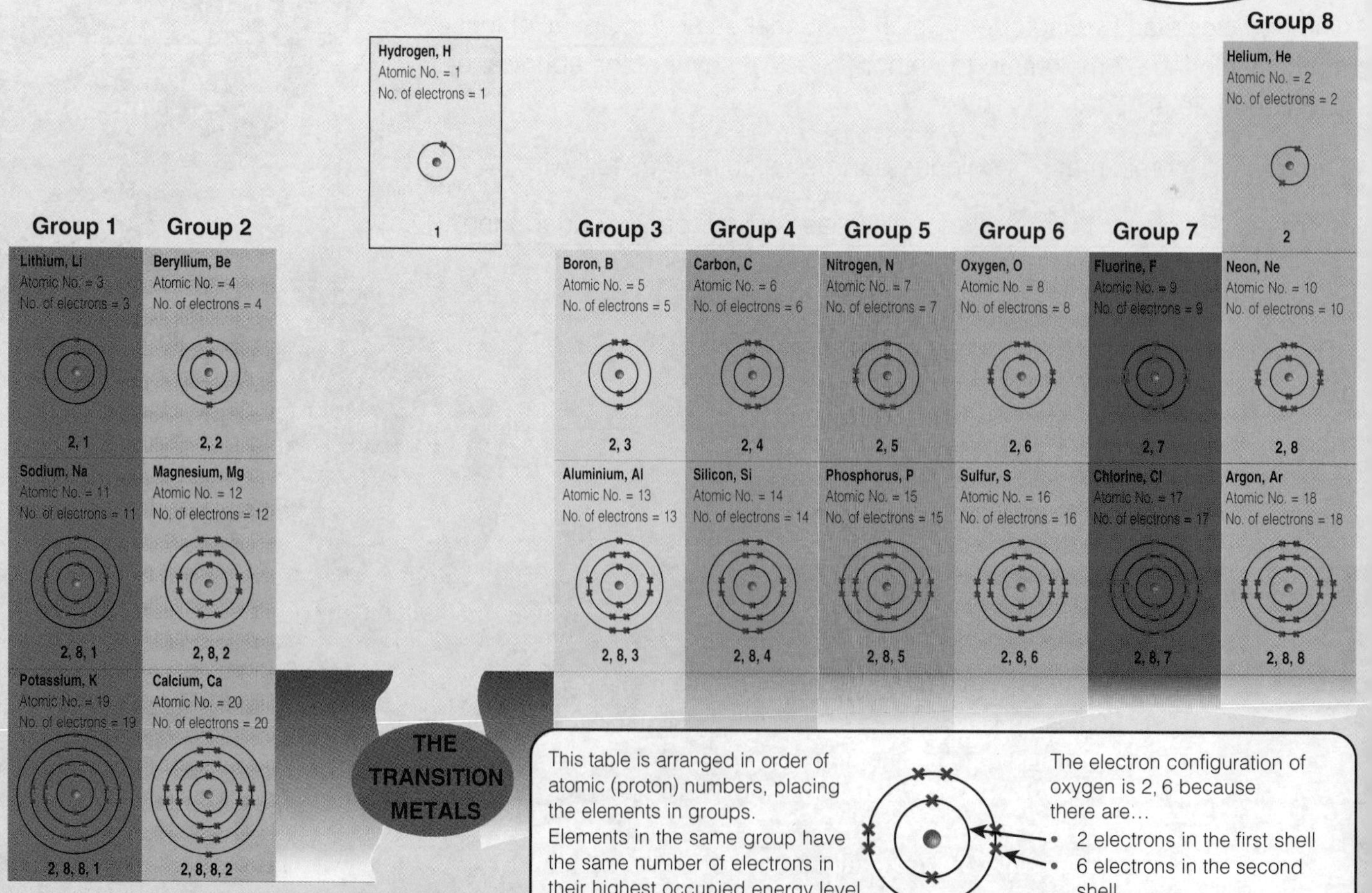

Hydrogen, H
Atomic No. = 1
No. of electrons = 1
1
Group 1
Group 2
Group 3
Group 4
Group 5
Group 6
Group 7
Group 8
Helium, He
Atomic No. = 2
No. of electrons = 2
2
Lithium, Li
Atomic No. = 3
No. of electrons = 3
2, 1
Beryllium, Be
Atomic No. = 4
No. of electrons = 4
2, 2
Boron, B
Atomic No. = 5
No. of electrons = 5
2, 3
Carbon, C
Atomic No. = 6
No. of electrons = 6
2, 4
Nitrogen, N
Atomic No. = 7
No. of electrons = 7
2, 5
Oxygen, O
Atomic No. = 8
No. of electrons = 8
2, 6
Fluorine, F
Atomic No. = 9
No. of electrons = 9
2, 7
Neon, Ne
Atomic No. = 10
No. of electrons = 10
2, 8
Sodium, Na
Atomic No. = 11
No. of electrons = 11
2, 8, 1
Magnesium, Mg
Atomic No. = 12
No. of electrons = 12
2, 8, 2
Aluminium, Al
Atomic No. = 13
No. of electrons = 13
2, 8, 3
Silicon, Si
Atomic No. = 14
No. of electrons = 14
2, 8, 4
Phosphorus, P
Atomic No. = 15
No. of electrons = 15
2, 8, 5
Sulfur, S
Atomic No. = 16
No. of electrons = 16
2, 8, 6
Chlorine, Cl
Atomic No. = 17
No. of electrons = 17
2, 8, 7
Argon, Ar
Atomic No. = 18
No. of electrons = 18
2, 8, 8
Potassium, K
Atomic No. = 19
No. of electrons = 19
2, 8, 8, 1
Calcium, Ca
Atomic No. = 20
No. of electrons = 20
2, 8, 8, 2
THE TRANSITION METALS

This table is arranged in order of atomic (proton) numbers, placing the elements in groups.
Elements in the same group have the same number of electrons in their highest occupied energy level (outer shell).

The electron configuration of oxygen is 2, 6 because there are…

- 2 electrons in the first shell
- 6 electrons in the second shell.

The periodic table

The elements in the periodic table are arranged in order of increasing atomic (proton) number.
The table is called a **periodic table** because similar properties occur at regular intervals.

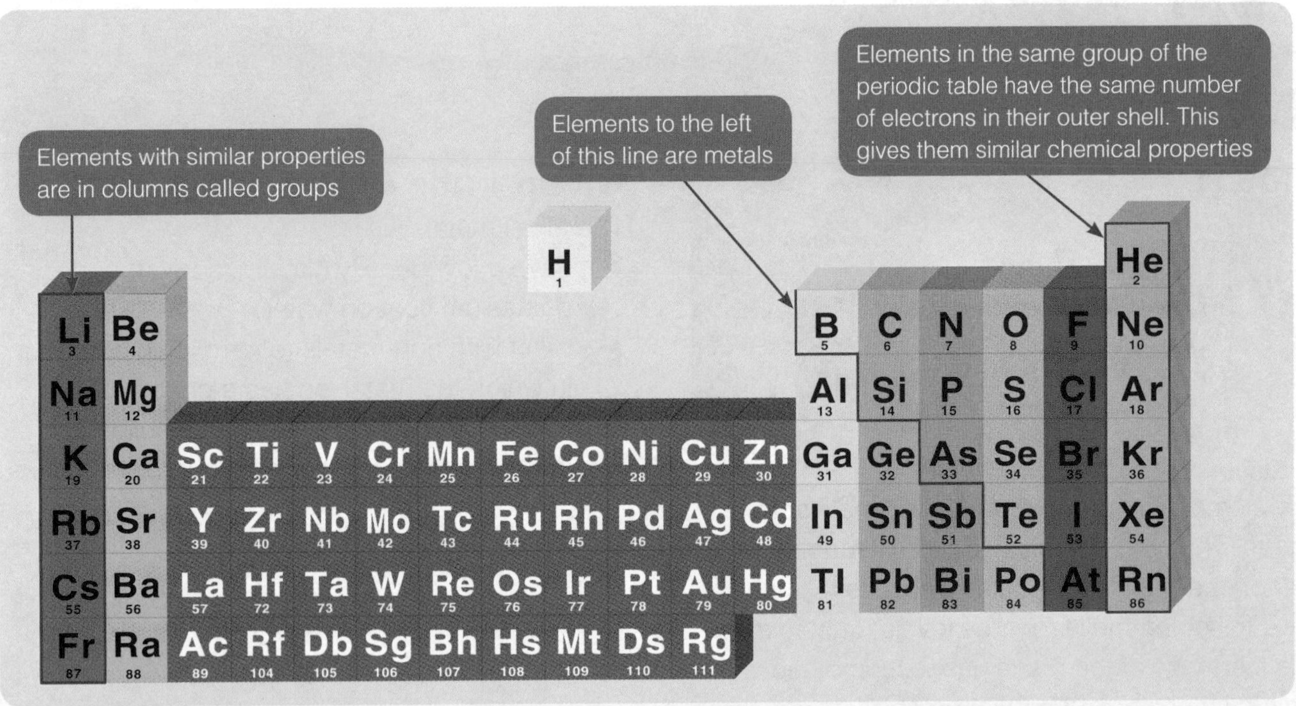

Development of the periodic table

Before the discovery of protons, neutrons and electrons, early attempts to classify the elements involved placing them in order of their atomic weights. These early attempts resulted in incomplete tables and the placing of some elements in appropriate groups based on their chemical properties.

Dmitri Mendeleev overcame some of these problems by leaving gaps for elements that he predicted were yet to be discovered. He also changed the order for some elements based on atomic weights. Knowledge of isotopes made it possible to explain why the order based on atomic weights was not always correct.

Metals and non-metals

- Metals are elements that react to form positive ions.
- Elements that do not form positive ions are non-metals.

Typical properties of metals and non-metals	
Metals	**Non-metals**
Have high melting / boiling points	Have low melting / boiling points
Conduct heat and electricity	Thermal and electrical insulators
React with oxygen to form alkalis	React with oxygen to form acids
Shiny	Dull
Malleable and ductile	Brittle

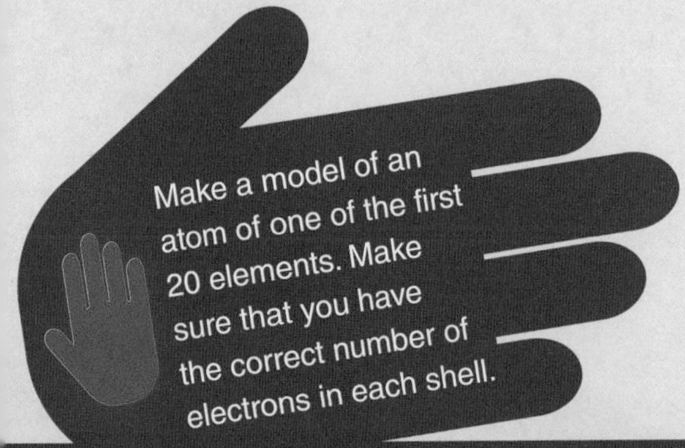

1. Sodium has the atomic number 11. What is the electronic structure of sodium?
2. Why did Mendeleev leave gaps in his periodic table?
3. Element X has a high melting point, is malleable and conducts electricity. Is X a metal or a non-metal?

Groups 0, 1 and 7

4

Group 0

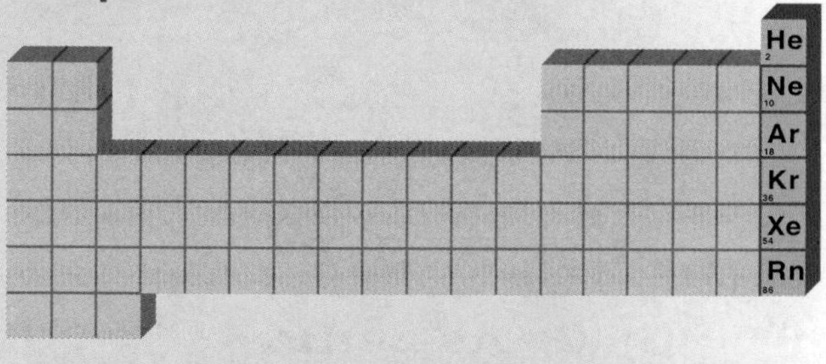

He
2
Ne
10
Ar
18
Kr
36
Xe
54
Rn
86

The elements in group 0 are called the **noble gases**. They are chemically inert (unreactive) and do not easily form molecules because their atoms have full outer shells (energy levels) of electrons. The inertness of the noble gases, combined with their low density and non-flammability, mean that they can be used in airships, balloons, light bulbs, lasers and advertising signs.

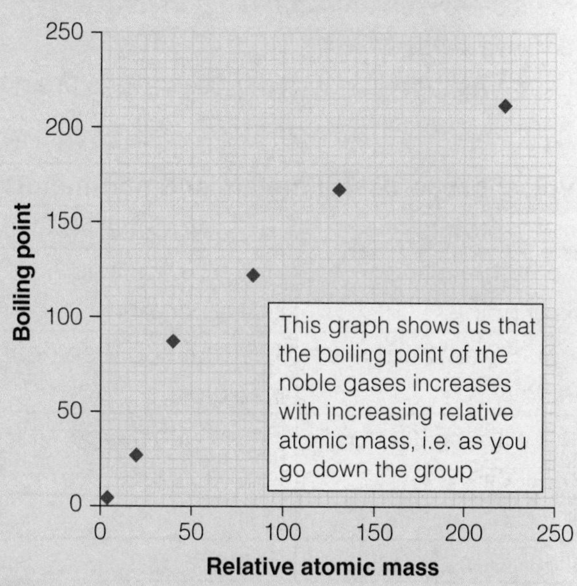

250
200
150
100
50
0
Boiling point
0
50
100
150
200
250
Relative atomic mass
This graph shows us that the boiling point of the noble gases increases with increasing relative atomic mass, i.e. as you go down the group

Write each property of the alkali metals and the halogens on separate cards. Shuffle the cards. Now try to place them into the correct two piles: **alkali metals** and **halogens**.

Group 1 (the alkali metals)

The alkali metals…

- ➤ have a low density (lithium, sodium and potassium float on water)
- ➤ react with non-metals to form ionic compounds in which the metal ion has a charge of +1
- ➤ form compounds that are white solids and dissolve in water to form colourless solutions.

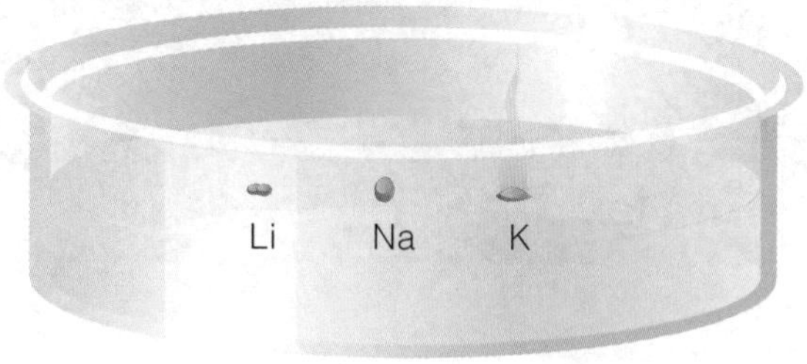

Li
Na
K

The alkali metals react with water forming metal hydroxides which dissolve in water to form alkaline solutions and hydrogen gas. For example, for the reaction between sodium and water:

$$2Na_{(s)} + 2H_2O_{(l)} \rightarrow 2NaOH_{(aq)} + H_{2(g)}$$

The alkali metals become more reactive as you go down the group because the outer shell gets further away from the positive attraction of the nucleus. This makes it easier for an atom to lose an electron from its outer shell.

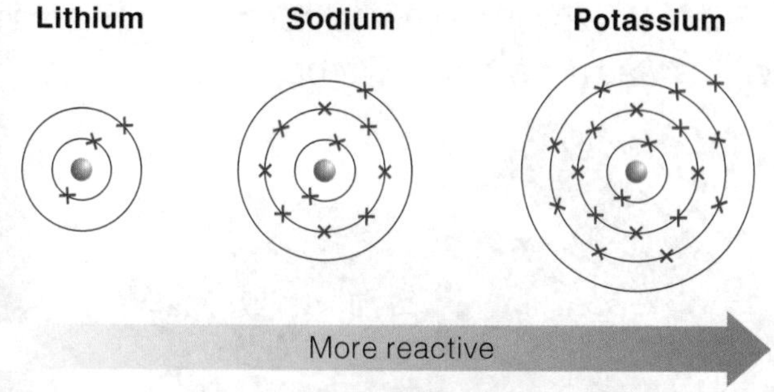

Lithium
Sodium
Potassium
More reactive

Keywords

Halogen ➤ One of the five non-metals in group 7 of the periodic table

Displacement reaction ➤ A reaction in which a more reactive element takes the place of a less reactive element in a compound

Group 7 (the halogens)

The **halogens**…

- are non-metals
- consist of diatomic molecules (molecules made up of two atoms)
- react with metals to form ionic compounds where the halide ion has a charge of –1
- form molecular compounds with other non-metals
- form hydrogen halides (e.g. HCl), which dissolve in water, forming acidic solutions.

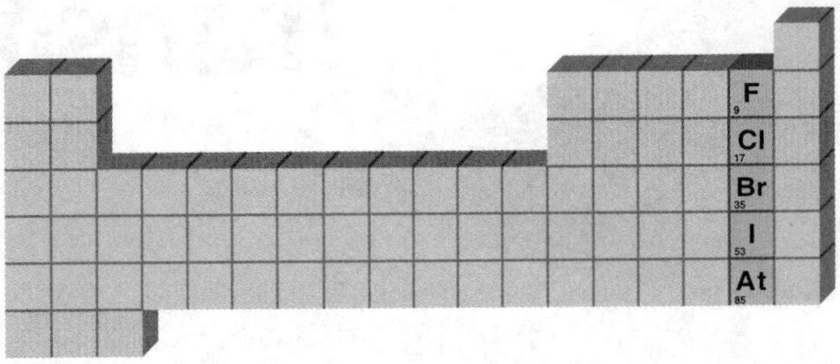

F
9
Cl
17
Br
35
I
53
At
85

Crystals of natural fluorite

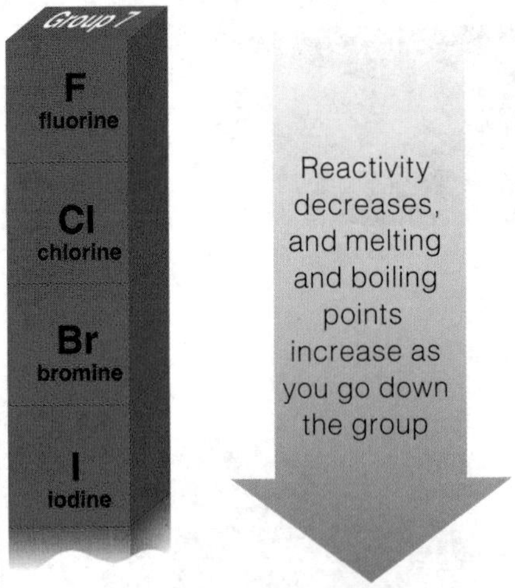

Group 7
F
fluorine
Cl
chlorine
Br
bromine
I
iodine
Reactivity decreases, and melting and boiling points increase as you go down the group

Halogen	State of matter at room temperature	Colour
Fluorine	Gas	Yellow
Chlorine	Gas	Green
Bromine	Liquid	Red / orange
Iodine	Solid	Grey / black

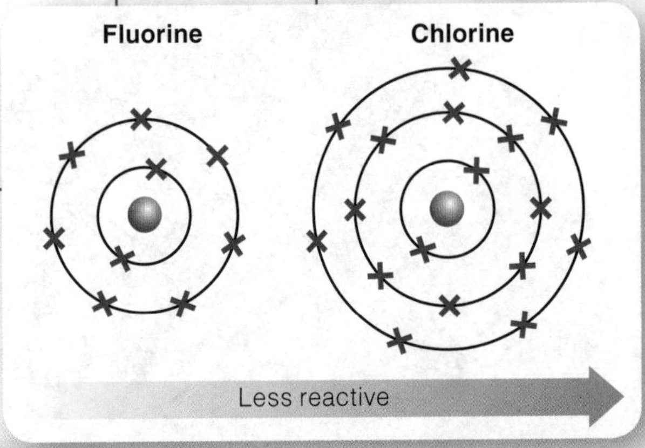

Fluorine
Chlorine
Less reactive

Halogens become less reactive as you go down the group because the outer electron shell gets further away from the attraction of the nucleus, and so an electron is gained less easily.

Displacement reactions of halogens

A more reactive halogen will **displace** a less reactive halogen from an aqueous solution of its metal halide.

For example:

chlorine + potassium bromide → potassium chloride + bromine

$$Cl_2 + 2KBr \rightarrow 2KCl + Br_2$$

The products of reactions between halogens and aqueous solutions of halide ion salts are as follows.

Halogens	Halide salts: Potassium chloride, KCl	Potassium bromide, KBr	Potassium iodide, KI
Chlorine, Cl_2	No reaction	Potassium chloride + bromine	Potassium chloride + iodine
Bromine, Br_2	No reaction	No reaction	Potassium bromide + iodine
Iodine, I_2	No reaction	No reaction	No reaction

1. Why are the noble gases so unreactive?
2. What are the products of the reaction between lithium and water?
3. What is the trend in reactivity of the halogens as you go down the group?
4. What are the products of the reaction between bromine and potassium iodide?

Transition metals

5

Comparison with group 1 elements

Typical transition metals are chromium, manganese, iron, cobalt, nickel and copper.

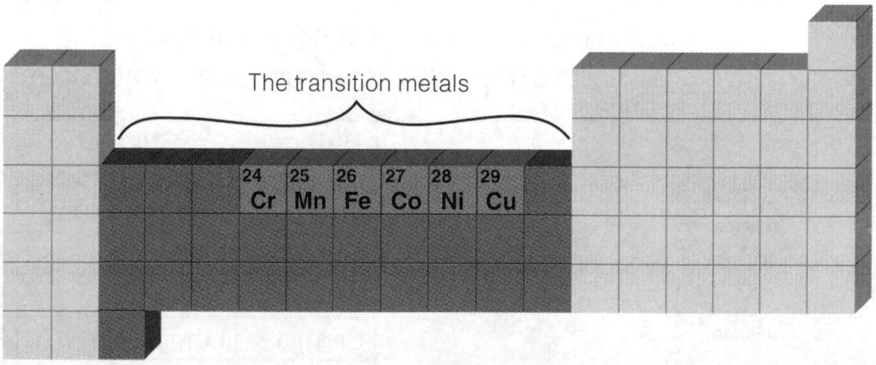

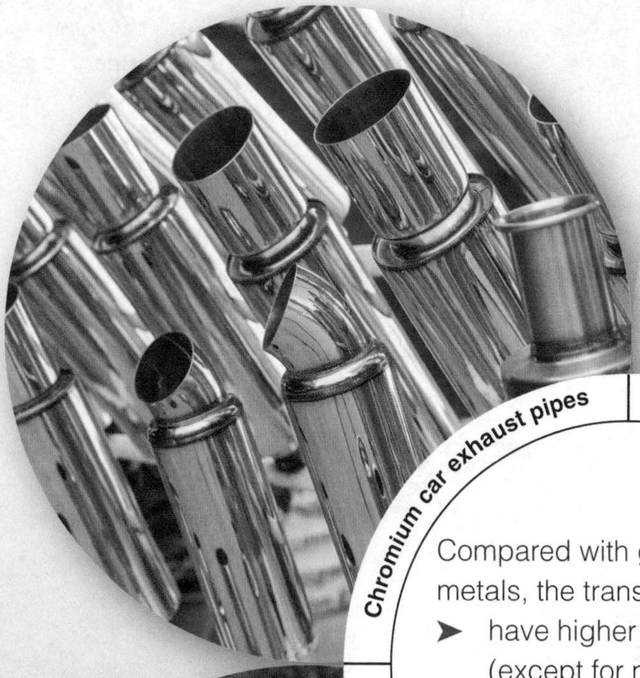
Chromium car exhaust pipes

Manganese

Compared with group 1 metals, the transition metals....

- have higher melting points (except for mercury)
- are more dense
- are less reactive with water and oxygen

Copper

Nickel coins

Properties of transition metals

Many transition elements have ions with different charges. For example, $FeCl_2$ is a compound that contains Fe^{2+} ions and $FeCl_3$ is a compound that contains Fe^{3+} ions.

Compounds of transition metals are also often coloured. For example, potassium manganate(VII), $KMnO_4$, is purple and copper(II) sulfate, $CuSO_4$, is blue.

Keywords

Catalyst ➤ A substance that changes the rate of a chemical reaction without being used up or chemically changed at the end of the reaction

Haber process ➤ A process used to make ammonia, NH_3

The purple colour of potassium manganate(VII) solution

The colours of some other transition metal ions

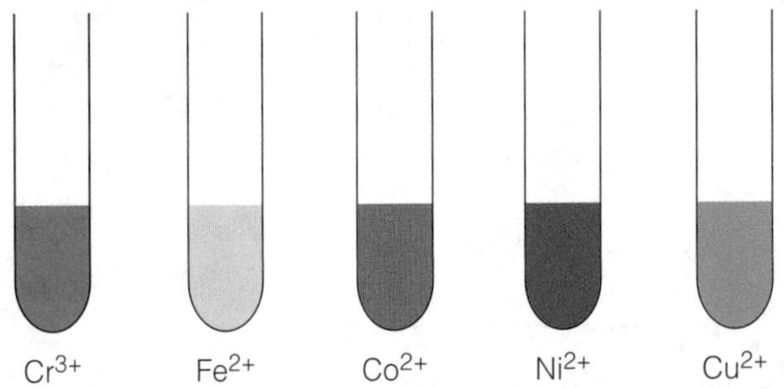
Cr3+
Fe2+
Co2+
Ni2+
Cu2+

Transition metals are also frequently used as **catalysts**, such as iron in the **Haber process** (see Module 40) and nickel used in the manufacture of margarine.

Margarine

Iron ore

Colour paper in different colours corresponding to the colours of the different transition metal ions shown on this page. On the reverse of the paper, write the ion that provides this colour.

1. Give two contrasting properties of transition metals when compared with group 1 metals.
2. Give the name and colour of a transition metal compound.
3. Which transition metal is used as a catalyst in the Haber process?

Mind map

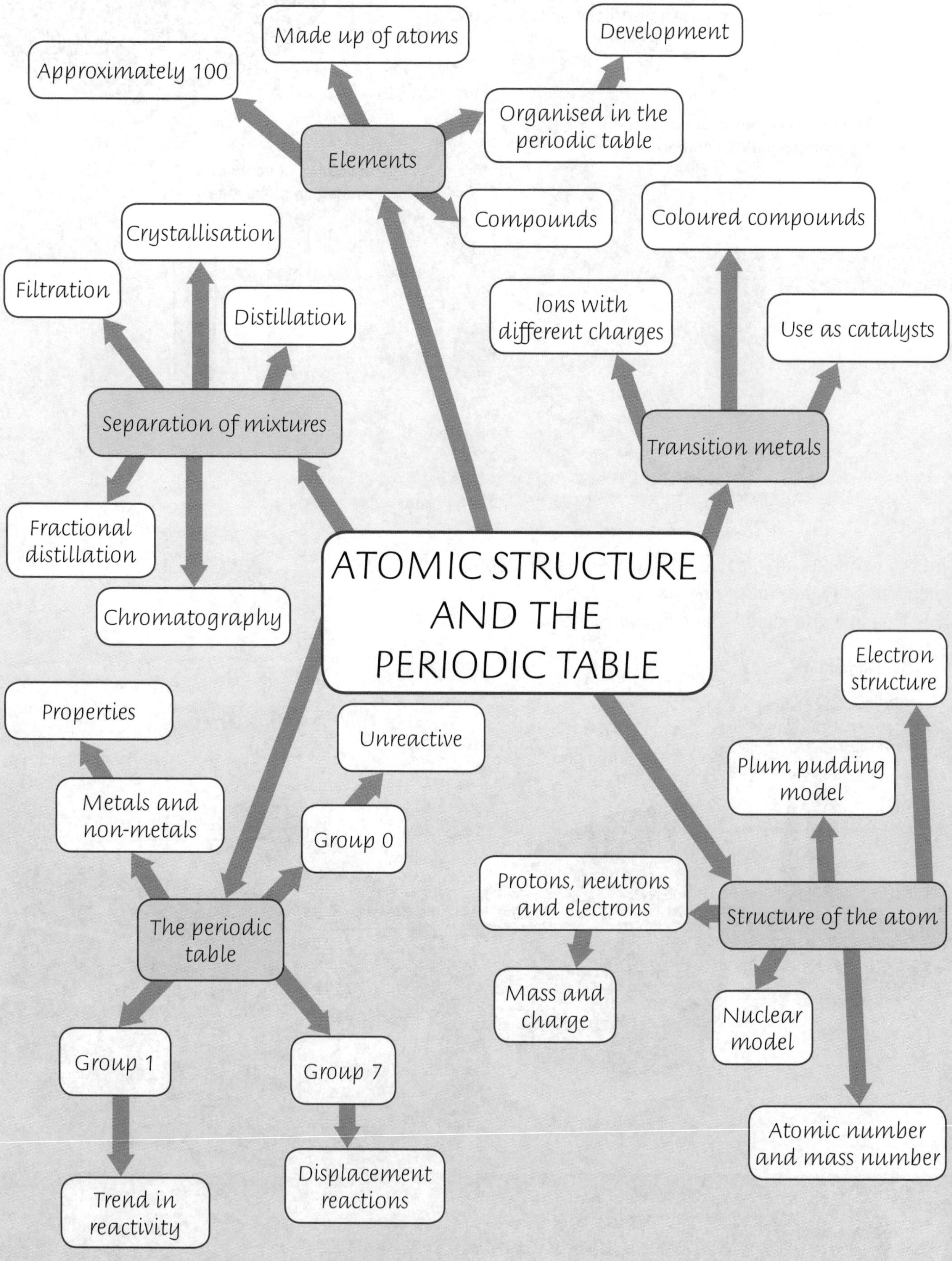
ATOMIC STRUCTURE AND THE PERIODIC TABLE
Elements
Approximately 100
Made up of atoms
Organised in the periodic table
Development
Compounds
Separation of mixtures
Filtration
Crystallisation
Distillation
Fractional distillation
Chromatography
Transition metals
Ions with different charges
Coloured compounds
Use as catalysts
The periodic table
Metals and non-metals
Properties
Group 0
Unreactive
Group 1
Trend in reactivity
Group 7
Displacement reactions
Structure of the atom
Protons, neutrons and electrons
Mass and charge
Nuclear model
Plum pudding model
Electron structure
Atomic number and mass number

Practice questions

1. This question is about the non-metal chlorine.

   An atom of chlorine can be represented as:

   $$^{35}_{17}Cl$$

   a) Give the number of protons, neutrons and electrons in an atom of chlorine. **(3 marks)**

   b) What is the electronic structure of chlorine? **(1 mark)**

   c) Chlorine exists as two isotopes.
   The other isotope of chlorine is represented as:

   $$^{37}_{17}Cl$$

   Give one similarity and one difference between the two isotopes of chlorine. **(2 marks)**

   d) Give one property of chlorine that is characteristic of it being a non-metal. **(1 mark)**

   e) Write a balanced symbol equation for the reaction between chlorine and sodium iodide solution. **(2 marks)**

   f) Explain why chlorine does not react with sodium fluoride solution. **(2 marks)**

2. Sand does not dissolve in water but salt does.

   a) How can sand be separated from water? **(1 mark)**

   b) Draw and label a diagram to show how water can be collected from a salt water solution. **(3 marks)**

   c) Why is crystallisation not a suitable method for obtaining water from a salt water solution? **(1 mark)**

3. The element boron exists as two naturally occurring isotopes. The mass and abundance (amount) of each isotope of boron is shown below.

Mass number of isotope	% abundance
10	20
11	80

   Use the above information to calculate the relative atomic mass of boron.
   Give your answer to three significant figures. **(3 marks)**

Chemical bonding

6

There are three types of chemical bond:

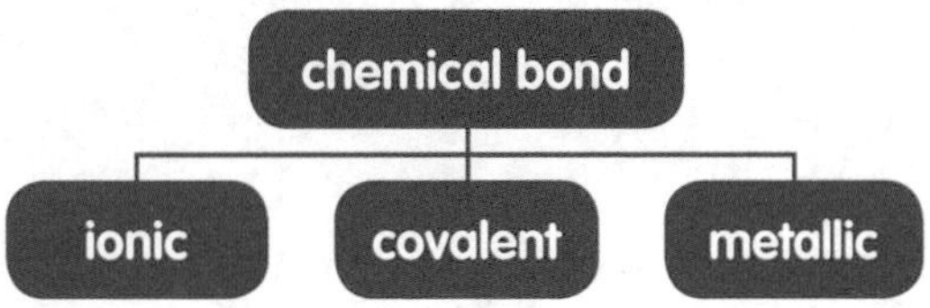
chemical bond
ionic
covalent
metallic

Ionic bonding

Ionic bonds occur between metals and non-metals. An ionic bond is the electrostatic force of attraction between two oppositely charged **ions** (called **cations** and **anions**).

Ionic bonds are formed when metal atoms transfer electrons to non-metal atoms. This is done so that each atom forms an ion with a full outer shell of electrons.

Example 1: The formation of an ionic bond between sodium and chlorine

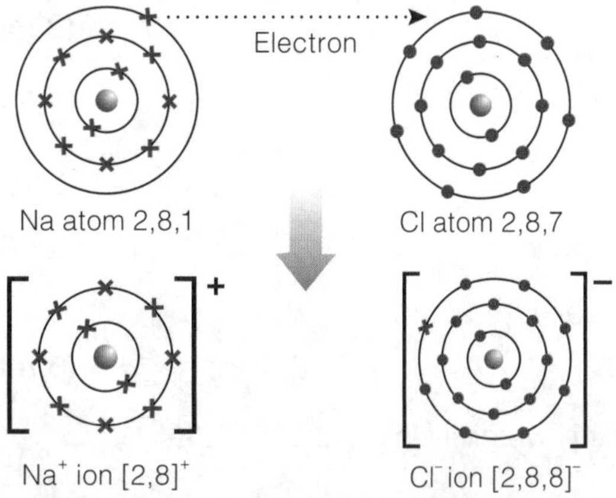
Electron
Na atom 2,8,1
Cl atom 2,8,7
+
−
Na⁺ ion [2,8]⁺
Cl⁻ ion [2,8,8]⁻

Example 2: The formation of the ionic bond between magnesium and oxygen

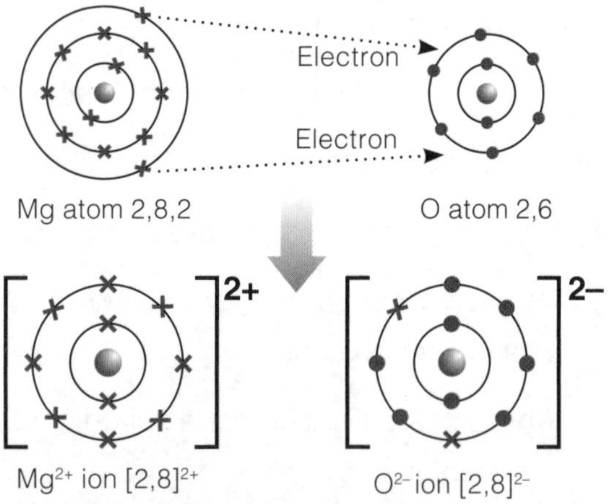
Electron
Electron
Mg atom 2,8,2
O atom 2,6
2+
2−
Mg²⁺ ion [2,8]²⁺
O²⁻ ion [2,8]²⁻

Covalent bonding

Covalent bonds occur between two non-metal atoms. Atoms share a pair of electrons so that each atom ends up with a full outer shell of electrons, such as:

- the formation of a covalent bond between two hydrogen atoms

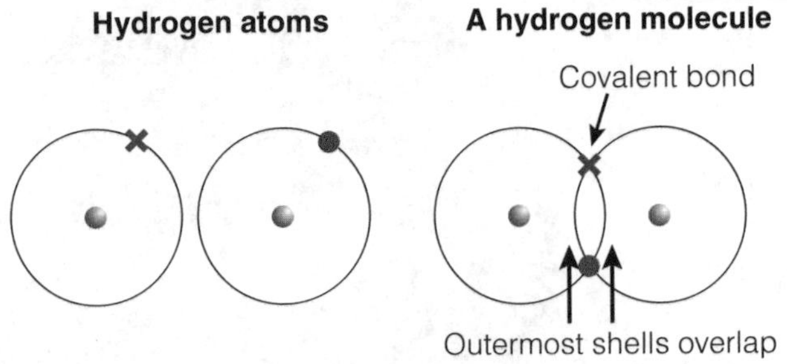
Hydrogen atoms
A hydrogen molecule
Covalent bond
Outermost shells overlap

- the covalent bonding in methane, CH_4.

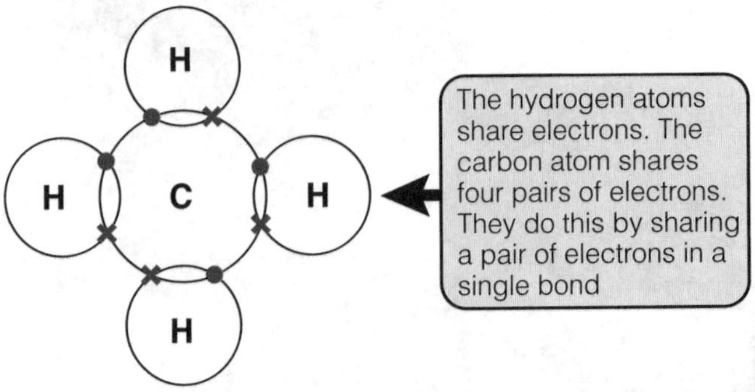
H
H
C
H
H
The hydrogen atoms share electrons. The carbon atom shares four pairs of electrons. They do this by sharing a pair of electrons in a single bond

Double covalent bonds occur when two pairs of electrons are shared between atoms, for example in carbon dioxide.

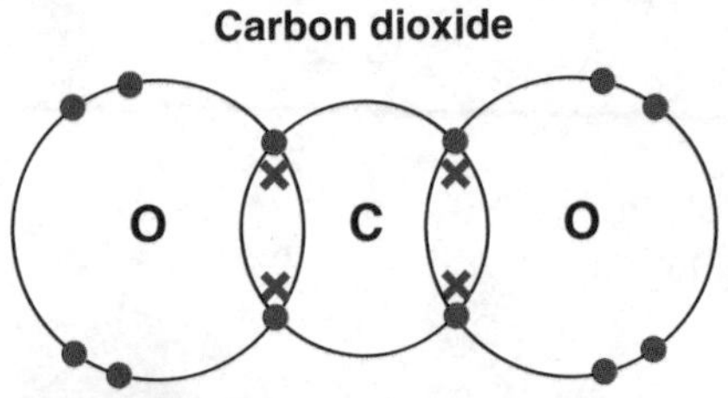
Carbon dioxide
O
C
O

Keywords

Ion ➤ An atom or group of atoms that has gained or lost one or more electrons in order to gain a full outer shell

Cation ➤ A positive ion

Anion ➤ A negative ion

Delocalised electrons ➤ Free-moving electrons

Metallic bonding

Metals consist of giant structures. Each atom loses its outer shell electrons and these electrons become **delocalised**, i.e. they are free to move through the structure. The metal cations are arranged in a regular pattern called a lattice (see below).

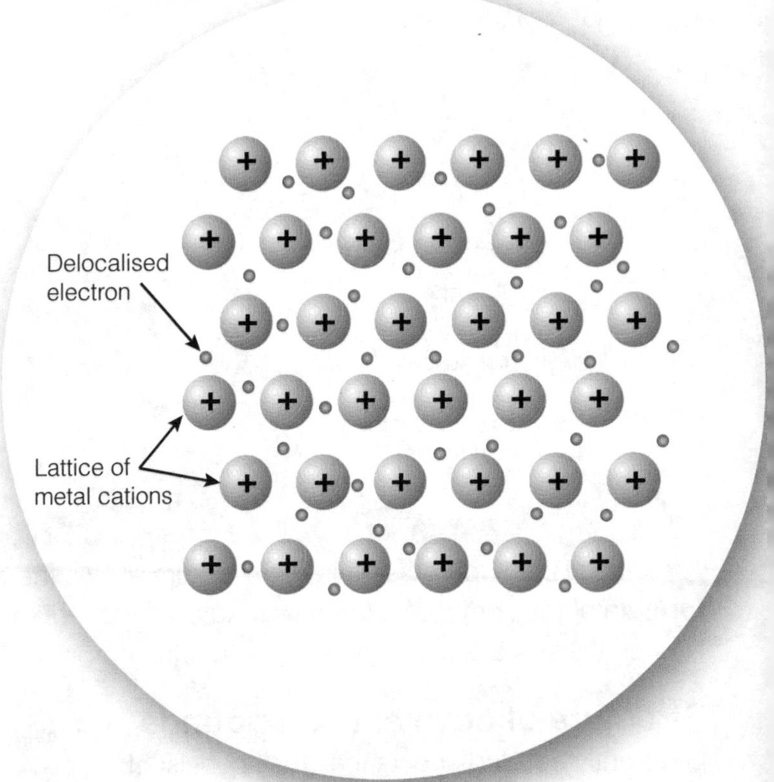
Delocalised electron
Lattice of metal cations

Use the models of atoms you have previously made to try to work out what happens when different atoms bond together. Make sure that each atom ends up with a full outer shell. Remember that you might need more than one of each type of atom.

What type of bonding occurs between a metal and non-metal atom?
How many electrons are present in every covalent bond?
Describe the structure of a metal.

Ionic and covalent structures

7

Sodium chloride

Structure of ionic compounds

Compounds containing ionic bonds form giant structures. These are held together by strong electrostatic forces of attraction between the oppositely charged ions. These forces act in all directions throughout the lattice.

The diagrams below represent a typical giant ionic structure, sodium chloride.

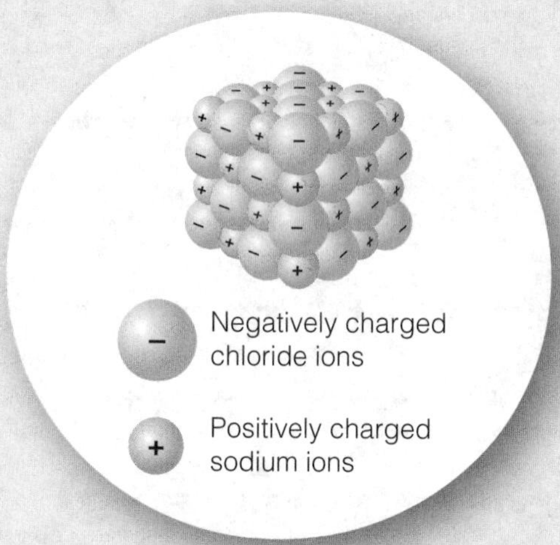
Negatively charged chloride ions
Positively charged sodium ions

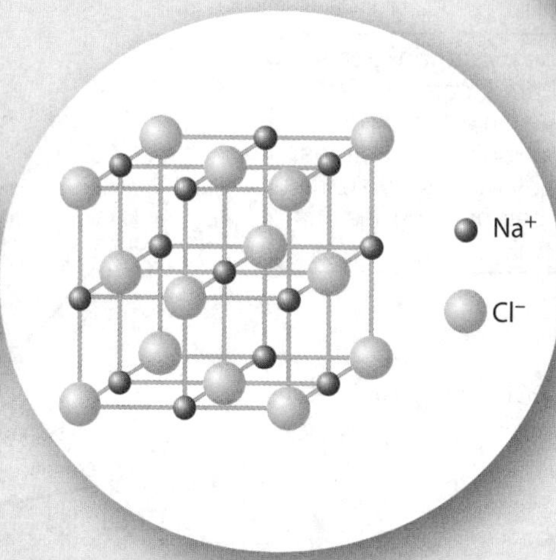
Na+
Cl−

The ratio of each ion present in the structure allows the **empirical formula** of the compound to be worked out. In the diagram above, for every Na^+ ion there is a Cl^- ion. This means that the empirical formula is NaCl.

Structure of covalent compounds

Covalently bonded substances may consist of....

- small molecules / simple molecular structures (e.g. Cl_2, H_2O and CH_4)
- large molecules (e.g. **polymers** – see Module 28)
- giant covalent structures (e.g. diamond, graphite and silicon dioxide).

Small molecular structures

The bonding between hydrogen and carbon in methane can be represented in several ways, as shown here.

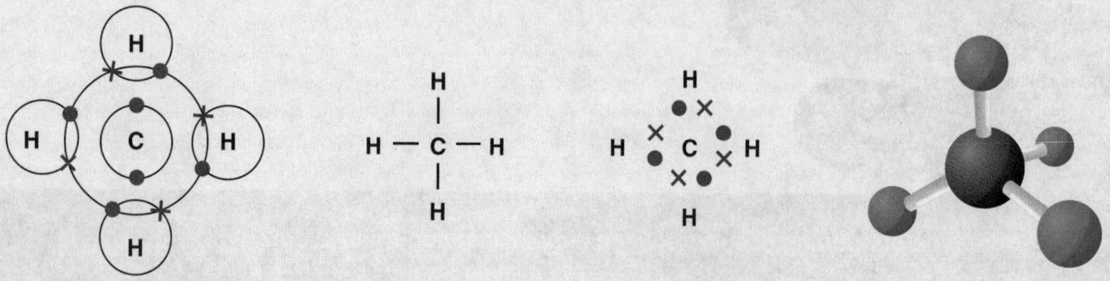
H
H
C
H
H

Large molecules

Polymers can be represented in the form:

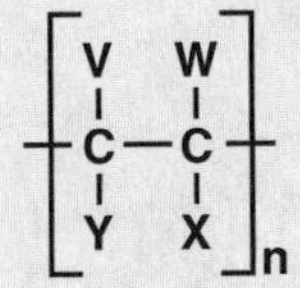

V
W
C
C
Y
X
n

V, W, X and Y represent the atoms bonded to the carbon atoms

For example, poly(ethene) can be represented as:

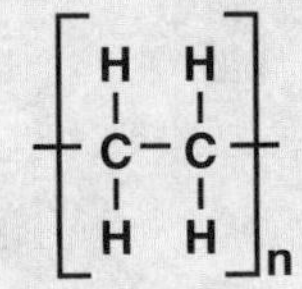

H
H
C
C
H
H
n

Giant covalent structures

This is the giant covalent structure of silicon dioxide.

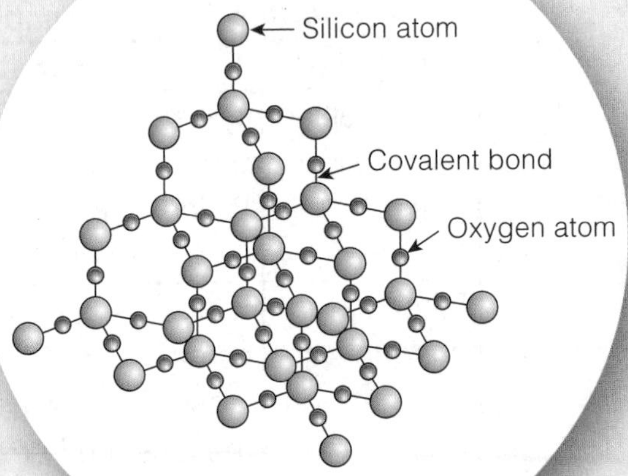

Silicon atom
Covalent bond
Oxygen atom

The formula of silicon dioxide is SiO_2 – this can be deduced by looking at the ratio of Si to O atoms in the diagram above.

Models, such as dot-and-cross diagrams, ball-and-stick diagrams and two- / three-dimensional diagrams to represent structures, are limited in value, as they do not accurately represent the structures of materials. For example, a chemical bond is not a solid object as depicted in some models, it is actually an attraction between particles. The relative size of different atoms is often not shown when drawing diagrams.

Keywords

Empirical formula ➤ The simplest whole number ratio of each kind of atom present in a compound

Polymer ➤ A large, long-chained molecule

Make a model that represents sodium chloride or silicon dioxide. Count the number of each particle and then work out the simplest whole number ratio of each particle present. This is the empirical formula.

Diamond

Graphite

What forces hold ionic structures together?
What are the three types of covalent substance?
Draw a diagram to show the structure of sodium chloride.

States of matter: properties of compounds

States of matter

The three main states of matter are **solids**, **liquids** and **gases**. Individual atoms do not have the same properties as these bulk substances. The diagram below shows how they can be interconverted and also how the particles in the different states of matter are arranged.

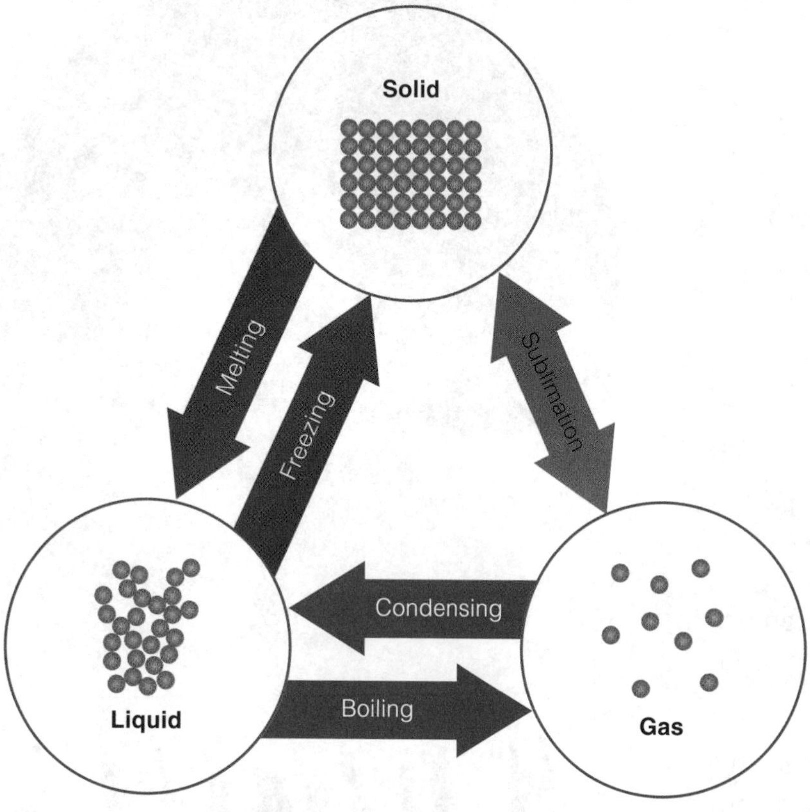

These are physical changes because the particles are either gaining or losing energy and are not undergoing a chemical reaction. Particles in a gas have more energy than in a liquid; particles in a liquid would have more energy than in a solid.

Melting and freezing occur at the same temperature. Condensing and boiling also occur at the same temperature. The amount of energy needed to change state depends on the strength of the forces between the particles of the substance.

The stronger the forces between the particles, the higher the melting and boiling points of the substance.

Properties of ionic compounds	
Property	**Explanation**
High melting and boiling points	There are lots of strong bonds throughout an ionic lattice which require lots of energy to break.
Electrical conductivity	Ionic compounds conduct electricity when molten or dissolved in water because the ions are free to move and carry the charge. Ionic solids do not conduct electricity because the ions are in a fixed position and are unable to move.

HT The model on the left is limited in value because....

- ➤ it does not indicate that there are forces between the spheres
- ➤ all particles are represented as spheres
- ➤ the spheres are solid.

Keyword

Intermolecular forces ➤ The weak forces of attraction that occur between molecules

Properties of small molecules

Substances made up of small molecules are usually gases or liquids at room temperature. They have relatively low melting and boiling points because there are weak (intermolecular) forces that act between the molecules. It is these weak forces and not the strong covalent bonds that are broken when the substance melts or boils.

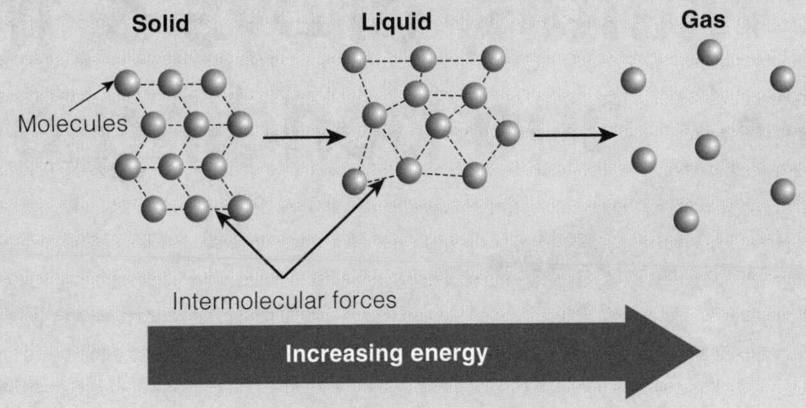

Solid
Liquid
Gas
Molecules
Intermolecular forces
Increasing energy

Substances made up of small molecules do not normally conduct electricity. This is because the molecules do not have an overall electric charge or delocalised electrons.

Polymers

Polymers are very large molecules made up of atoms joined together by strong covalent bonds. The **intermolecular forces** between polymer molecules are much stronger than in small molecules because the molecules are larger. This is why most polymers are solid at room temperature.

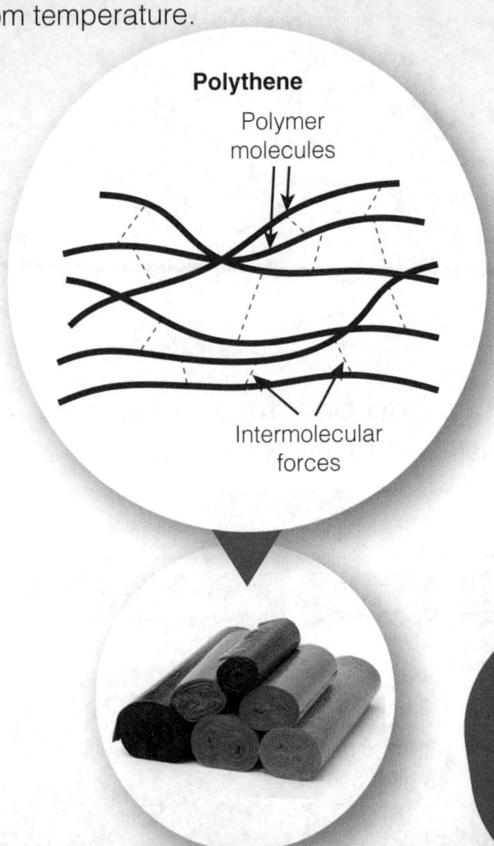

Polythene
Polymer molecules
Intermolecular forces

Giant covalent structures

Substances with a giant covalent structure are solids at room temperature. They have relatively high melting and boiling points. This is because there are lots of strong covalent bonds that need to be broken.

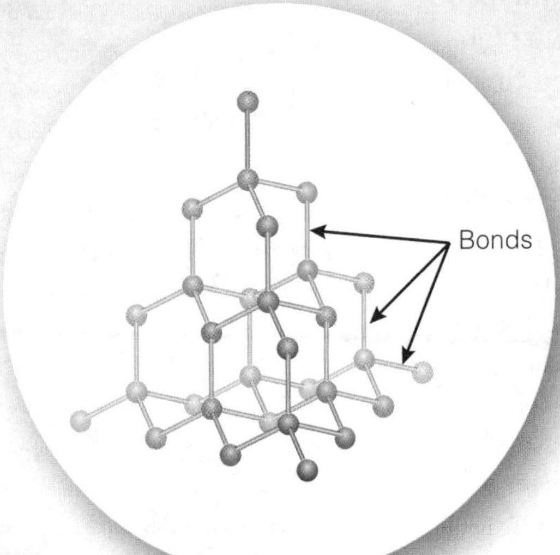

Bonds

At home, find some salt (ionic), a plastic bag (polymer) and a pencil lead (giant covalent). Compare the differences and similarities between these objects.

8

What is the main factor that determines the melting point of a solid?
Why do ionic compounds have relatively high melting points?
What needs to be broken in order to melt a substance made up of small molecules such as water?
Why do polymers have higher melting points than substances made up of small molecules?
Why do substances with giant covalent structures have relatively high melting points?

Metals, alloys & the structure and bonding of carbon

9

Structure and properties of metals

Metals have giant structures. Metallic bonding (the attraction between the cations and the delocalised electrons) is strong meaning that most metals have high melting and boiling points.

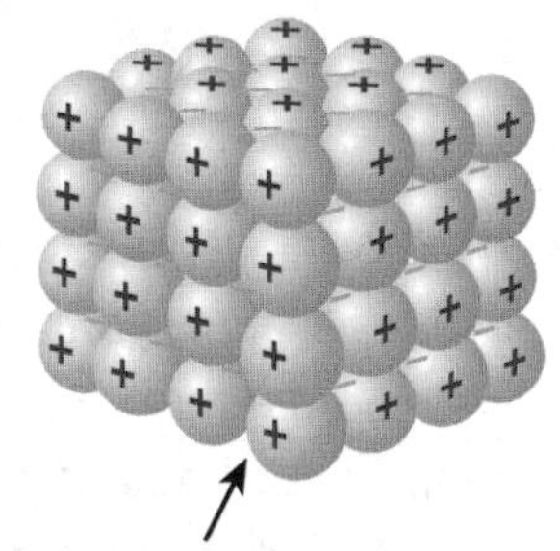

High melting point
Strong forces of attraction between cations and electrons

The layers are able to slide over each other, which means that metals can be bent and shaped.

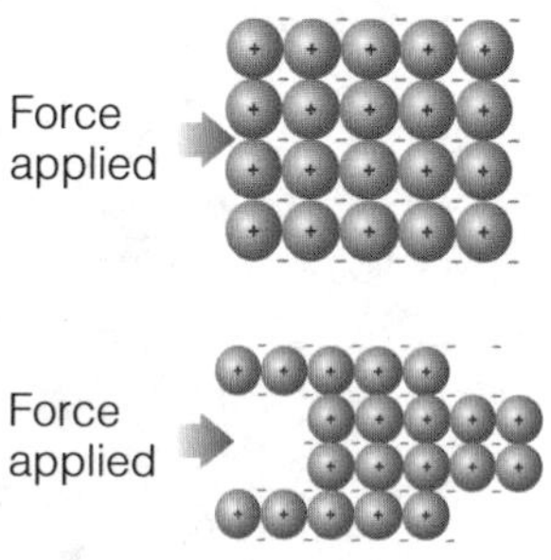

Malleable
Force applied
Force applied
Rows of ions slide over each other

Metals are good conductors of electricity because the delocalised electrons are able to move.

The delocalised electrons also transfer energy meaning that they are good thermal conductors.

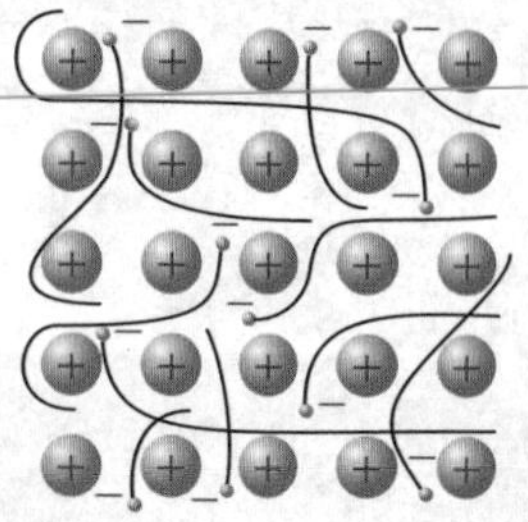

Electrons moving between the cations

Alloys

Most metals we use are **alloys**. Many pure metals (such as gold, iron and aluminium) are too soft for many uses and so are mixed with other materials (usually metals) to make alloys.

The different sizes of atoms in alloys make it difficult for the layers to slide over each other. This is why alloys are harder than pure metals.

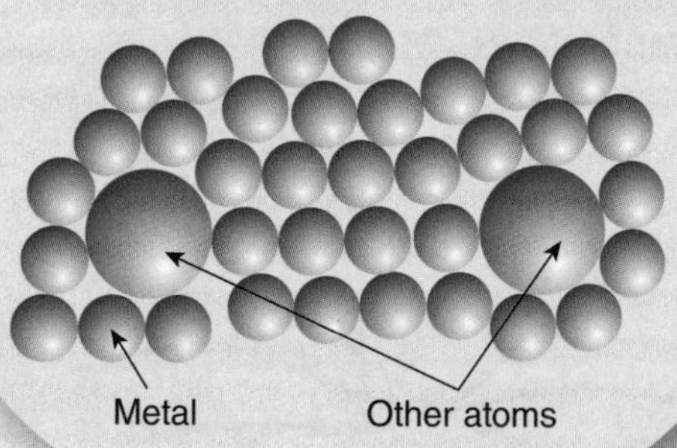

Typical alloy structure
Metal
Other atoms

Structure and bonding of carbon

Carbon has four different structures.

- carbon
  - diamond
  - graphite
  - graphene
  - fullerenes

Keywords

Alloy ➤ A mixture of two or more metals, or a mixture of a metal and a non-metal

Fullerene ➤ A molecule made of carbon atoms arranged as a hollow sphere

Nanotube ➤ A molecule made of carbon atoms arranged in a tubular structure

High tensile strength ➤ Does not break easily when stretched

Diamond

Diamond is a giant covalent structure (or macromolecule) where each carbon atom is bonded to four others.

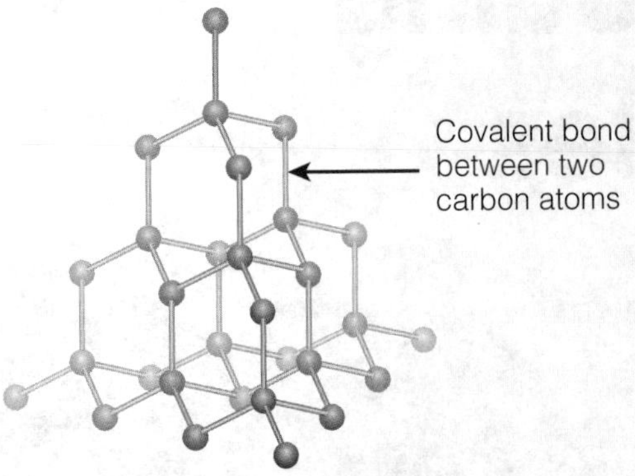
Covalent bond
between two
carbon atoms

In diamond, there are lots of very strong covalent bonds so diamond...

- is hard
- has a high melting point.

For these reasons, diamond is used in making cutting tools.

There are no free electrons in diamond so it does not conduct electricity.

Graphite

Graphite is also a giant covalent structure, with each carbon atom forming three covalent bonds, resulting in layers of hexagonal rings of carbon atoms. Carbon has four electrons in its outer shell and as only three are used for bonding the other one is delocalised.

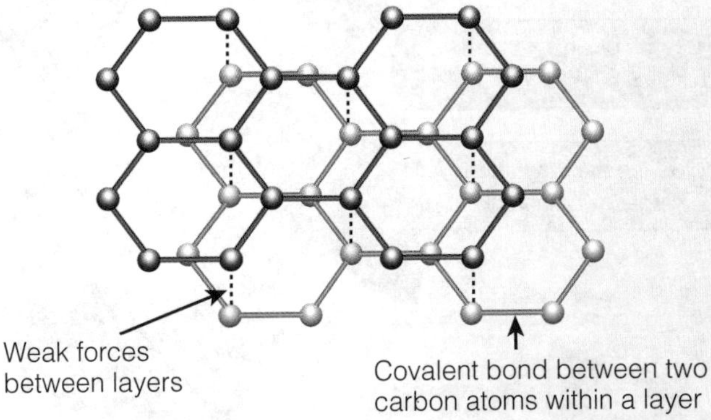
Weak forces
between layers
Covalent bond between two
carbon atoms within a layer

The layers in graphite are able to slide over each other because there are only weak intermolecular forces holding them together. This is why graphite is soft and slippery. These properties make graphite suitable for use as a lubricant.

Like diamond, there are lots of strong covalent bonds in graphite so it has a high melting point.

The delocalised electrons allow graphite to conduct electricity and heat.

Graphene and fullerenes

Graphene is a single layer of graphite and so it is one atom thick.

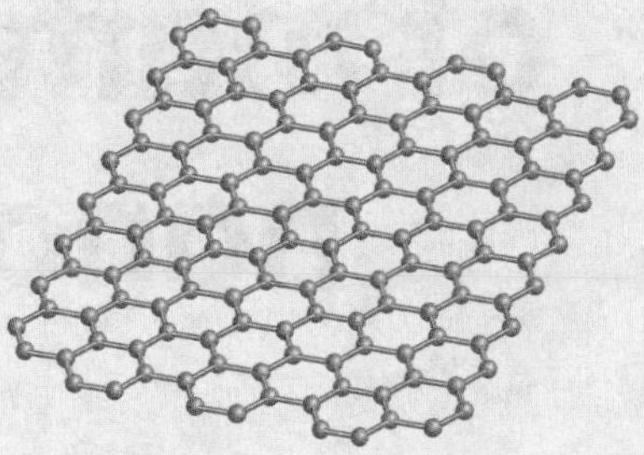

Fullerenes are molecules made up of carbon atoms and they have hollow shapes. The structure of fullerenes is based on hexagonal rings of carbon atoms but they may also contain rings with five or seven carbon atoms.

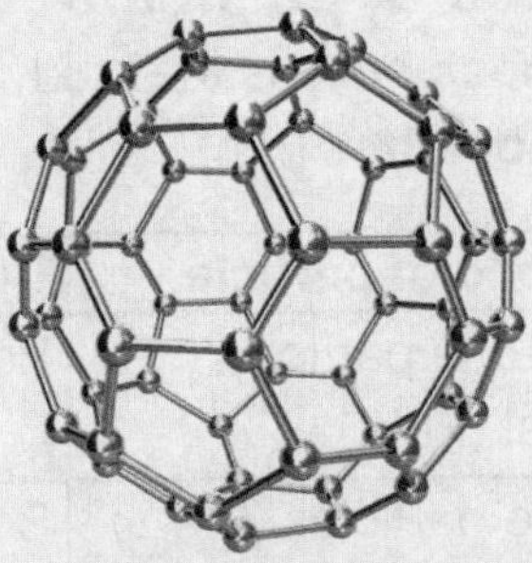

buckminsterfullerene (C_{60}) was the first fullerene to be discovered

Carbon **nanotubes** are cylindrical fullerenes.

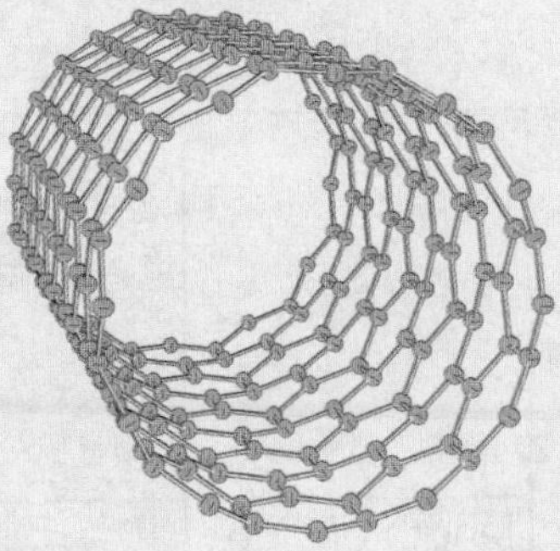

Fullerenes have **high**...

- **tensile strength**
- electrical conductivity
- thermal conductivity.

Fullerenes can be used...

- for drug delivery into the body
- as lubricants
- for reinforcing materials, e.g. tennis rackets.

Make flash cards with the four different structures of carbon on one side and the properties / uses on the reverse. Use these cards to test your knowledge.

Why do metals generally have high melting points?
Why are alloys harder than pure metals?
Why does graphite conduct electricity?
State two properties of fullerenes.
Give two uses of fullerenes.

Bulk and surface properties of matter, including nanoparticles

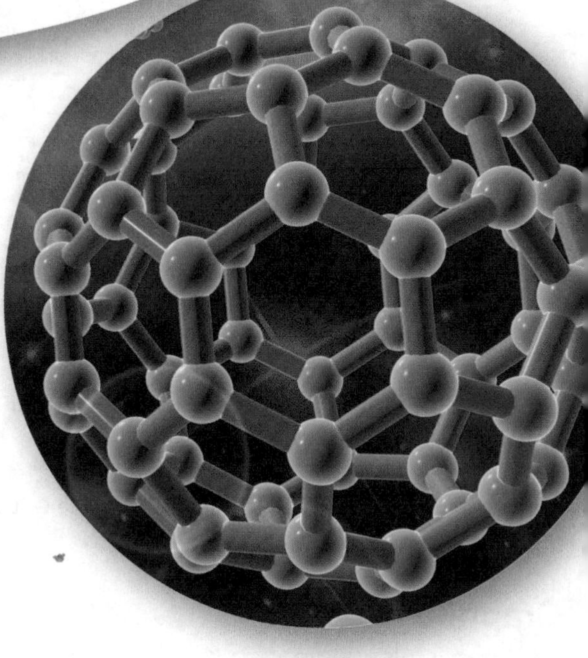

Sizes of particles

Nanoscience is the study of structures that are 1–100 **nanometres** (nm) in size, i.e. a few hundred atoms.

Name of particle	Diameter of particles
Coarse particles / dust (PM_{10})	Between 1×10^{-5} and 2.5×10^{-6} m
Fine particles ($PM_{2.5}$)	Between 1×10^{-7} and 2.5×10^{-6} m (100 and 250 nm)
Nanoparticles	Less than 1×10^{-7} m (100 nm)

PM = particulate matter

As the side of a cube decreases by a factor of 10, the surface area to volume ratio $\left(\frac{\text{surface area}}{\text{volume}}\right)$ increases by a factor of 10.

	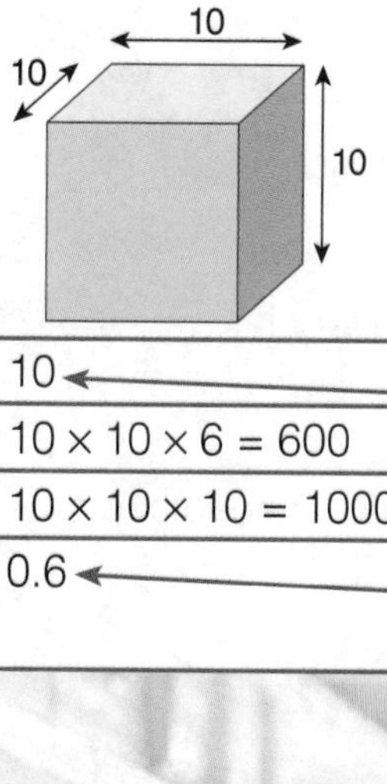	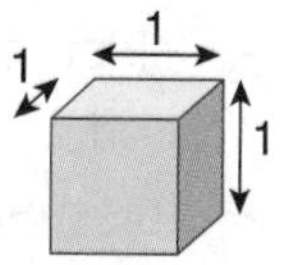
length of side	10	1
surface area	$10 \times 10 \times 6 = 600$	$1 \times 1 \times 6 = 6$
volume	$10 \times 10 \times 10 = 1000$	$1 \times 1 \times 1 = 1$
$\frac{\text{surface area}}{\text{volume}}$	0.6	6

Length of side decreases by a factor of 10

Surface area to volume ratio increases by a factor of 10

10

Properties of nanoparticles

Nanoparticles may have properties that are different from larger amounts of the same material because of their higher surface area to volume ratio. This may mean that smaller quantities are needed to be effective when compared with materials which have normal-sized particles.

Keywords

Nanoscience ➤ The study of structures that are 1–100 nm in size (i.e. a few hundred atoms)

Nanometre ➤ 1×10^{-9} (0.000 000 001) m

Nanoparticles ➤ Particles that are less than 100 nm in size

Uses of nanoparticles

Uses of nanoparticles

- In deodorants and fabrics to prevent the growth of bacteria
- Controlled drug delivery
- Cosmetics and sun creams
- Electronics
- Synthetic skin
- Development of new catalysts for fuel cell materials

Use of nanoparticles in sun creams	
Advantages	**Disadvantages**
Better skin coverage	Potential cell damage in the body
More effective protection from the Sun's ultraviolet rays	Potentially harmful effects on the environment

Make one small and one large cube out of paper. Now calculate the total surface area, volume of each cube and the surface area to volume ratio.

1. What size are nanoparticles?
2. What happens to the surface area to volume ratio of a cube when the side of a cube decreases by a factor of 10?
3. State two uses of nanoparticles.
4. Give one advantage and one disadvantage of using nanoparticles in sun creams.

Mind map

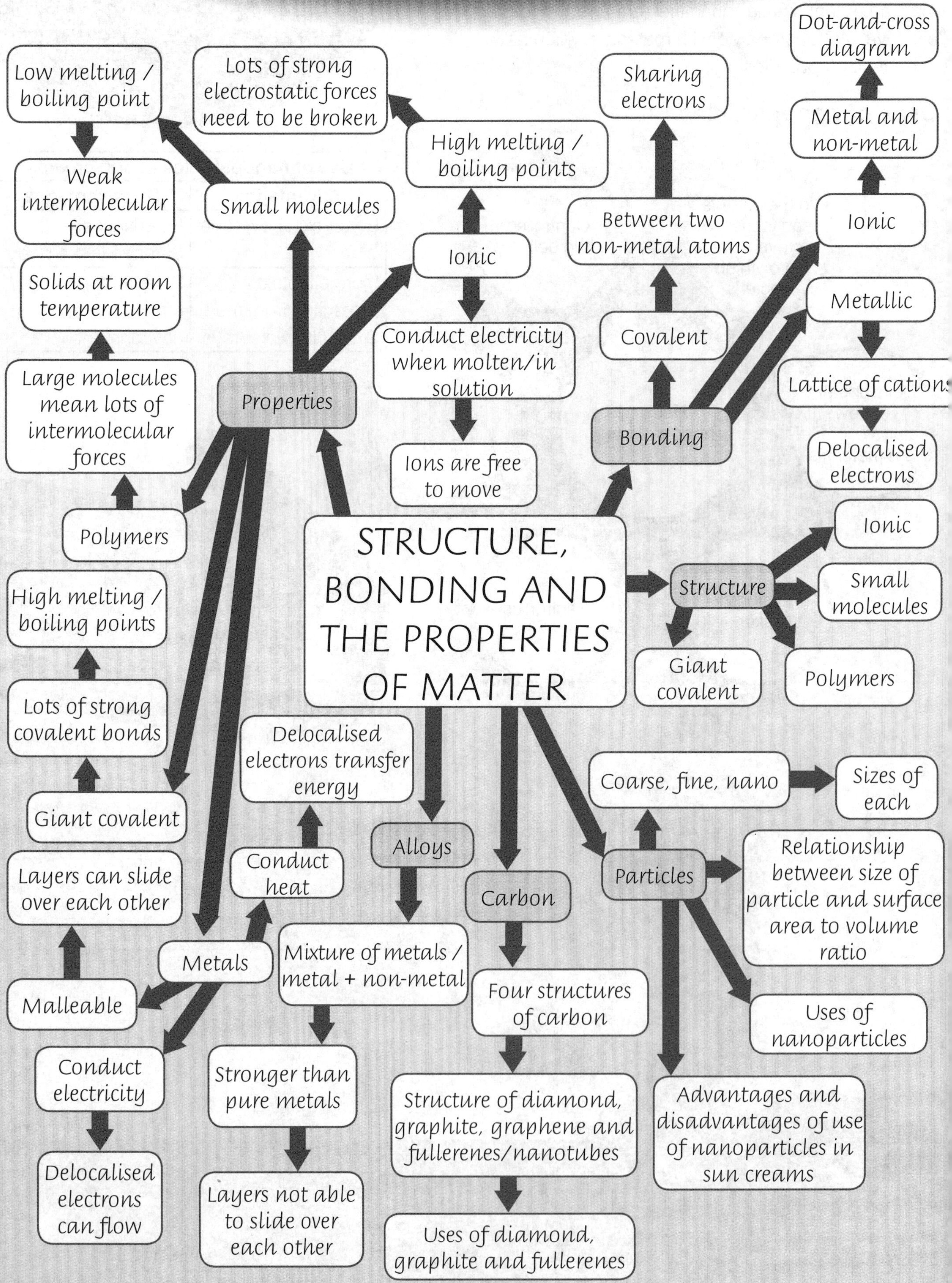
STRUCTURE, BONDING AND THE PROPERTIES OF MATTER
Properties
Small molecules
Low melting / boiling point
Weak intermolecular forces
Lots of strong electrostatic forces need to be broken
High melting / boiling points
Ionic
Conduct electricity when molten/in solution
Ions are free to move
Polymers
Large molecules mean lots of intermolecular forces
Solids at room temperature
Giant covalent
Lots of strong covalent bonds
High melting / boiling points
Metals
Malleable
Layers can slide over each other
Conduct heat
Delocalised electrons transfer energy
Conduct electricity
Delocalised electrons can flow
Alloys
Mixture of metals / metal + non-metal
Stronger than pure metals
Layers not able to slide over each other
Carbon
Four structures of carbon
Structure of diamond, graphite, graphene and fullerenes/nanotubes
Uses of diamond, graphite and fullerenes
Bonding
Covalent
Between two non-metal atoms
Sharing electrons
Ionic
Metal and non-metal
Dot-and-cross diagram
Metallic
Lattice of cations
Delocalised electrons
Structure
Ionic
Small molecules
Giant covalent
Polymers
Particles
Coarse, fine, nano
Sizes of each
Relationship between size of particle and surface area to volume ratio
Uses of nanoparticles
Advantages and disadvantages of use of nanoparticles in sun creams

Practice questions

1. This question is about the structure and bonding of sodium chloride and the properties that it has.
   a) What type of bonding is present in sodium chloride? **(1 mark)**
   b) Draw a dot-and-cross diagram to show the formation of the bond in sodium chloride. Draw the electronic structure of the atoms before the bond has formed and the ions after the bond has formed. **(3 marks)**
   c) Explain how the ions in sodium chloride are held together. **(2 marks)**
   d) Does sodium chloride have a high or a low boiling point? Explain your answer. **(2 marks)**
   e) Draw a diagram showing the positions of the ions in a crystal of sodium chloride. **(1 mark)**
2. Carbon dioxide and silicon dioxide have different structures.
   a) What type of bonding is present in both carbon dioxide and silicon dioxide? **(1 mark)**
   b) The diagram below shows the bonding in carbon dioxide.

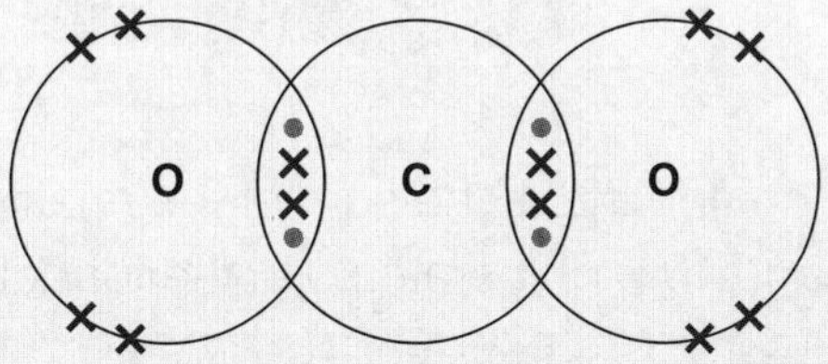

O
C
O

   i) How many covalent bonds are there between the carbon atom and each oxygen atom? **(1 mark)**
   ii) Does carbon dioxide have a simple molecular or giant covalent (macromolecular) structure? **(1 mark)**

   c) The structure of silicon dioxide is shown below.

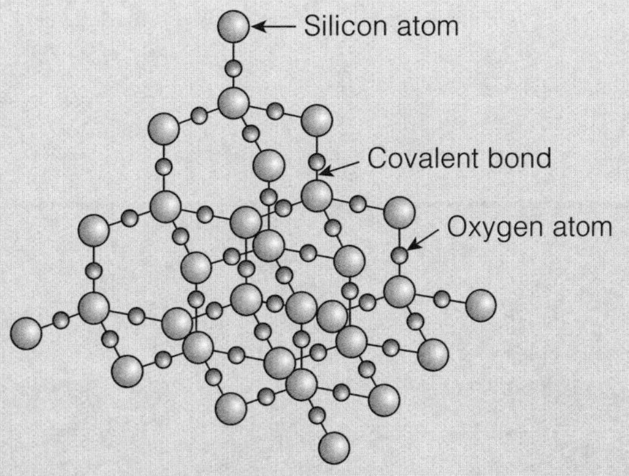

Silicon atom
Covalent bond
Oxygen atom

   i) Does silicon dioxide have a simple molecular or a giant covalent (macromolecular) structure? **(1 mark)**
   ii) In terms of structure, what is the difference between a simple molecular structure and a giant covalent (macromolecular) structure? **(2 marks)**

   d) Would you expect silicon dioxide to have a higher or lower boiling point than carbon dioxide? Explain your answer. **(2 marks)**

Mass and equations

11

Keywords

Relative formula mass ➤ The sum of the atomic masses of the atoms in a formula

Thermal decomposition ➤ The breakdown of a chemical substance due to the action of heat

Conservation of mass

The total mass of reactants in a chemical reaction is equal to the total mass of the products because atoms are not created or destroyed.

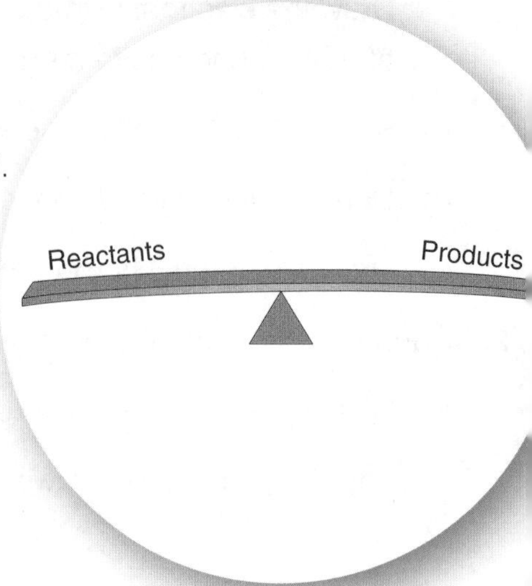

Chemical reactions are represented by balanced symbol equations.

For example:

$$4Na + TiCl_4 \rightarrow 4NaCl + Ti$$

This means there are four atoms of Na

This means there are four atoms of chlorine in $TiCl_4$

Relative formula mass

The **relative formula mass** (M_r) of a compound is the sum of the relative atomic masses (see the periodic table on page 104) of the atoms in the formula.

For example:

- The M_r of MgO is 40 (24 + 16)
- The M_r of H_2SO_4 is 98 [(2 × 1) + 32 + (4 × 16)]

In a balanced symbol equation, the sum of the relative formula masses of the reactants equals the sum of the relative formula masses of the products.

Example: $CaCO_3 + 2HCl \rightarrow CaCl_2 + H_2O + CO_2$

Sum of relative formula masses: 100 + (2 × 36.5) = 173 111 + 18 + 44 = 173

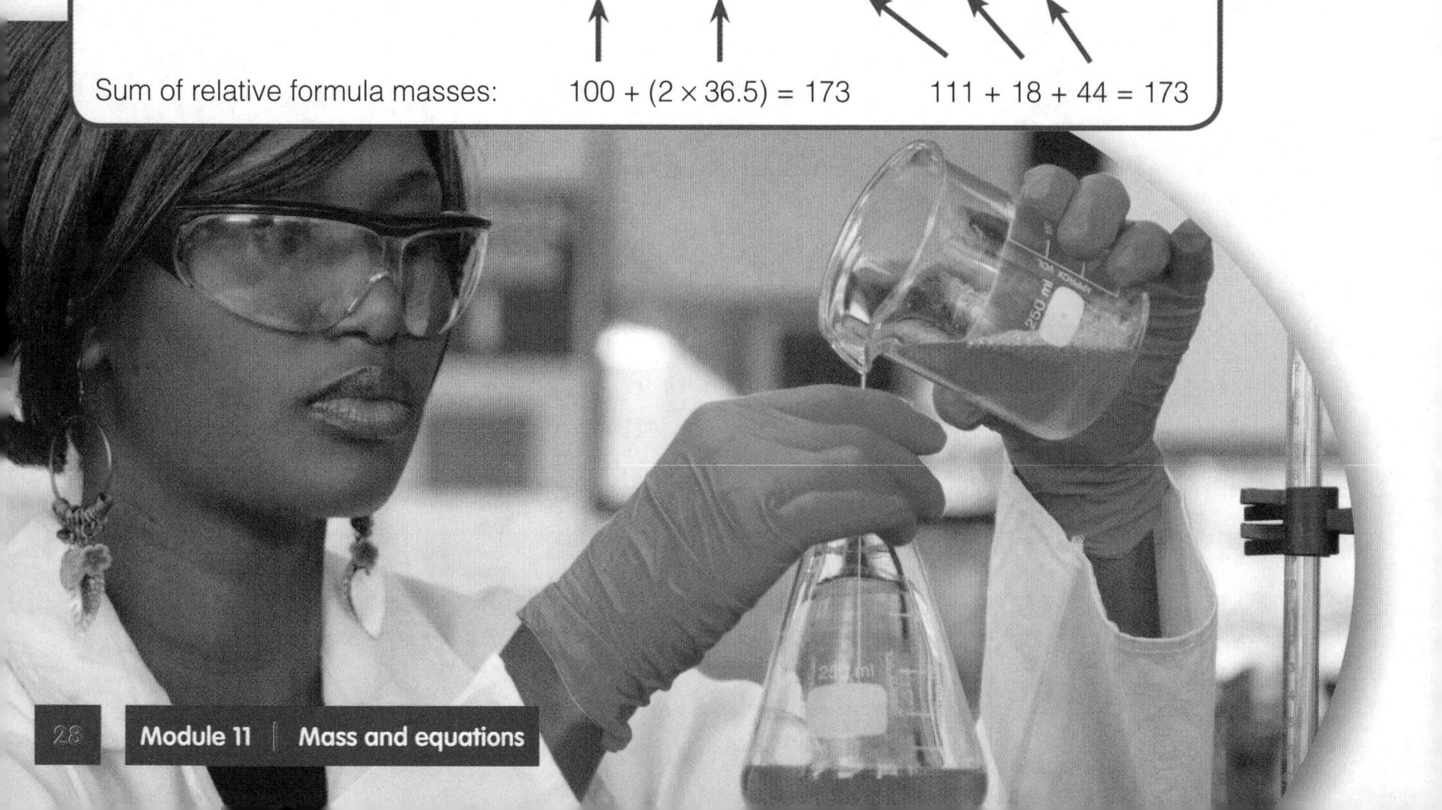

Mass changes when a reactant or product is a gas

During some chemical reactions, there can appear to be a change in mass. When copper is heated its mass actually increases because oxygen is being added to it.

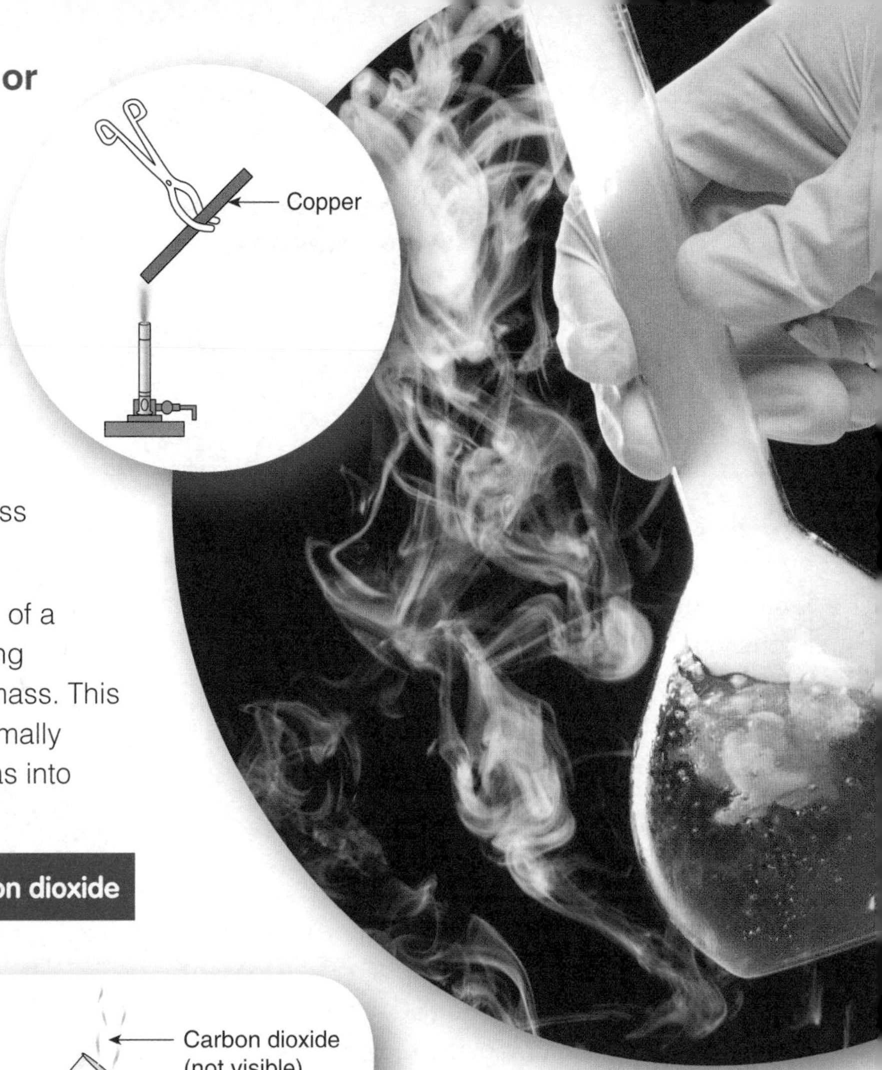
Copper

copper + oxygen → copper oxide

The mass of copper oxide formed is equal to the starting mass of copper plus the mass of the oxygen that has been added to it.

During a **thermal decomposition** reaction of a metal carbonate, the final mass of remaining metal oxide solid is less than the starting mass. This is because when the metal carbonate thermally decomposes it releases carbon dioxide gas into the atmosphere.

copper carbonate → copper oxide + carbon dioxide

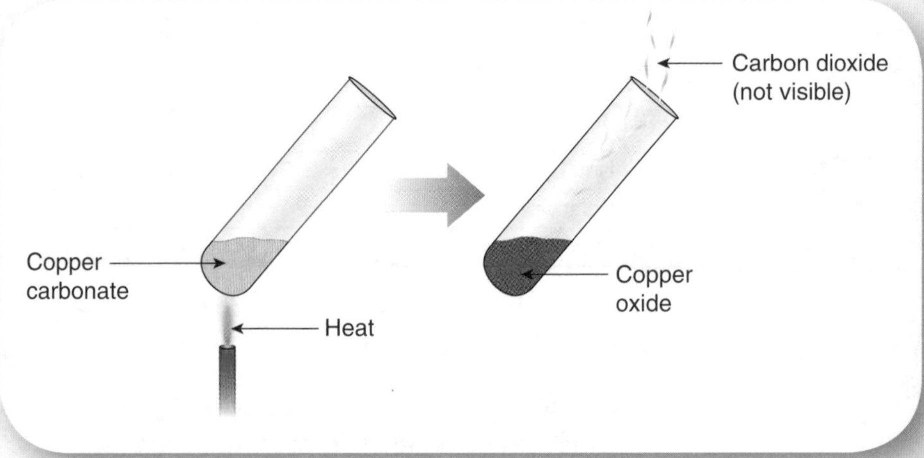
Carbon dioxide
(not visible)
Copper
carbonate
Heat
Copper
oxide

Example:

Starting mass of copper carbonate	= 8.00 g
Final mass of copper oxide	= 5.15 g
Therefore, mass of carbon dioxide released to the atmosphere	= 2.85 g (8.00 g – 5.15 g)

Make cards with the symbol of the element on one side and the relative atomic mass on the reverse.
Use these cards to work out the relative formula mass of the compounds you find in this book.

1. In a chemical reaction the total mass of reactants is 13.60 g. Will the expected mass of all the products be lower, higher or the same as 13.60 g?
2. With reference to the periodic table on page 104 work out the relative formula mass of the following compounds.
   a) NH_4NO_3
   b) $Mg(OH)_2$
3. When 5.0 g of zinc carbonate is heated will the mass of remaining metal oxide be lower, higher or the same as 5.0 g?

Moles and masses

12

Keywords

HT **Mole** ➤ The amount of material containing 6×10^{23} particles

HT **Avogadro's constant** ➤ 6×10^{23} (the number of particles in one mole)

HT Moles and Avogadro's constant

Amounts of chemicals are measured in **moles** (mol). The number of atoms, molecules or ions in a mole of a given substance is 6.02×10^{23}. This value is known as **Avogadro's constant**.

Avogadro's constant = 602 000 000 000 000 000 000 000

For example:

➤ 1 mole of carbon contains 6.02×10^{23} carbon atoms

➤ 1 mole of sulfur dioxide (SO_2) contains 6.02×10^{23} sulfur dioxide molecules.

Moles and relative formula mass

The mass of one mole of a substance in grams is equal to its relative formula mass (M_r).

For example:

➤ The mass of one mole of carbon is 12 g.

➤ The mass of one mole of sulfur dioxide is 64 g.

The number of moles can be calculated using the following formula:

$$\text{moles} = \frac{\text{mass}}{M_r}$$

For example, the number of moles of carbon in 48 g = $\frac{48}{12} = 4$

By rearranging the above equation, the relative formula mass of a compound can be worked out from the number of moles and mass.

Example: Calculate the relative formula mass of the compound given that 0.23 moles has a mass of 36.8 g.

$$M_r = \frac{\text{mass}}{\text{moles}} \qquad M_r = \frac{36.8}{0.23} = 160$$

Amounts of substances in equations

Balanced symbol equations give information about the number of moles of reactants and products. For example:

$$2Mg + O_2 \rightarrow 2MgO$$

This equation tells us that 2 moles of magnesium react with one mole of oxygen to form 2 moles of magnesium oxide.

This means that 48 g of Mg (the mass of 2 moles of Mg) reacts with 32 g of oxygen to form 2 moles of magnesium oxide.

	2Mg	+	O_2	→	2MgO
Number of moles reacting	2		1		2
Relative formula mass	24		32		40
Mass reacting/formed (g)	48		32		80

We can use this relationship between mass and moles to calculate reacting masses.

Example: Calculate the mass of magnesium oxide formed when 12 g of magnesium reacts with an excess of oxygen.

	2Mg	+	O_2	→	2MgO
Number of moles reacting	2		1		2
Relative formula mass	24		32		40
Mass reacting/formed (g)	48		32		80
Reacting mass (g)	12				

To get from 48 to 12 we divide by 4

Therefore to find the mass of magnesium oxide formed we divide 80 by 4

The mass of magnesium oxide formed is therefore 20 g.

Chemical measurements

When a measurement is made during a chemical experiment there is always some uncertainty about the result obtained.

For example, in an experiment to investigate the volume of hydrogen produced when a 2 cm strip of magnesium was reacted with 10 cm^3 of acid, the following results were obtained:

Experiment	1	2	3	4
Volume of hydrogen collected / cm^3	29	28	33	34

The **mean** volume of hydrogen collected is $(29 + 28 + 33 + 34) \div 4 = 31$ cm^3

The **range** of results is 28 cm^3 to 34 cm^3 = 6 cm^3

Therefore, a reasonable estimate of uncertainty is half the range of results. In this case we can say that the average volume of hydrogen collected was 31 cm^3 ± 3 cm^3.

The level of uncertainty can be shown when plotting results on a graph.

The graph below shows experimental results and how the uncertainty can be indicated by drawing **error bars** (ignoring outliers).

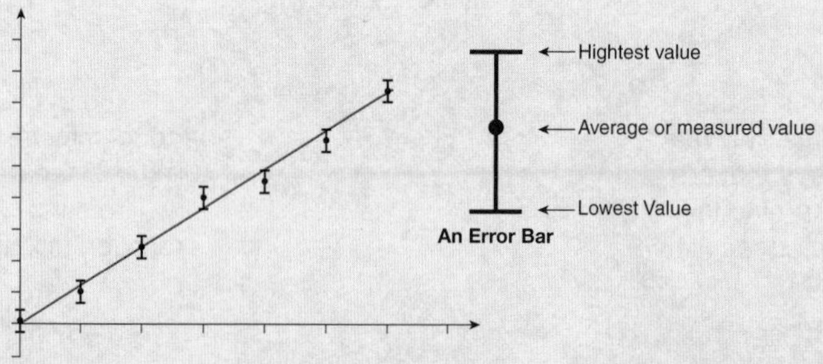

The line of best fit doesn't need to go through all of the data points, but it should go through all of the error bars.

There are also errors associated with any measuring instrument, e.g. a balance. The uncertainty is usually half the smallest scale division.

A balance reads to 0.01g.
The uncertainty is therefore ± 0.005g.

HT Limiting reactants

The reactant that gets used up first in a reactant is called the **limiting reactant**.

For example, when neutralising an acid an excess of metal oxide might be used. The acid is the limiting reactant and determines the amount of products formed in the reaction.

Example 1: 1 mole of magnesium is reacted with 1.5 moles of chlorine and the following reaction occurs.

$$Mg_{(s)} + Cl_{2(g)} \rightarrow MgCl_{2(s)}$$

Which is the limiting reactant and how much product will be formed?

According to the equation, one mole of magnesium reacts with one mole of chlorine. Therefore, the chlorine is in excess / the magnesium is the limiting reactant. One mole of magnesium chloride will be formed.

Example 2: 3g of carbon is reacted with 4g of oxygen as shown in the following equation.

$$C + O_2 \rightarrow CO_2$$

Which is the limiting reactant and what mass of carbon dioxide will be formed?

The equation tells us the reacting ratio of moles. The question gives masses, therefore we need to convert the masses into moles.

Moles of carbon = $3 \div 12 = 0.25$
Moles of oxygen = $4 \div 32 = 0.125$

0.25 moles of carbon requires 0.25 moles of oxygen to react with. As only 0.125 moles of oxygen are available to react, the oxygen is the limiting reactant. Therefore, only 0.125 moles of carbon dioxide will be formed.

HT Use Avogadro's constant to work out how many atoms are in one mole of each of the compounds on this page.

1. HT What is the mass of one mole of $CaCO_3$?
2. HT Using the equation below, calculate the mass sodium oxide formed when 92 g of sodium reacts an excess of oxygen.

$$4Na + O_2 \rightarrow 2Na_2O$$

3. A burette reads to 0.10 cm^3. What is the level of uncertainty in this measurement?
4. HT In the reaction below, 0.3 moles of sodium were added to 0.2 moles of bromine.

$$2Na + Br_2 \rightarrow 2NaBr$$

Which was the limiting reactant?

Percentage yield and atom economy

13

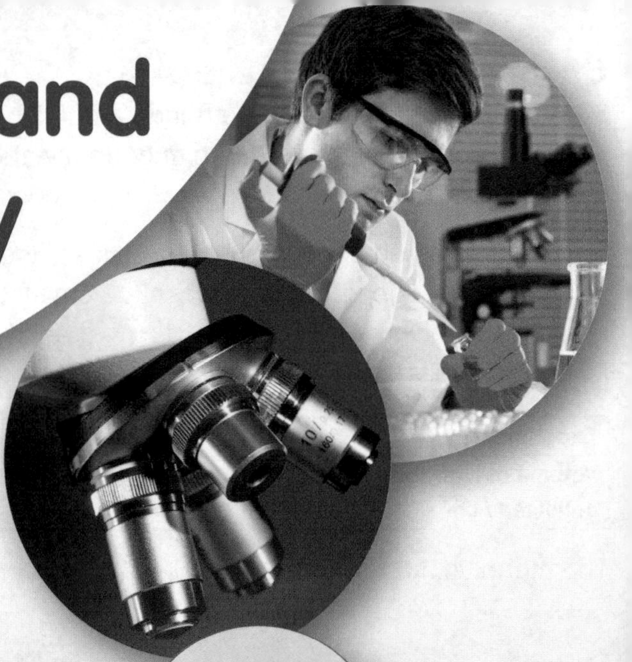

Percentage yield

Balanced symbol equations allow us to work out the mass of products (**yield**) we expect to obtain in a chemical reaction. This is known as the 'theoretical yield'. However, the calculated amount of product may not always be obtained, i.e. the **percentage yield** may not always be 100%.

The actual yield (i.e. the mass of products actually made) compared with the theoretical yield is known as the percentage yield.

$$\% \text{ yield} = \frac{\text{mass of products actually made}}{\text{maximum theoretical mass of product}} \times 100$$

Example: In a chemical reaction the theoretical mass of product is 8.4 g. The mass of product actually obtained was 3.2 g. Calculate the percentage yield for the reaction.

$\% \text{ yield} = \frac{3.2}{8.4} \times 100 = 38\%$

Reasons why the calculated amount of product is not always obtained:

- The reaction may not go to completion because it is reversible
- Some of the reactants may react in ways that are different to the expected reaction
- Some of the product may be lost when it is separated from the reaction mixture

HT

Example: In the following reaction 12.6 g of nitric acid (HNO_3) reacted with an excess of ammonia (NH_3) to form 12.3 g of ammonium nitrate (NH_4NO_3). Calculate the percentage yield for the reaction.

$HNO_3 + NH_3 \rightarrow NH_4NO_3$

Step 1: To calculate the theoretical yield we calculate the expected mass. This is the same calculation as shown on page 30.

The theoretical / expected mass of ammonium nitrate is 16 g.

	NH_3	+ NH_3	→ NH_4NO_3
Number of moles reacting	1	1	1
M_r	63	17	80
Mass reacting / formed in equation (g)	63	÷ 5	80 ÷ 5
Reacting mass (g)	12.6		16

Step 2: Calculate the percentage yield.

$\% \text{ yield} = \frac{12.3}{16} \times 100$

$= 76.9\%$ (to 1 d.p.)

Atom economy

Atom economy is a measure of the amount of starting materials that end up as useful products, i.e. a measure of how much starting material is not wasted.

Reactions with a high atom economy are important for sustainable development and are more economic because of the lack of waste formed and the smaller demand for raw materials.

The percentage atom economy of a reaction is calculated from the balanced equation of the reaction and using the following equation:

Keywords

Yield ➤ The amount of product obtained in a reaction

Percentage yield ➤ The ratio of mass of product obtained to mass of product expected

Atom economy ➤ A measure of the amount of starting materials that end up as useful products

$$\frac{\text{relative formula mass of desired product from equation}}{\text{sum of relative formula masses of all reactants from equation}} \times 100$$

Example 1:

Calculate the atom economy for the production of hydrogen from the following reaction.

$$Mg + 2HCl \rightarrow MgCl_2 + H_2$$

In this case, the 'desired product' is hydrogen. Hydrogen has a relative formula mass (M_r) of 2.

Magnesium chloride is the other product in this reaction. Magnesium chloride has an M_r of 95.

The sum of the relative formula masses of the products is 2 + 95 = 97.

Atom economy $= \frac{2}{97} \times 100$

$= 2.1\%$ (to 1 d.p.)

Example 2:

Ethene (C_2H_4) can be made by the cracking of decane ($C_{10}H_{22}$) according to the equation:

$$C_{10}H_{22} \rightarrow 2C_2H_4 + C_6H_{14}$$

Calculate the atom economy for this method of producing ethene.

The ratios in the balanced equation need to be taken into account:

M_r ethene = 28

M_r hexane (C_6H_{14}) = 86

We need to multiply by 2 because there is a 2 in front of C_2H_4 in the balanced equation for the reaction

Atom economy $= \frac{2 \times 28}{142} \times 100$

Atom economy = 39.4% (to 1 d.p.)

Write each expression from the percentage yield and the atom economy equations on a separate piece of paper. Mix up the pieces of paper and then arrange them so that they show the correct equations.

1. Calculate the percentage yield for a reaction where the actual yield is 3.6g and the expected yield is 5.0 g.
2. Give one reason why the percentage yield for a reaction may not be 100%.
3. Calculate the atom economy for the production of iron in the reaction below.

$$Fe_2O_{3(s)} + 3CO_{(g)} \rightarrow 2Fe_{(l)} + 3CO_{2(g)}$$

Moles, solutions and masses

Concentration of solutions in g/dm³

Many chemical reactions take place in solutions. The concentration of a solution can be measured in mass of **solute** per given volume of solution, e.g. grams per dm^3 ($1\ dm^3 = 1000\ cm^3$).

For example, a solution of 5 g/dm^3 has 5 g of solute dissolved in 1 dm^3 of water. It has half the concentration of a 10 g/dm^3 solution of the same solute.

The mass of solute in a solution can be calculated if the concentration and volume of solution are known.

Example: Calculate the mass of solute in 250 cm^3 of a solution whose concentration is 8 g/dm^3.

Step 1: Divide the mass by 1000 (this gives you the mass of solute in 1 cm^3).

$8 \div 1000 = 0.008\ g/cm^3$

Step 2: Multiply this value by the volume specified.

$0.008 \times 250 = 2\ g$

HT Concentrations of solutions in mol/dm³

Solution concentrations can also be measured in mol/dm^3 (i.e. how many moles of a solute are dissolved in 1 dm^3 (1000 cm^3) of water).

$$\text{moles} = \frac{\text{mass}}{\text{relative formula mass}}$$

If we know the concentration of a solution in g/dm^3, we can work out the concentration in mol/dm^3.

Example: What is the concentration in mol/dm^3 of a 5 g/dm^3 solution of NaOH?

The relative formula mass of NaOH is 40.
The number of moles of NaOH present in 5 g is $\frac{5}{40} = 0.125$.

Therefore the concentration is 0.125 mol/dm^3.

WS Acid–alkali titrations

A **titration** is an accurate technique that you can use to find out *how much* of an acid is needed to neutralise an alkali of known concentration (called a standard solution).

When neutralisation takes place, the hydrogen ions (H^+) from the acid join with the hydroxide ions (OH^-) from the alkali to form water (neutral pH).

hydrogen ion + hydroxide ion ⟶ water molecule

$$H^+_{(aq)} + OH^-_{(aq)} \longrightarrow H_2O_{(l)}$$

Use the following titration method:

1. Wash and rinse a pipette with the alkali that you will use.
2. Use the pipette to measure out a known and accurate volume of the alkali.
3. Place the alkali in a clean, dry conical flask. Add a few drops of a suitable indicator, e.g. phenolphthalein.
4. Place the acid in a burette that has been carefully washed and rinsed with the acid. Take a reading of the volume of acid in the burette (initial reading). Ensure the jet space is filled with acid.
5. Carefully add the acid to the alkali (with swirling of the flask) until the indicator changes colour to show neutrality. This is called the end point. Take a reading of the volume of acid in the burette (final reading).
6. Calculate the volume of acid added (i.e. subtract the initial reading from the final reading).

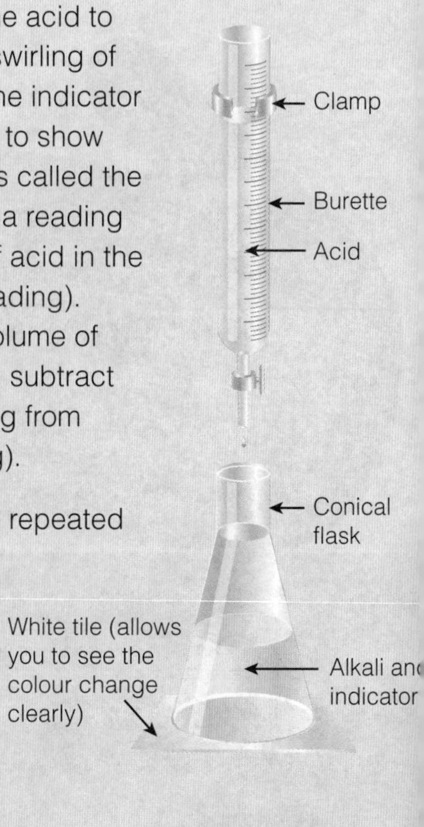

Clamp
Burette
Acid
Conical flask
White tile (allows you to see the colour change clearly)
Alkali and indicator

This method can be repeated to check results.

Keywords

Solute ➤ A solid that dissolves in a liquid to form a solution

Titration ➤ A method used to find the concentration of an acid or alkali

14

HT **Titrations** can also be used to find the **concentration** of an **acid** or **alkali** providing you know either…

- the relative **volumes** of acid and alkali used

or

- the **concentration** of the other acid or alkali.

It will help if you break down the calculation.

1. Write down a **balanced equation** for the reaction to determine the ratio of moles of acid to alkali involved.
2. Calculate the number of moles in the solution of known volume and concentration. (You will know the number of moles in the other solution from your previous calculation.)
3. Calculate the concentration of the other solution using this formula:

$$\text{concentration of solution } (\text{mol/dm}^3 \text{ or M}) = \frac{\text{number of moles of solute (mol)}}{\text{volume of solution } (\text{dm}^3)}$$

Example: A titration is carried out and 0.04 dm^3 hydrochloric acid neutralises 0.08 dm^3 sodium hydroxide of concentration 1 mol dm^{-3}. Calculate the concentration of the hydrochloric acid.

Write the balanced symbol equation for the reaction

$$HCl_{(aq)} + NaOH_{(aq)} \rightarrow NaCl_{(aq)} + H_2O_{(l)}$$

You can see that 1 mol of HCl neutralises 1 mol of NaOH

Rearrange the formula:

number of moles of NaOH = concentration of NaOH × volume of NaOH

$$= 1 \text{ mol/dm}^3 \times 0.08 \text{ dm}^3$$
$$= 0.08 \text{ mol}$$

Number of moles of HCl used up in the reaction is also 0.08 mol

Now calculate the concentration of HCl:

$$\textbf{concentration of HCl} = \frac{\textbf{number of moles of HCl}}{\textbf{volume of HCl}}$$

$$= \frac{0.08 \text{ mol}}{0.04 \text{ dm}^3}$$
$$= 2 \text{ mol/dm}^3$$

Write out each of the steps involved in performing a titration on separate pieces of paper.
Mix them all up and then put them in the correct order.

1. Calculate the mass of solute in 125 cm^3 of a solution whose concentration is 18.4 g/dm^3.
2. HT What is the concentration in mol/dm^3 of a 19.6 g/dm^3 solution of H_2SO_4?
3. HT During a titration, 25.0 cm^3 of sodium hydroxide solution is neutralised by 22.4 cm^3 of 0.8 mol/dm^3 nitric acid. Calculate the concentration of the sodium hydroxide solution in mol/dm^3.
   The equation for the reaction taking place during the titration is:
   $NaOH_{(aq)} + HNO_{3(aq)} \rightarrow NaNO_{3(aq)} + H_2O_{(l)}$

Moles and gases

HT

15

Volumes of gases

The volume of one mole of any gas measured at room temperature and pressure (20°C and 1 atmosphere pressure) is 24 dm^3. Based on this fact, equal volumes of gases contain the same number of moles (when compared under the same temperature and pressure).

number of moles of gas = $\dfrac{\textbf{volume}}{\textbf{24}}$ ← measured in dm^3

Example: At 20°C and 1 atmosphere pressure, how many moles are present in 18 dm^3 of carbon dioxide gas?

$$\text{number of moles of gas} = \frac{18}{24} = 0.75$$

Gas volumes and equations

The volumes of gaseous reactants and products can be calculated from the balanced equation for the reaction.

Example: Calculate the volume of hydrogen gas formed (at room temperature and pressure) when 3 g of magnesium reacts with excess hydrochloric acid. The equation for the reaction is:

$$Mg_{(s)} + 2HCl_{(aq)} \rightarrow MgCl_{2(aq)} + H_{2(g)}$$

Step 1: Work out the mass of hydrogen formed.

The calculations on page 30 show how to work out the mass of hydrogen formed.

Number of moles reacting	1	2	1	1
Relative formula mass	24	36.5	95	2
Mass reacting / formed in equation (g)	24 ÷8	73	95	2
Reacting mass (g)	3			

The mass of hydrogen formed = $\frac{2}{8}$ = 0.25 g

Step 2: Work out the number of moles of hydrogen formed.

$$\text{moles} = \frac{\text{mass}}{M_r}$$

Therefore the number of moles of hydrogen formed = $\frac{0.25}{2}$ = 0.125

Step 3: Work out the volume of hydrogen formed, by rearranging:

$$\text{number of moles of gas} = \frac{\text{volume}}{24}$$

We can work out the volume of hydrogen formed.

number of moles × 24 = volume

0.125 × 24 = 3 dm^3

Therefore, the volume of hydrogen formed in this experiment is 3 dm^3 (3000 cm^3).

Using moles to balance equations

The masses of reactants / products in an equation and the M_r values can be used to work out the balancing numbers in a symbol equation.

Example: Balance the equation below given that 8 g of CH_4 reacts with 32 g of oxygen to form 22 g of CO_2 and 18 g of H_2O

$$...CH_4 + ...O_2 \rightarrow ...CO_2 + ...H_2O$$

Chemical	CH_4	O_2	CO_2	H_2O
Mass (from question)	8	32	22	18
M_r	16	32	44	18
Moles = $\frac{\text{mass}}{M_r}$	$\frac{8}{16} = 0.5$	$\frac{32}{32} = 1$	$\frac{22}{44} = 0.5$	$\frac{18}{18} = 1$

We can make this a whole number ratio by dividing all answers by the smallest answer

÷ 0.5	$\frac{0.5}{0.5} = 1$	$\frac{1}{0.5} = 2$	$\frac{0.5}{0.5} = 1$	$\frac{1}{0.5} = 2$

The balanced equation is therefore:

$$.......CH_4 + ..2...O_2 \rightarrow ....CO_2 + ..2...H_2O$$

0 — 100 ml
APPROX.
20 — 80
40 — 60
60 — 40

Collect 73 empty 330 ml drinks cans. You will be able to picture the volume of one mole of gas at room temperature and pressure. Actually this is slightly more than one mole but only by approximately a quarter of one can!

1. At 20 °C and 1 atmosphere pressure, how many moles are present in 1.5 dm^3 of neon gas?
2. Calculate the volume of carbon dioxide gas formed (at room temperature and pressure) when 40 g of calcium carbonate reacts with excess hydrochloric acid. The equation for the reaction is shown below.

$$CaCO_{3(s)} + 2HCl_{(aq)} \rightarrow CaCl_{2(aq)} + H_2O_{(l)} + CO_{2(g)}$$

3. Balance the equation below for the reaction that occurs when 7 g of silicon reacts with 35.5 g of chlorine to form 42.5 g of silicon chloride.

$$..........Si + ...Cl_2 \rightarrow ....SiCl_4$$

Mind map

QUANTITATIVE CHEMISTRY

- **Mass in equations**
  - Conservation of mass → Total mass of reactants = total mass of products
  - Relative formula mass → The sum of the individual atomic masses in a molecule
  - Mass of solid reactants may increase during a reaction, e.g. copper + oxygen
  - Mass of solid reactants may decrease during a reaction, e.g. thermal decomposition
  - Percentage yield → $\% \text{ yield} = \dfrac{\text{mass of products actually made}}{\text{maximum theoretical mass of product}} \times 100$
  - Atom economy → $\dfrac{\text{relative formula mass of desired product from equation}}{\text{sum of relative formula masses of all reactants from equation}} \times 100$
- **Moles**
  - HT Avogadro's constant (the number of particles in one mole) → 6.02×10^{23}
  - HT Limiting reactants
  - HT $\text{moles} = \dfrac{\text{mass}}{\text{relative formula mass}}$
  - HT $\text{moles of a gas} = \dfrac{\text{volume (in dm}^3\text{)}}{24}$
  - HT $\text{moles in solution} = \dfrac{\text{volume} \times \text{concentration}}{1000}$ → Use to perform titration calculations
  - Chemical measurement → Estimating uncertainty

Practice questions

1. Calcium carbonate thermally decomposes when heated to form calcium oxide and carbon dioxide gas.

   The equation for the reaction is shown below.

   $$CaCO_{3(s)} \rightarrow CaO_{(s)} + CO_{2(g)}$$

   In an experiment, a student placed 10 g of $CaCO_3$ in a crucible and heated it strongly for 10 minutes.

   a) Will the mass of solid in the crucible at the end of the experiment be higher or lower than 10 g? Explain your answer. **(2 marks)**

   b) With reference to the periodic table (see page 104), what is the relative formula mass of calcium carbonate? **(1 mark)**

   HT **c)** Calculate the mass of carbon dioxide that would be produced in this experiment. **(2 marks)**

   In another experiment, the student investigated the reaction of magnesium with oxygen.

   The equation for the reaction is shown below.

   $$2Mg_{(s)} + O_{2(g)} \rightarrow 2\,MgO_{(s)}$$

   The student heated 0.15 g of magnesium and at the end of the experiment she had made 0.20 g of magnesium oxide.

   HT **d)** How many atoms of magnesium are there in 0.15 g of magnesium? (Avogadro's constant is 6×10^{23}) **(2 marks)**

   e) The teacher said that 0.25 g of magnesium oxide was expected to have been made in this experiment.

   Calculate the percentage yield. **(1 mark)**

2. During a titration, 22.50 cm³ of 0.20 mol/dm³ hydrochloric acid neutralised 25.00 cm³ of sodium hydroxide solution.

   The equation for the reaction is shown below.

   $$NaOH_{(aq)} + HCl_{(aq)} \rightarrow NaCl_{(aq)} + H_2O_{(l)}$$

   a) How many moles are present in 22.50 cm³ of 0.20 mol/dm³ hydrochloric acid? **(1 mark)**

   b) How many moles of sodium hydroxide were present in the 25.00 cm³ of sodium hydroxide? Explain your answer. **(2 marks)**

   c) Calculate the concentration of the sodium hydroxide solution in mol/dm³. **(2 marks)**

   d) Calculate the concentration of the sodium hydroxide solution in g/dm³. **(2 marks)**

Reactivity of metals and metal extraction

16

Keywords

Oxidation ➤ A reaction involving the gain of oxygen (HT) or the loss of electrons

Reduction ➤ A reaction involving the loss of oxygen (HT) or the gain of electrons

Reaction of metals with oxygen

Many metals react with oxygen to form metal oxides, for example:

copper + oxygen ⟶ copper oxide

These reactions are called **oxidation** reactions. Oxidation reactions take place when a chemical gains oxygen.

When a substance loses oxygen it is called a **reduction** reaction.

The reactivity series

When metals react they form positive ions. The more easily the metal forms a positive ion the more reactive the metal.

Calcium and magnesium are both in group 2 of the periodic table so will form 2^+ ions when they react. Calcium is more reactive than magnesium so it has a greater tendency/is more likely to form the 2^+ ion.

Decreasing reactivity ↓

Metal	Reaction with water	Reaction with acid
Potassium	Very vigorous	Explosive
Sodium	Vigorous	Dangerous
Lithium	Steady	Very vigorous
Calcium	Steady fizzing and bubbling	Vigorous
Magnesium	Slow reaction	Steady fizzing and bubbling
***Carbon**		
Zinc	Very slow reaction	Gentle fizzing and bubbling
Iron	Extremely slow	Slight fizzing and bubbling
***Hydrogen**		
Copper	No reaction	No reaction
Gold	No reaction	No reaction

* included for comparison

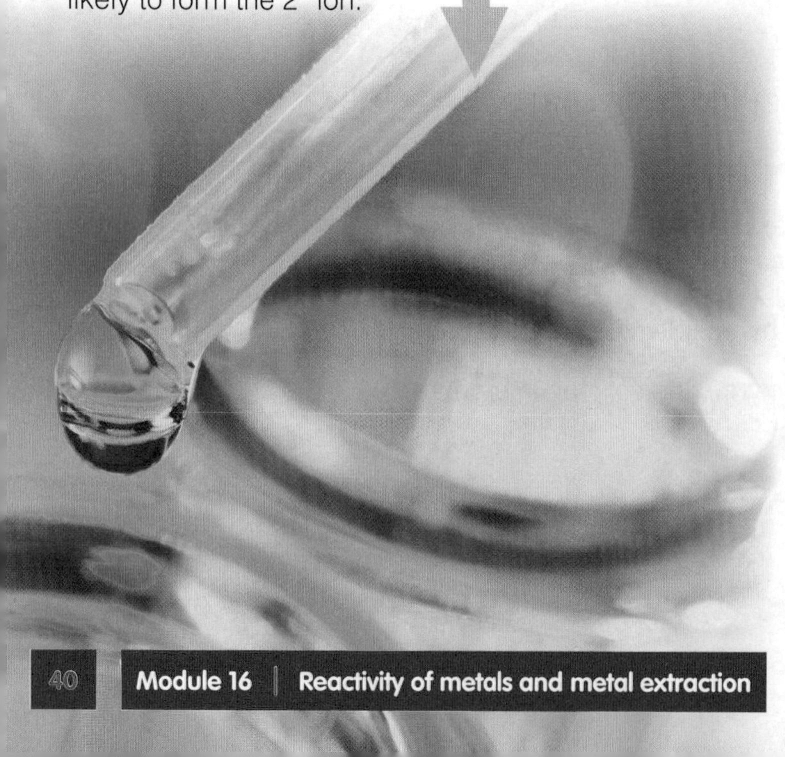

The reactivity series can also be used to predict displacement reactions.

zinc + copper oxide ⟶ zinc oxide + copper

In this reaction…

- zinc displaces (i.e. takes the place of) copper
- zinc is oxidised (i.e. it gains oxygen)
- copper oxide is reduced (i.e. it loses oxygen).

Extraction of metals and reduction

Unreactive metals, such as gold, are found in the Earth's crust as pure metals. Most metals are found as compounds and chemical reactions are required to extract the metal. The method of extraction depends on the position of the metal in the reactivity series.

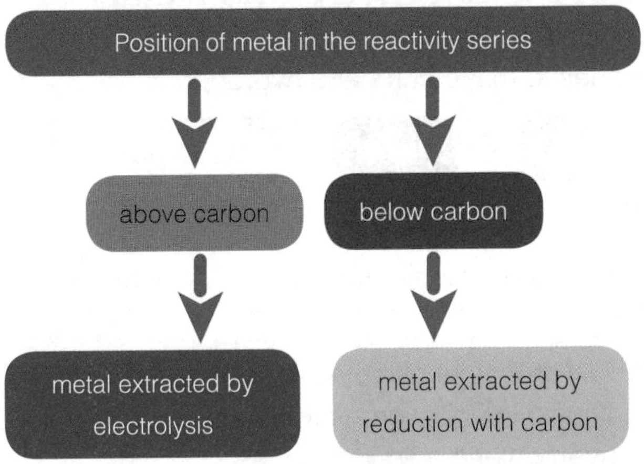

For example, iron is found in the earth as iron(III) oxide, Fe_2O_3. The iron(III) oxide can be reduced by reacting it with carbon.

The Fe_2O_3 is reduced to Fe

$$2Fe_2O_3 + 3C \rightarrow 4Fe + 3CO_2$$

The C is oxidised to CO_2

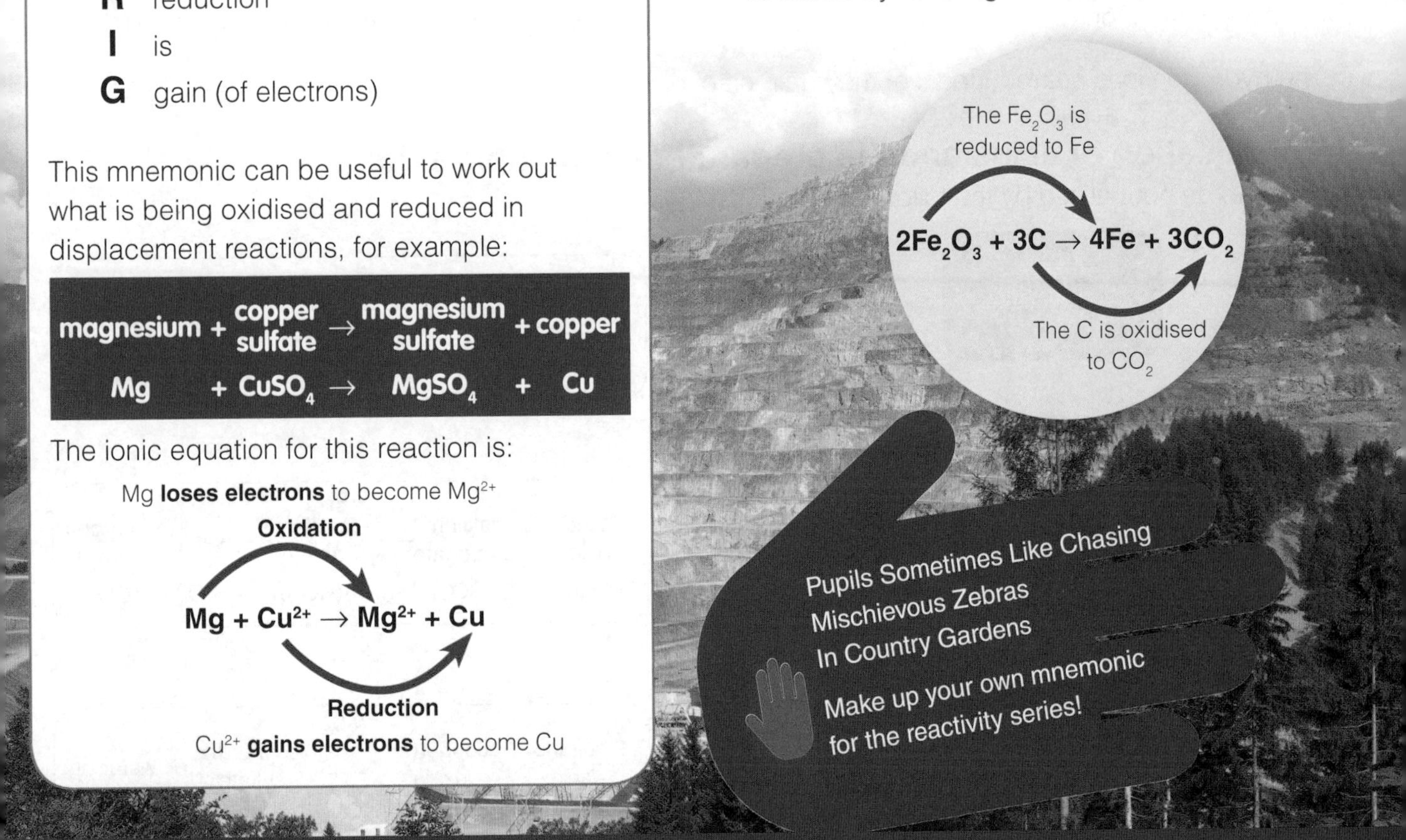

HT Oxidation and reduction in terms of electrons

Oxidation and reduction can also be defined in terms of electrons:

O oxidation
I is
L loss (of electrons)
R reduction
I is
G gain (of electrons)

This mnemonic can be useful to work out what is being oxidised and reduced in displacement reactions, for example:

magnesium	+	copper sulfate	$\rightarrow$	magnesium sulfate	+	copper
Mg	+	$CuSO_4$	$\rightarrow$	$MgSO_4$	+	Cu

The ionic equation for this reaction is:

Mg **loses electrons** to become Mg^{2+}

Oxidation

$$Mg + Cu^{2+} \rightarrow Mg^{2+} + Cu$$

Reduction

Cu^{2+} **gains electrons** to become Cu

Pupils Sometimes Like Chasing Mischievous Zebras In Country Gardens

Make up your own mnemonic for the reactivity series!

1. Write a word equation for the oxidation of magnesium to form magnesium oxide.
2. Both sodium and lithium react to form 1+ ions. Which one of these metals has a greater tendency/is more likely to form this ion?
3. Name two metals from the reactivity series that are extracted by reduction with carbon.
4. HT In the equation below, which species is oxidised and which one is reduced?

$$Mg + Zn^{2+} \rightarrow Mg^{2+} + Zn$$

Reactions of acids

Reactions of acids with metals

Acids react with metals that are above hydrogen in the reactivity series to make **salts** and hydrogen.

Acid + **Metal** → Salt + Hydrogen

For example:

magnesium + hydrochloric acid ⟶ magnesium chloride + hydrogen

(This is a salt → magnesium chloride)

HT

The reactions of metals with acids are **redox** reactions. The ionic equation for the reaction of magnesium with hydrochloric acid is:

$$Mg + 2H^+ \rightarrow Mg^{2+} + H_2$$

The metal (in this case magnesium) is oxidised, i.e. it loses electrons.

The hydrogen ions are reduced, i.e. they gain electrons.

Mg is **oxidised**, i.e. it loses electrons (to form Mg^{2+})

$$Mg + 2H^+ \rightarrow Mg^{2+} + H_2$$

H^+ is **reduced**, i.e. it gains electrons (to form H_2)

Neutralisation of acids and the preparation of soluble salts

Acids can be neutralised by the following reactions.

Acid +

- **Alkali** (soluble metal hydroxides) → Forms a salt + water → **e.g.** hydrochloric acid + sodium hydroxide ⟶ sodium chloride + water
  $HCl_{(aq)} + NaOH_{(aq)} \longrightarrow NaCl_{(aq)} + H_2O_{(l)}$
- **Metal carbonates** → Forms a salt + water + carbon dioxide → **e.g.** nitric acid + calcium carbonate ⟶ calcium nitrate + water + carbon dioxide
  $2HNO_{3\,(aq)} + CaCO_{3\,(s)} \longrightarrow Ca(NO_3)_{2\,(aq)} + H_2O_{(l)} + CO_{2\,(g)}$
- **Base** (insoluble metal hydroxides and metal oxides) → Forms a salt + water → **e.g.** sulfuric acid + copper(II) oxide ⟶ copper(II) sulfate + water
  $H_2SO_{4\,(aq)} + CuO_{(s)} \longrightarrow CuSO_{4\,(aq)} + H_2O_{(l)}$

The first part of the salt formed contains the positive ion (usually the metal) from the alkali, base or carbonate followed by…

- chloride if hydrochloric acid was used
- sulfate if sulfuric acid was used
- nitrate if nitric acid was used.

For example, when calcium hydroxide is reacted with sulfuric acid, the salt formed is calcium sulfate.

Preparation of soluble salts

Soluble salts can be prepared by the following method.

Add solid to the acid until no more reacts → Filter off the excess solid → Obtain the solid salt by **crystallisation**

Keywords

Salt ➤ A product of the reaction that occurs when an acid is neutralised

HT **Redox** ➤ A reaction in which both oxidation and reduction occur

Crystallisation ➤ A method used to separate a soluble solid from its solution when you want to collect the solid

For example, copper(II) sulfate crystals can be made by reacting copper(II) oxide with sulfuric acid.

Add copper(II) oxide to sulfuric acid → Filter to remove any unreacted copper(II) oxide → Evaporate to leave behind blue crystals of the 'salt' copper(II) sulfate

17

Write examples of neutralisation reactions on pieces of paper or card. Stick them on a wall near where you study, so that you regularly see them.

1. Write a word equation for the reaction that occurs when zinc reacts with sulfuric acid.
2. (HT) Identify the species that is oxidised in the following reaction.

$$Fe + 2H^{+} \longrightarrow Fe^{2+} + H_2$$

3. Other than an alkali, name a substance that can neutralise an acid.
4. Name the salt formed when lithium oxide reacts with nitric acid.
5. What are the three main steps in preparing a soluble salt from an acid and a metal oxide?

18

pH, neutralisation, acid strength and electrolysis

Indicators, the pH scale and neutralisation reactions

Indicators are useful dyes that become different colours in acids and alkalis.

Indicator	Colour in acid	Colour in alkali
Litmus	Red	Blue
Phenolphthalein	Colourless	Pink
Methyl orange	Pink	Yellow

The pH scale measures the acidity or alkalinity of a solution. The pH scale runs from 0 to 14 and the pH of a solution can be measured using universal indicator or a pH probe.

0 1 2 3 4 5 6 7 8 9 10 11 12 13 14
Neutral
Strongly acidic
Slightly acidic
Slightly alkaline
Strongly alkaline

Acids are solutions that contain hydrogen ions (H^+). The higher the concentration of hydrogen ions, the more acidic the solution (i.e. the lower the pH).

Alkalis are solutions that contain hydroxide ions (OH^-). The higher the concentration of hydroxide ions, the more alkaline the solution (i.e. the higher the pH).

When an acid is neutralised by an alkali, the hydrogen ions from the acid react with the hydroxide ions in the alkali to form water.

$$H^+_{(aq)} + OH^-_{(aq)} \rightarrow H_2O_{(l)}$$

HT **Strong acids**, such as hydrochloric, sulfuric and nitric acids, are those that completely ionise in aqueous solution. For example:

$$HCl_{(aq)} \rightarrow H^+_{(aq)} + Cl^-_{(aq)}$$

This means dissolved in water

Weak acids, such as ethanoic, citric and carbonic acids, only partially ionise in water. For example:

$$CH_3COOH_{(aq)} \rightleftharpoons CH_3COO^-_{(aq)} + H^+_{(aq)}$$

This sign means that the reaction is reversible, i.e. that the acid does not fully ionise

The pH of an acid is a measure of the concentration of hydrogen ions. When two different acids of the same concentration have different pH values the strongest acid will have the lowest pH.

The pH scale is a logarithmic scale. As the pH decreases by 1 unit (e.g. from 3 to 2) the hydrogen ion concentration increases by a factor of 10.

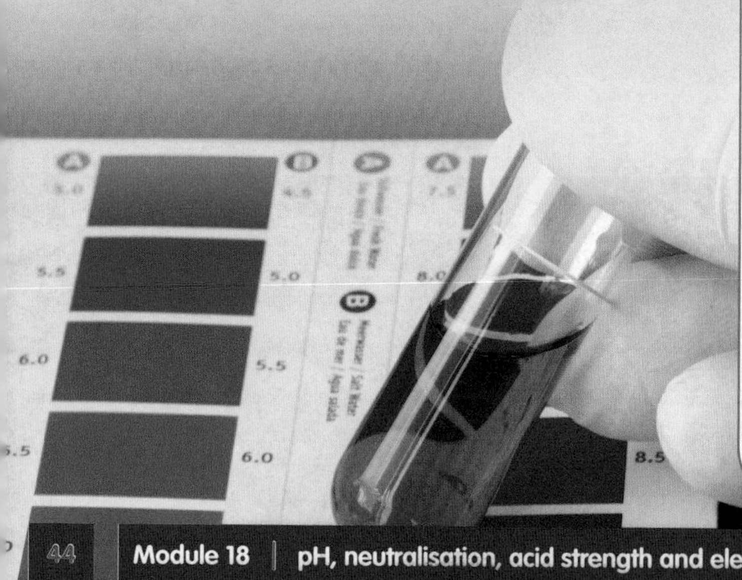

Electrolysis

An electric current is the flow of electrons through a conductor but it can also flow by the movement of ions through a solution or a liquid.

Covalent compounds do not contain free electrons or ions that can move. So they will not conduct electricity when solid, liquid, gas or in solution.

The ions in:

- an **ionic solid** are fixed and cannot move
- an **ionic substance** that is **molten** or in **solution** are free to move.

Electrolysis is a chemical reaction that involves passing electricity through an **electrolyte**. An electrolyte is a liquid that conducts electricity. Electrolytes are either molten ionic compounds or solutions of ionic compounds. Electrolytes are decomposed during electrolysis.

- The positive ions (**cations**) move to, and discharge at, the negative electrode (**cathode**).
- The negative ions (**anions**) move to, and discharge at, the positive electrode (**anode**).

Electrons are removed from the anions at the anode. These electrons then flow around the circuit to the cathode and are transferred to the cations.

Keywords

HT **Strong acid** ➤ An acid that fully ionises when dissolved

HT **Weak acid** ➤ An acid that partially ionises when dissolved in water

Electrolyte ➤ A liquid or solution containing ions that is broken down during electrolysis

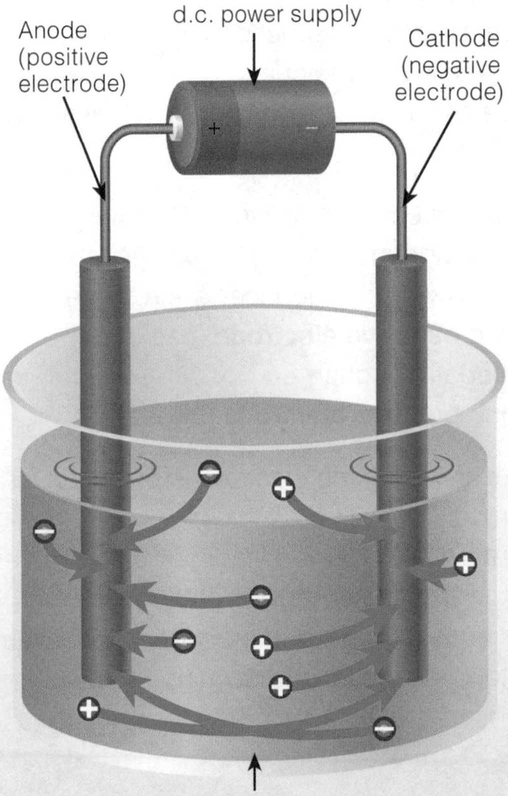

Colour pieces of paper in different colours on the pH scale. On the back of each, write the pH number that each colour corresponds to.
Mix up the pieces of paper, then practise putting them into the right order.

1. What type of substance has a pH of less than 7?
2. Which ion is responsible for solutions being alkaline?
3. Write an ionic equation for the reaction that takes place when an acid is neutralised by an alkali.
4. HT What is the difference between a strong acid and a weak acid?
5. Why must electrolytes be in the liquid state?

Applications of electrolysis

19

Keywords
Cathode ➤ The negative electrode
Anode ➤ The positive electrode

Electrolysis of molten ionic compounds

When an ionic compound melts, electrostatic forces between the charged ions in the crystal lattice are broken down, meaning that the ions are free to move.

When a direct current is passed through a molten ionic compound:

- positively charged ions are attracted towards the **negative electrode** (cathode)
- negatively charged ions are attracted towards the **positive electrode** (anode).

For example, in the electrolysis of molten lead bromide:

- positively charged lead ions are attracted towards the **cathode**, forming lead
- negatively charged bromide ions are attracted towards the **anode**, forming bromine.

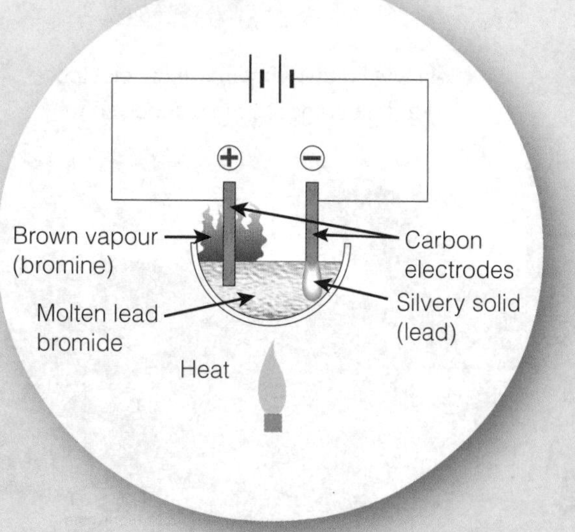
+
−
Brown vapour (bromine)
Carbon electrodes
Silvery solid (lead)
Molten lead bromide
Heat

When ions get to the oppositely charged electrode they are **discharged** – they lose their charge. For example, in the electrolysis of molten lead bromide, the non-metal ion loses electrons to the positive electrode to form a bromine atom. The bromine atom then bonds with a second atom to form a bromine molecule.

WS Using electrolysis to extract metals

Aluminium is the most abundant metal in the Earth's crust. It must be obtained from its ore by electrolysis because it is too reactive to be extracted by heating with carbon. The electrodes are made of graphite (a type of carbon). The aluminium ore (bauxite) is purified to leave aluminium oxide, which is then melted so that the ions can move. Cryolite is added to increase the conductivity and lower the melting point.

When a current passes through the molten mixture:

- positively charged aluminium ions move towards the negative electrode (**cathode**) and form aluminium
- negatively charged oxygen ions move towards the positive electrode (**anode**) and form oxygen.

The positive electrodes gradually wear away (because the graphite electrodes react with the oxygen to form carbon dioxide gas). This means they have to be replaced every so often. Extracting aluminium can be quite an expensive process because of the cost of the large amounts of electrical energy needed to carry it out.

Bauxite

Aluminium rods

Electrolysis of aqueous solutions

When a solution undergoes electrolysis, there is also water present. During electrolysis water molecules break down into hydrogen ions and hydroxide ions.

$$H_2O_{(l)} \rightarrow H^+_{(aq)} + OH^-_{(aq)}$$

This means that when an aqueous compound is electrolysed there are two cations present (H^+ from water and the metal cation from the compound) and two anions present (OH^- from water and the anion from the compound).

Solution	Product at cathode	Product at anode
copper chloride	copper	chlorine
sodium sulfate	hydrogen	oxygen
water (diluted with sulfuric acid to aid conductivity)	hydrogen	oxygen

For example, in copper(II) sulfate solution...

- cations present: Cu^{2+} and H^+
- anions present: SO_4^{2-} and OH^-

At the positive electrode (anode): *Oxygen is produced unless the solution contains halide ions.* In this case the oxygen is produced.

At the negative electrode (cathode): *The least reactive element is formed.* The reactivity series in Module 16 will be helpful here. In this case, hydrogen is formed.

HT Half-equations

During electrolysis, the cation that is discharged at the cathode gains electrons (is reduced) to form the element. For example:

$$Cu^{2+} + 2e^- \rightarrow Cu$$

$$2H^+ + 2e^- \rightarrow H_2$$

At the anode the anion loses electrons (is oxidised). For example:

$$2Cl^- \rightarrow Cl_2 + 2e^-$$

this can also be written as $2Cl^- - 2e^- \rightarrow Cl_2$

$$4OH^- \rightarrow O_2 + 2H_2O + 4e^-$$

or $4OH^- - 4e^- \rightarrow O_2 + 2H_2O$

Try making a model to show how the ions move during electrolysis.

Example:

What are the three products of the electrolysis of sodium chloride solution?

Cations present: Na^+ and H^+

Q. What happens at the cathode?

A. Hydrogen is less reactive than sodium therefore hydrogen gas is formed.

Anions present: Cl^- and OH^-

Q. What happens at the anode?

A. A halide ion (Cl^-) is present therefore chlorine will be formed.

The sodium ions and hydroxide ions stay in solution (i.e. sodium hydroxide solution remains).

WS How aqueous solutions can be electrolysed in the laboratory

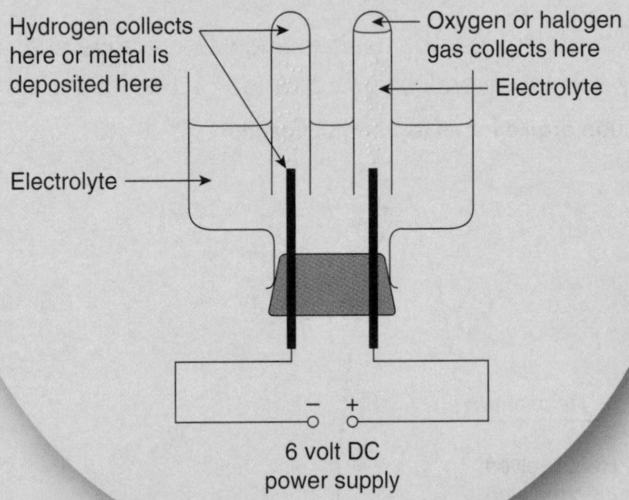
Hydrogen collects here or metal is deposited here
Oxygen or halogen gas collects here
Electrolyte
Electrolyte
–
+
6 volt DC power supply

1. When molten potassium iodide is electrolysed, what will be formed at the cathode and anode?
2. When aqueous potassium iodide is electrolysed, what will be formed at the cathode and anode?
3. HT When aqueous copper(II) sulfate is electrolysed, oxygen gas is formed at the anode. Write a half-equation for this oxidation reaction.

Energy changes in reactions

20

Keywords

Exothermic ➤ A reaction in which energy is given out

Endothermic ➤ A reaction in which energy is taken in

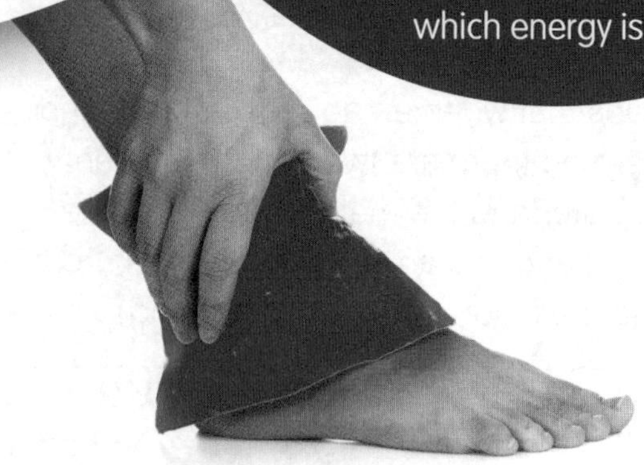

Exothermic and endothermic reactions

Energy is not created or destroyed during chemical reactions, i.e. the amount of energy in the universe at the end of a chemical reaction is the same as before the reaction takes place.

Type of reaction	Is energy given out or taken in?	What happens to the temperature of the surroundings?
Exothermic	out	increases
Endothermic	in	decreases

Examples of **exothermic** reactions include…
- combustion
- neutralisation
- many oxidation reactions
- precipitation reactions
- displacement reactions.

Everyday applications of exothermic reactions include self-heating cans and hand warmers.

Examples of **endothermic** reactions include…
- thermal decomposition
- the reaction between citric acid and sodium hydrogen carbonate.

Some changes, such as dissolving salts in water, can be either exothermic or endothermic. Some sports injury packs are based on endothermic reactions.

Reaction profiles

For a chemical reaction to occur, the reacting particles must collide together with sufficient energy. The minimum amount of energy that the particles must have in order to react is known as the 'activation energy'.

Reaction profiles can be used to show the relative energies of reactants and products, the activation energy and the overall energy change of a reaction.

Reaction profile for an exothermic reaction

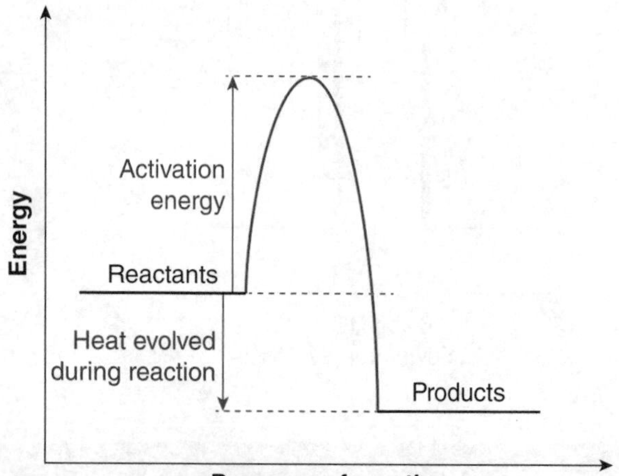
Energy
Activation energy
Reactants
Heat evolved during reaction
Products
Progress of reaction

Reaction profile for an endothermic reaction

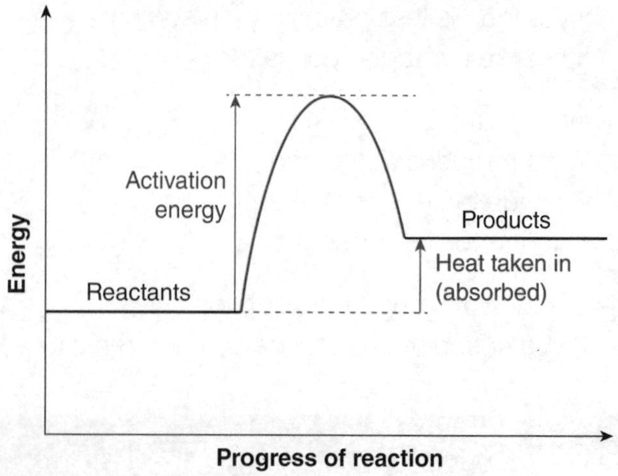
Energy
Activation energy
Reactants
Products
Heat taken in (absorbed)
Progress of reaction

Chemical reactions in which more energy is made when new bonds are made than was used to break the existing bonds are **exothermic**.

Chemical reactions in which more energy is used to break the existing bonds than is released in making the new bonds are **endothermic**.

HT The energy change of reactions

During a chemical reaction:

- bonds are broken in the reactant molecules – this is an endothermic process

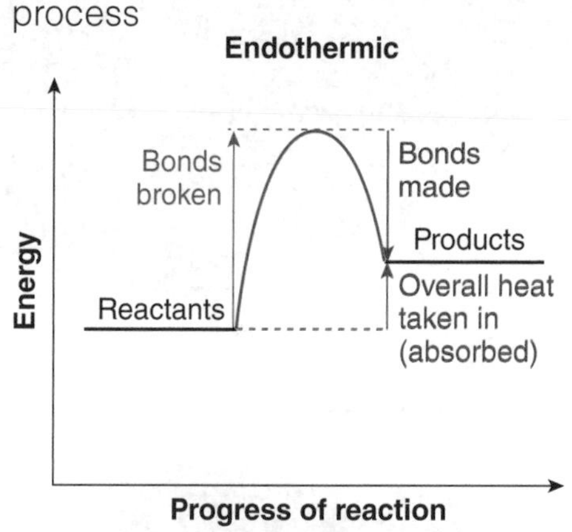
Endothermic
Energy
Bonds broken
Bonds made
Products
Reactants
Overall heat taken in (absorbed)
Progress of reaction

- bonds are made to form the product molecules – this is an exothermic process.

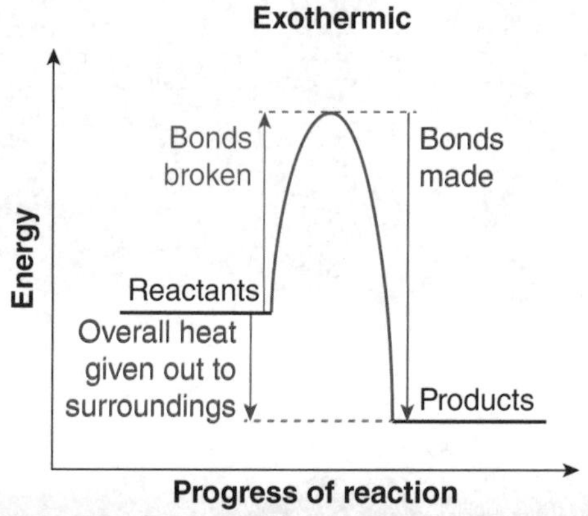
Exothermic
Energy
Bonds broken
Bonds made
Reactants
Overall heat given out to surroundings
Products
Progress of reaction

Example:

Hydrogen is burned in oxygen to produce water:

$$\text{hydrogen} + \text{oxygen} \rightarrow \text{water}$$

$$2H_{2(g)} + O_{2(g)} \rightarrow 2H_2O_{(l)}$$

$$2H{-}H + O{=}O \rightarrow 2H{-}O{-}H$$

The following are **bond energies** for the **reactants** and **products**:

H–H is 436 kJ   O=O is 496 kJ   O–H is 463 kJ

Calculate the energy change.

You can calculate the energy change using this method:

1. Calculate the energy used to break bonds:

$(2 \times H{-}H) + O{=}O = (2 \times 436) + 496 =$ **1368 kJ**

2. Calculate the energy released when new bonds are made:

(Water is made up of 2 × O–H bonds.)

$2 \times H{-}O{-}H = 2 \times (2 \times 463) =$ **1852 kJ**

Energy change (ΔH) = energy used to break bonds – energy released when new bonds are made

$\Delta H = 1368 - 1852$

$\Delta H =$ **–484 kJ**

The reaction is **exothermic** because the energy from making the bonds is **more than** the energy needed to break the bonds.

Pull apart 'things' that are 'bonded' together, such as a pen from its lid. You have to use energy to separate the pen from the lid just like you have to use energy to break chemical 'things' that are 'bonded' together!

1. What happens to the temperature of the surroundings when an endothermic reaction takes place?
2. Draw and label a reaction profile for an exothermic reaction.
3. The energy required to break the bonds in a reaction is 2314 kJ. The energy released when the new bonds are made is 3613 kJ. What is the energy change for this reaction?
4. Is the reaction in question 3 exothermic or endothermic? Explain your answer.

Chemical cells and fuel cells

21

Keywords

Chemical cell ➤ A system containing chemicals that react together to produce electricity

Battery ➤ A combination of cells connected in series

Fuel cell ➤ A chemical cell where the source of fuel is supplied externally

Cells and batteries

Cells contain chemicals which react to produce electricity. A typical cell consists of two different metals in contact with an electrolyte.

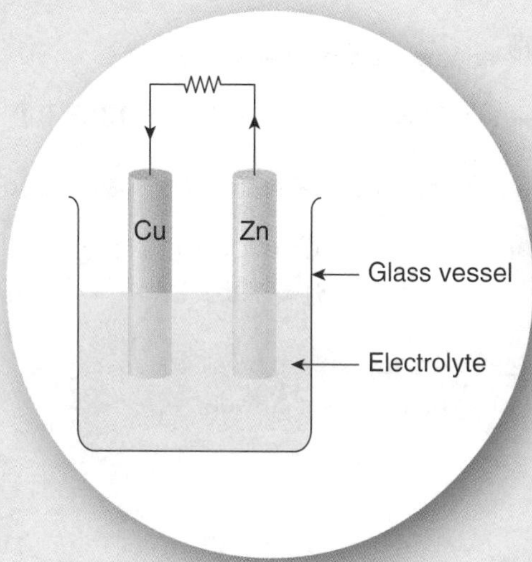

Everyday chemical 'cells'

Electricity flows from the more reactive metal to the less reactive metal. In the above case, electricity would flow through the wire from the zinc to the copper.

The voltage produced by a cell depends upon many factors including…

- the type of metal used as the electrode
- the chemical used as the electrolyte.

A battery consists of two or more **chemical cells** connected together in series to provide a greater voltage.

In non-rechargeable cells and **batteries**, such as alkaline batteries, when one of the reactants has been used up the chemical reactions stop, meaning that electricity is no longer produced.

Look at old batteries in your home. Can you see what chemicals they contain?

Fuel cells

Fuel cells differ from cells in that they are supplied by an external source of fuel, for example, hydrogen together with oxygen or air. The fuel is oxidised electrochemically within the cell to produce a potential difference.

The diagram on the right shows a simple fuel cell.

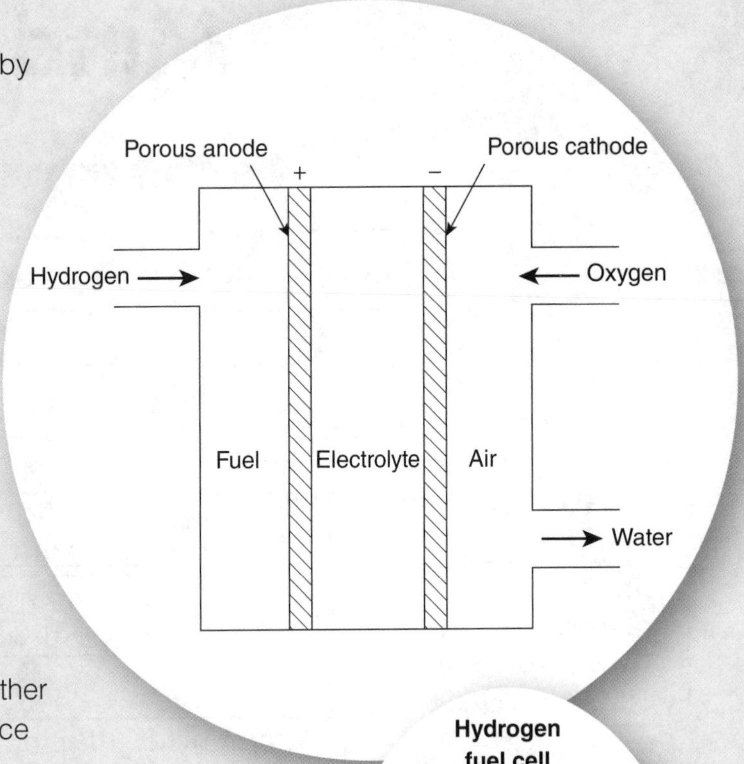

The overall reaction in a hydrogen fuel cell (a fuel cell where hydrogen is the fuel) involves the oxidation of hydrogen to produce water.

$$2H_{2(g)} + O_{2(g)} \rightarrow 2H_2O_{(g)}$$

As water is the only waste product, fuel cells can be said to be more environmentally friendly than some other sources of energy (such as fossil fuels), which produce carbon dioxide.

Hydrogen fuel cell

Fuel cells, provided that they are constantly supplied with fuel and oxygen, do not run out in the same way that alkaline batteries do and while they are limited in their use they represent a potential alternative to rechargeable cells and batteries.

Half-equations for the reactions taking place in the hydrogen fuel cell

Where hydrogen is the fuel used in a fuel cell, the following reactions take place at the electrodes.

Anode: $H_{2(g)} \rightarrow 2H^+_{(aq)} + 2e^-$

Cathode: $4H^+_{(aq)} + O_{2(g)} + 4e^- \rightarrow 2H_2O_{(g)}$

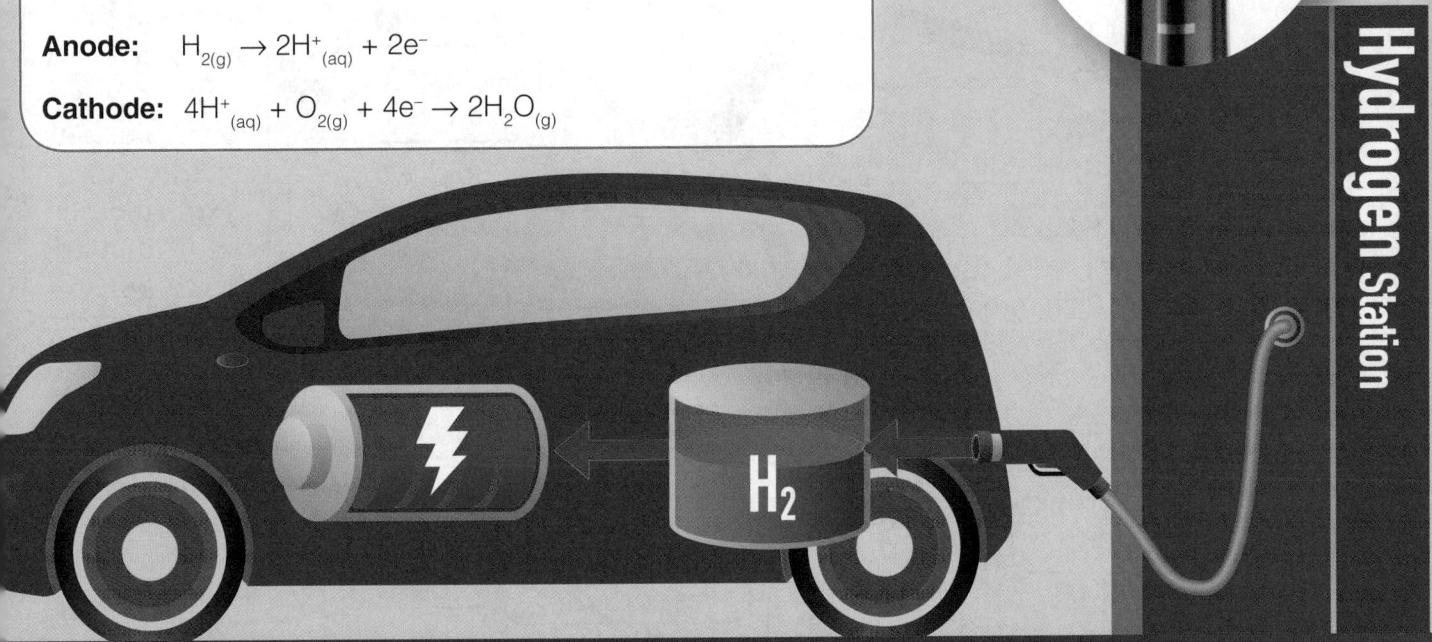

1. What is a 'chemical cell'?
2. What is the main difference between a fuel cell and a chemical cell?
3. What is the waste product from a hydrogen fuel cell?
4. Write the half-equation for the reaction that takes place at the cathode of a hydrogen fuel cell.

Mind map

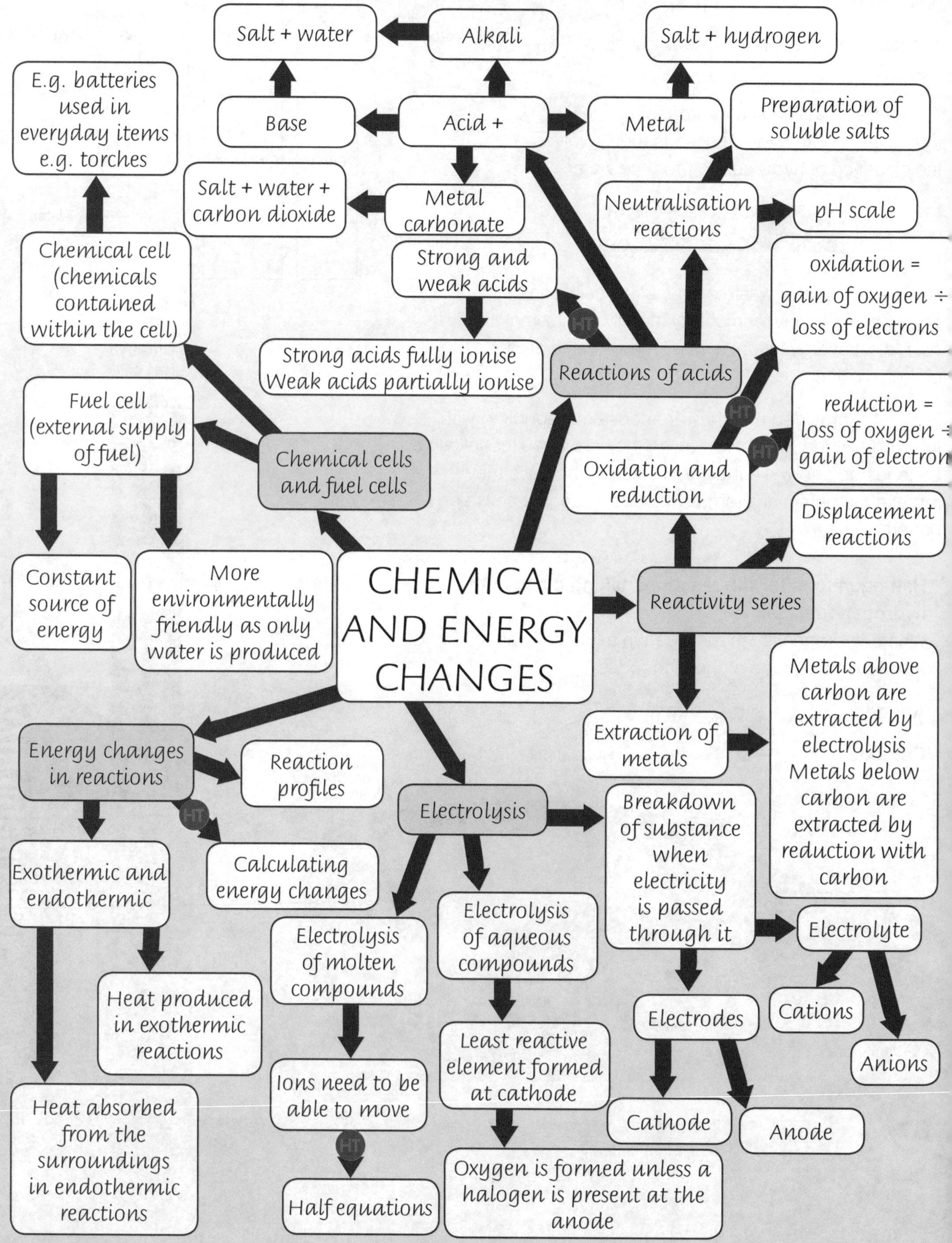
CHEMICAL AND ENERGY CHANGES
Reactions of acids
Acid +
Alkali
Salt + water
Base
Salt + water
Metal
Salt + hydrogen
Metal carbonate
Salt + water + carbon dioxide
Strong and weak acids
Strong acids fully ionise Weak acids partially ionise
Neutralisation reactions
Preparation of soluble salts
pH scale
Oxidation and reduction
oxidation = gain of oxygen ÷ loss of electrons
reduction = loss of oxygen ÷ gain of electron
HT
Reactivity series
Displacement reactions
Extraction of metals
Metals above carbon are extracted by electrolysis Metals below carbon are extracted by reduction with carbon
Chemical cells and fuel cells
Chemical cell (chemicals contained within the cell)
E.g. batteries used in everyday items e.g. torches
Fuel cell (external supply of fuel)
Constant source of energy
More environmentally friendly as only water is produced
Energy changes in reactions
Reaction profiles
Calculating energy changes
Exothermic and endothermic
Heat produced in exothermic reactions
Heat absorbed from the surroundings in endothermic reactions
Electrolysis
Breakdown of substance when electricity is passed through it
Electrolyte
Cations
Anions
Electrodes
Cathode
Anode
Electrolysis of molten compounds
Ions need to be able to move
Half equations
Electrolysis of aqueous compounds
Least reactive element formed at cathode
Oxygen is formed unless a halogen is present at the anode

Practice questions

1. Zinc is found in the Earth's crust as zinc oxide.

   a) Write a balanced symbol equation for the reaction between zinc and oxygen to form zinc oxide. **(1 mark)**

   b) Zinc can be extracted by reacting the zinc oxide with magnesium, as shown in the equation below.

   $Mg + ZnO \rightarrow MgO + Zn$

   Which species has been reduced in this reaction?
   Explain your answer. **(2 marks)**

   c) Is zinc more or less reactive than magnesium?
   Explain your answer with reference to the above equation. **(2 marks)**

   d) Would you expect zinc metal to normally be extracted from its ore by electrolysis or by reduction with carbon? Explain your answer. **(2 marks)**

   HT **e)** Zinc will react with copper solutions according to the ionic equation below.

   $Zn_{(s)} + Cu^{2+}_{(aq)} \rightarrow Zn^{2+}_{(aq)} + Cu_{(s)}$

   Which species is oxidised in this reaction?
   Explain your answer. **(2 marks)**

2. In a methane fuel cell the equation for the overall reaction is:

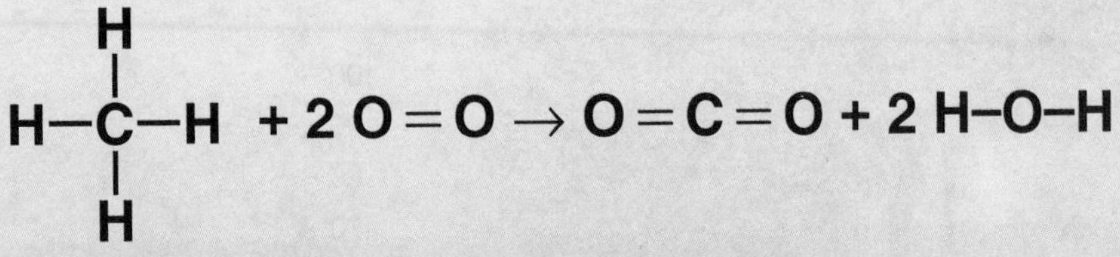

   a) What is a fuel cell? **(1 mark)**

   b) What is the main difference between a fuel cell and a chemical cell? **(1 mark)**

   c) The reaction between methane and oxygen is exothermic. Draw and label a reaction profile for this reaction. **(3 marks)**

   HT **d)** Use the bond energy values in the table below to calculate the value of ΔH for the reaction between methane and oxygen. **(3 marks)**

Bond	Energy kJ/mol
C–H	413
O=O	498
C=O	805
O–H	464

Rates of reaction

22

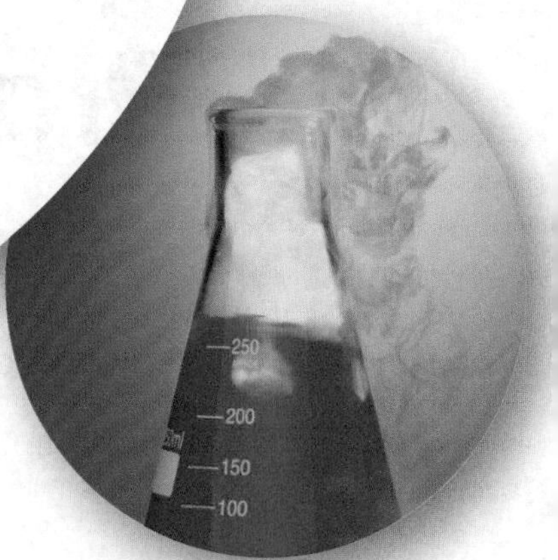

Calculating rates of reactions

The **rate** of a chemical reaction can be determined by measuring the quantity of a reactant used or (more commonly) the quantity of a product formed over time.

$$\text{mean rate of reaction} = \frac{\text{quantity of reactant used}}{\text{time taken}}$$

$$\text{mean rate of reaction} = \frac{\text{quantity of product formed}}{\text{time taken}}$$

For example, if 46 cm^3 of gas is produced in 23 seconds then the mean rate of reaction is 2 cm^3/s.

Rates of reaction can also be determined from grap

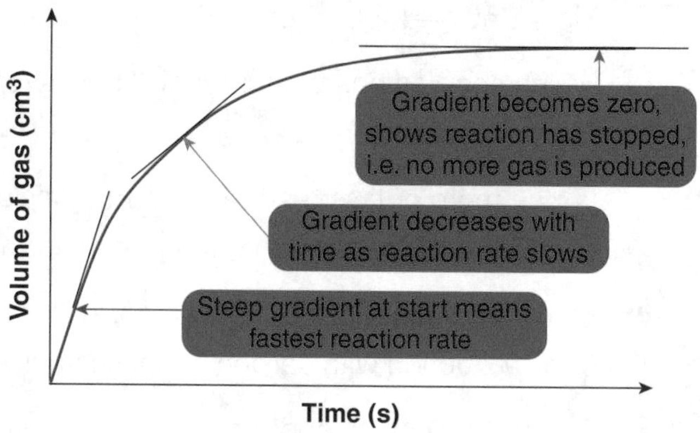

Volume of gas (cm3)
Time (s)
Gradient becomes zero, shows reaction has stopped, i.e. no more gas is produced
Gradient decreases with time as reaction rate slows
Steep gradient at start means fastest reaction rate

HT If the gradient of the tangent is calculated, this give a numerical measure of the rate of reaction. For example:

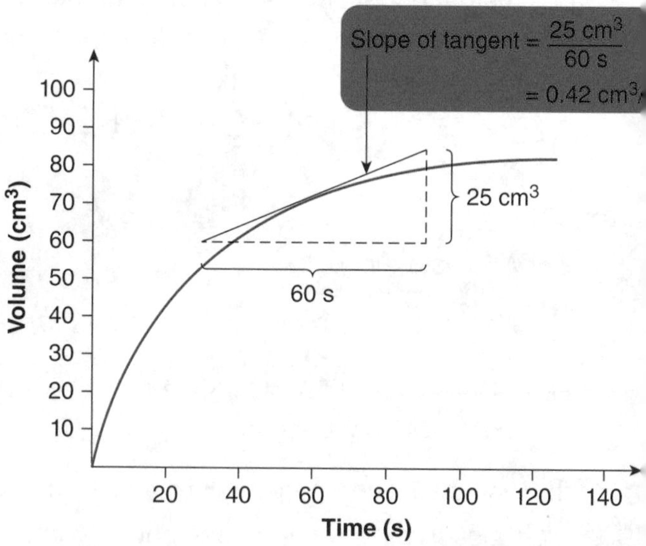

Slope of tangent = 25 cm3 / 60 s
= 0.42 cm3
100
90
80
70
60
50
40
30
20
10
Volume (cm3)
25 cm3
60 s
20
40
60
80
100
120
140
Time (s)

A measure of the speed of a chemical reaction

A species that alters the rate of a reaction without being used up or chemically changed at the end

Factors affecting the rates of reactions

There are five factors that affect the rate of chemical reactions:

- concentrations of the reactants in solution
- pressure of reacting gases
- surface area of any solid reactants
- temperature
- presence of a **catalyst**.

During experiments the rate of a chemical reaction can be found by…

- measuring the mass of the reaction mixture (e.g. if a gas is lost during a reaction)
- measuring the volume of gas produced
- observing a solution becoming opaque or changing colour.

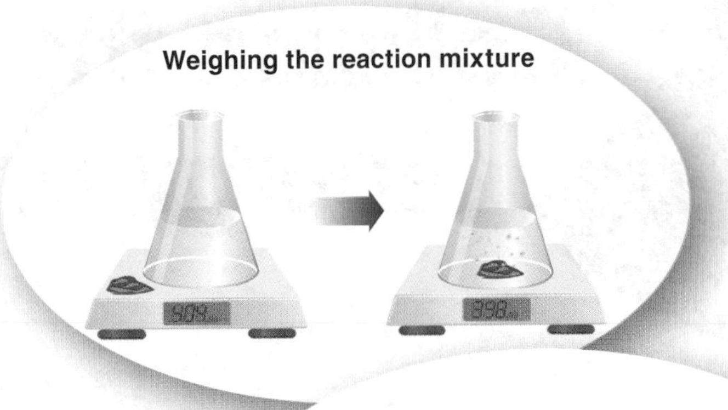

Weighing the reaction mixture

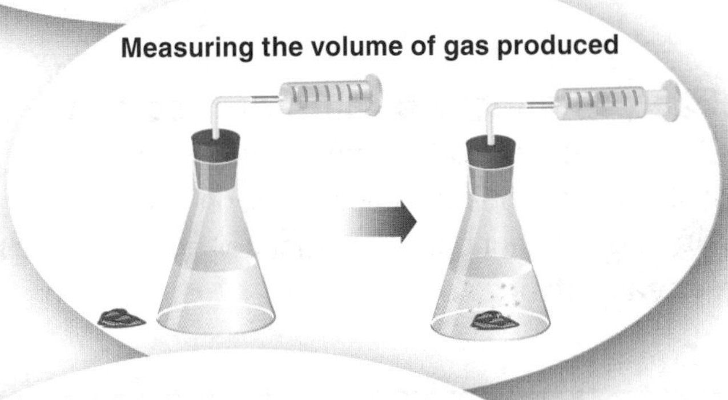

Measuring the volume of gas produced

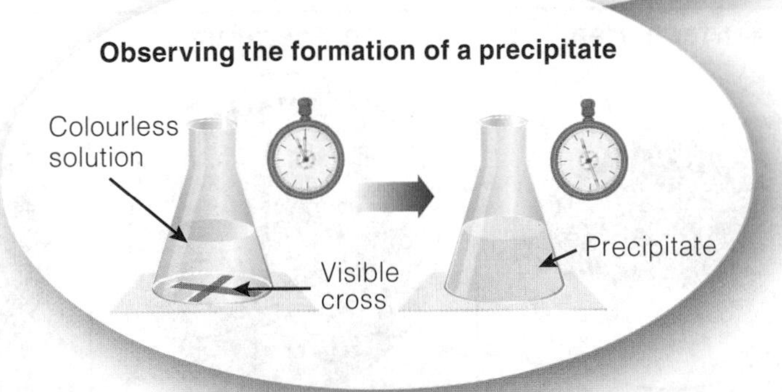

Observing the formation of a precipitate
Colourless solution
Visible cross
Precipitate

As particle size decreases → The surface area to volume ratio increases → and the rate of reaction increases

Add a teaspoon of sugar to a cup of tea or coffee and stir.
Time how long it takes for the sugar to dissolve.
Occasionally, lift the teaspoon to check that the sugar has all dissolved.
Make another cup of tea or coffee and repeat the experiment but using a cube of sugar instead.
Does sugar dissolve more quickly as a cube or as individual granules?
Dissolving is a physical process rather than a chemical reaction but the principle is the same!

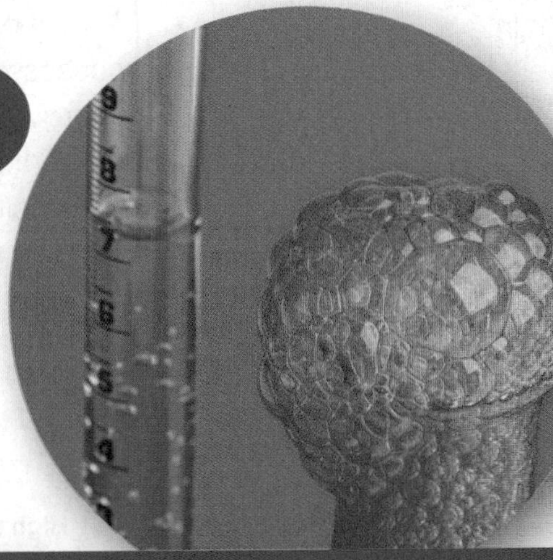

What is the rate of the reaction in which 12 g of reactant is used up over 16 seconds?
State two factors that affect the rate of reaction.
How would you measure the rate of a reaction where one of the products is hydrogen gas?
What is the effect on the rate of a reaction as the surface area to volume ratio of a solid reactant increases?

23 Collision theory, activation energy and catalysts

Factors affecting rates of reaction

Collision theory explains how various factors affect rates of reaction.

It states that, for a chemical reaction to occur…

1. The reactant particles must collide with each other.

AND

2. They must collide with sufficient energy – this amount of energy is known as the **activation energy**.

Surface area	Temperature	Pressure	Concentration
			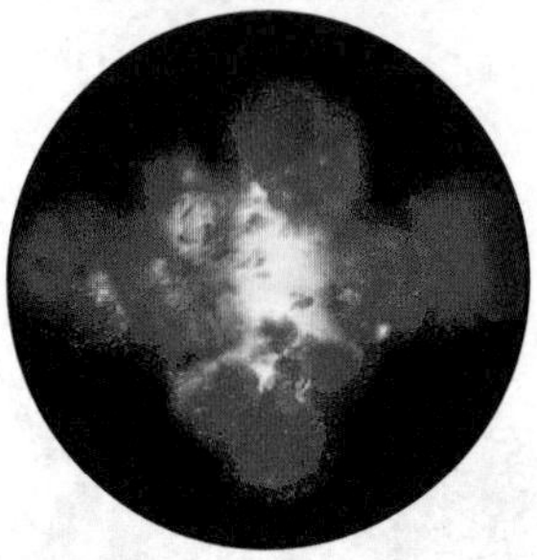
A smaller particle size means a higher surface area to volume ratio. With smaller particles, more collisions can take place, meaning a greater rate of reaction.	Increasing the temperature increases the rate of reaction because the particles are moving more quickly and so will collide more often. Also, more particles will possess the activation energy, so a greater proportion of collisions will result in a reaction.	At a higher pressure, the gas particles are closer together, so there is a greater chance of them colliding, resulting in a higher rate of reaction.	At a higher concentration, there are more reactant particles in the same volume of solution, which increases the chance of collisions and increases the rate of reaction.
Large pieces – small surface area to volume ratio 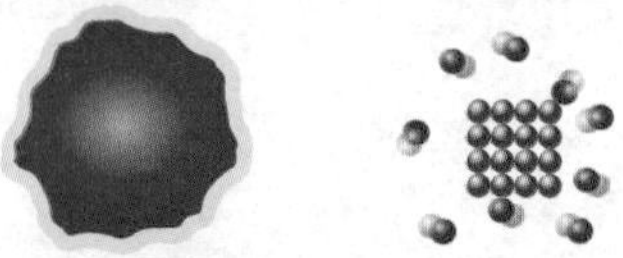 **Small pieces** – large surface area to volume ratio 	**Low temperature** 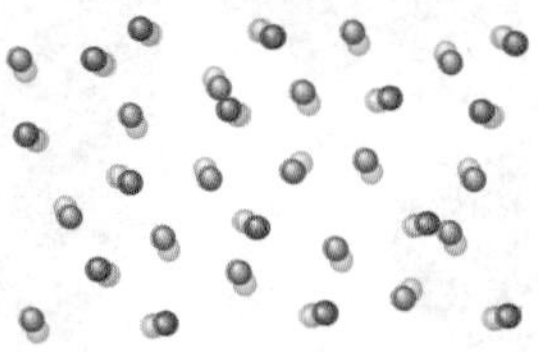 **High temperature** 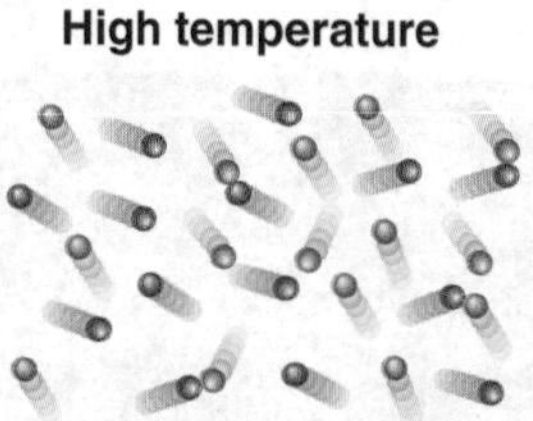	**Low pressure**  **High pressure** 	**Low concentration** 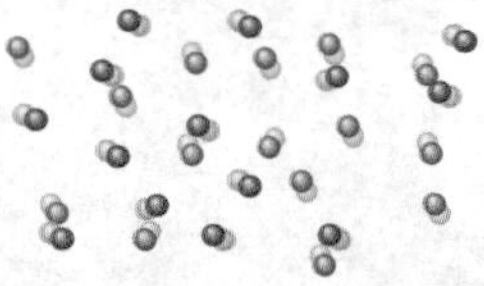 **High concentration** 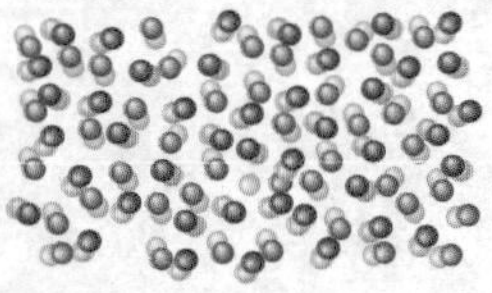

Enzyme (biological catalyst)

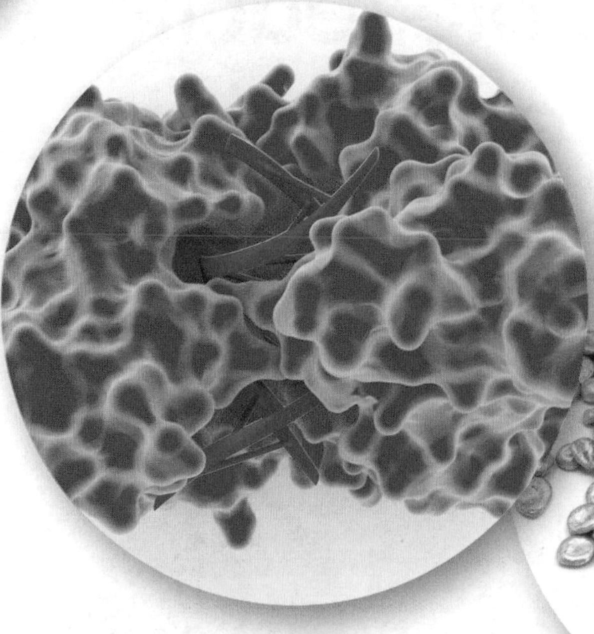

Keyword

Activation energy The minimum amount of energy that particles must collide with in order to react

Zinc catalyst

Part of car catalytic converter

Catalysts

Catalysts are chemicals that change the rate of chemical reactions but are not used up during the reaction. Different chemical reactions need different catalysts. In biological systems enzymes act as catalysts.

Catalysts work by providing an alternative reaction pathway of lower activation energy. This can be shown on a reaction profile.

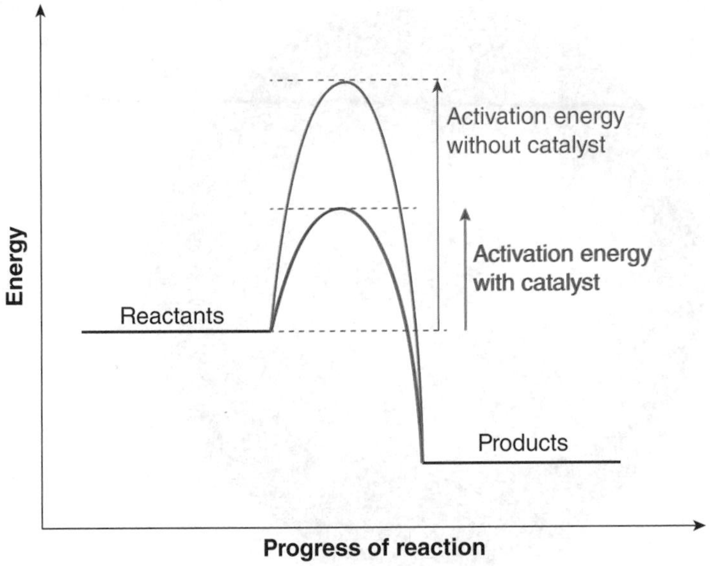

Catalysts are not reactants and so they are not included in the chemical equation.

Draw diagrams showing how the number of collisions can be increased at higher concentrations, higher temperatures, and when the particles have a greater surface area.

What is collision theory?
What is meant by the term 'activation energy'?
Why does a higher concentration of solution increase the rate of a chemical reaction?
What is a catalyst?
Explain how catalysts increase the rate of chemical reactions.

Keyword

Equilibrium ➤ A reversible reaction where the rate of the forward reaction is the same as the rate of the reverse reaction

Reversible reactions and equilibrium

24

Reversible reactions

In some reactions, the products of the reaction can react to produce the original reactants. These reactions are called reversible reactions. For example:

➤ Heating ammonium chloride:

ammonium chloride $\underset{\text{cool}}{\overset{\text{heat}}{\rightleftharpoons}}$ ammonia + hydrogen chloride

$NH_4Cl_{(s)} \rightleftharpoons NH_{3(g)} + HCl_{(g)}$

we use this symbol to represent a reversible reaction

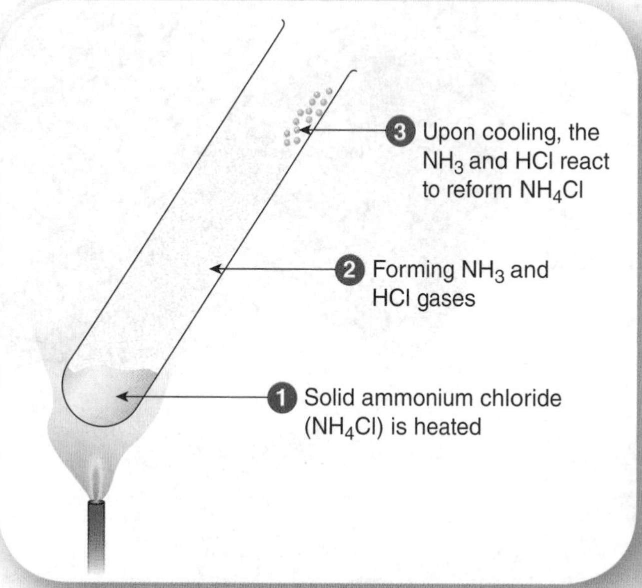

3 Upon cooling, the NH_3 and HCl react to reform NH_4Cl
2 Forming NH_3 and HCl gases
1 Solid ammonium chloride (NH_4Cl) is heated

➤ Heating hydrated copper(II) sulfate:

hydrated copper sulfate (blue) $\underset{\text{exothermic}}{\overset{\text{endothermic}}{\rightleftharpoons}}$ anhydrous copper sulfate (white) + water

Heat

$CuSO_4 \cdot 5H_2O_{(s)} \rightleftharpoons CuSO_{4(s)} + 5H_2O_{(g)}$

blue → white

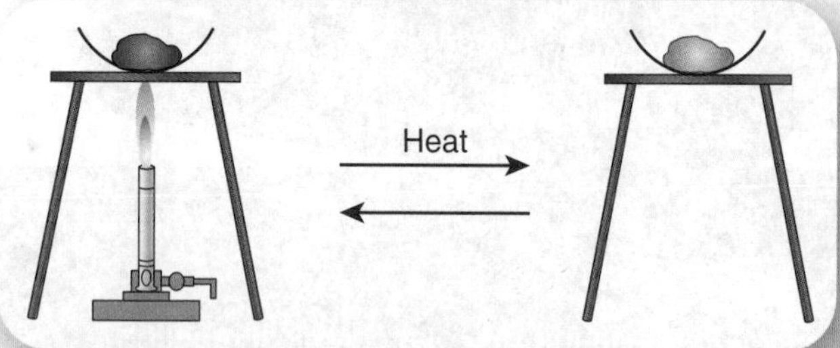

Heat

If the forward reaction is endothermic (absorbs heat) then the reverse reaction must be exothermic (releases heat).

HT

Write out the column and row headings from the table in the 'changing temperature' section on page 59.
Write out all of the four effects on separate pieces of paper and practise placing them in the right box.

Equilibrium

When a reversible reaction is carried out in a closed system (nothing enters or leaves) and the rate of the forward reaction is equal to the rate of the reverse reaction, the reaction is said to have reached **equilibrium**.

Equilibrium conditions

The relative amounts of reactants and products at equilibrium depend on the **reaction conditions**. The effect of changing conditions on reactions at equilibrium can be predicted by Le Chatelier's principle, which states that 'for a reversible reaction, if changes are made to the concentration, temperature or pressure (for gaseous reactions) then the system responds to counteract the change'.

Changing concentration

If the concentration of one of the reactants is increased, more products will be formed (to use up the extra reactant) until equilibrium is established again (i.e. the equilibrium moves to the right until a new equilibrium is established). Similarly, if the concentration of one of the products is increased, more reactants will be formed (i.e. the equilibrium moves to the left until a new equilibrium is established).

Changing temperature

Forward reaction	Effect of increasing temperature	Effect of decreasing temperature
Endothermic	Equilibrium moves to right-hand side (i.e. forward reaction)	Equilibrium moves to left-hand side (i.e. reverse reaction)
Exothermic	Equilibrium moves to left-hand side	Equilibrium moves to right-hand side

Changing pressure

In order to predict the effect of changing pressure, the number of molecules of gas on each side of the equation needs to be known:

there are two molecules of gas on the left-hand side of the equation → $2NO_{2(g)} \rightleftharpoons N_2O_{4(g)}$ ← there is one molecule of gas on the right-hand side of the equation

If the pressure on a reaction at equilibrium is **increased**, the equilibrium shifts to the side of the equation with the **fewer** molecules of gas. In this case, increasing the pressure will shift the reaction to the right-hand side (i.e. producing more N_2O_4).

Which symbol is used to represent a reversible reaction?

The forward reaction in a reversible reaction is exothermic. Is the reverse reaction exothermic or endothermic?

HT Consider the following reaction at equilibrium.

$$N_{2(g)} + 3H_{2(g)} \rightleftharpoons 2NH_{3(g)}$$

What is the effect on the amount of nitrogen at equilibrium of...

Increasing the concentration of hydrogen?

Increasing the pressure?

Mind map

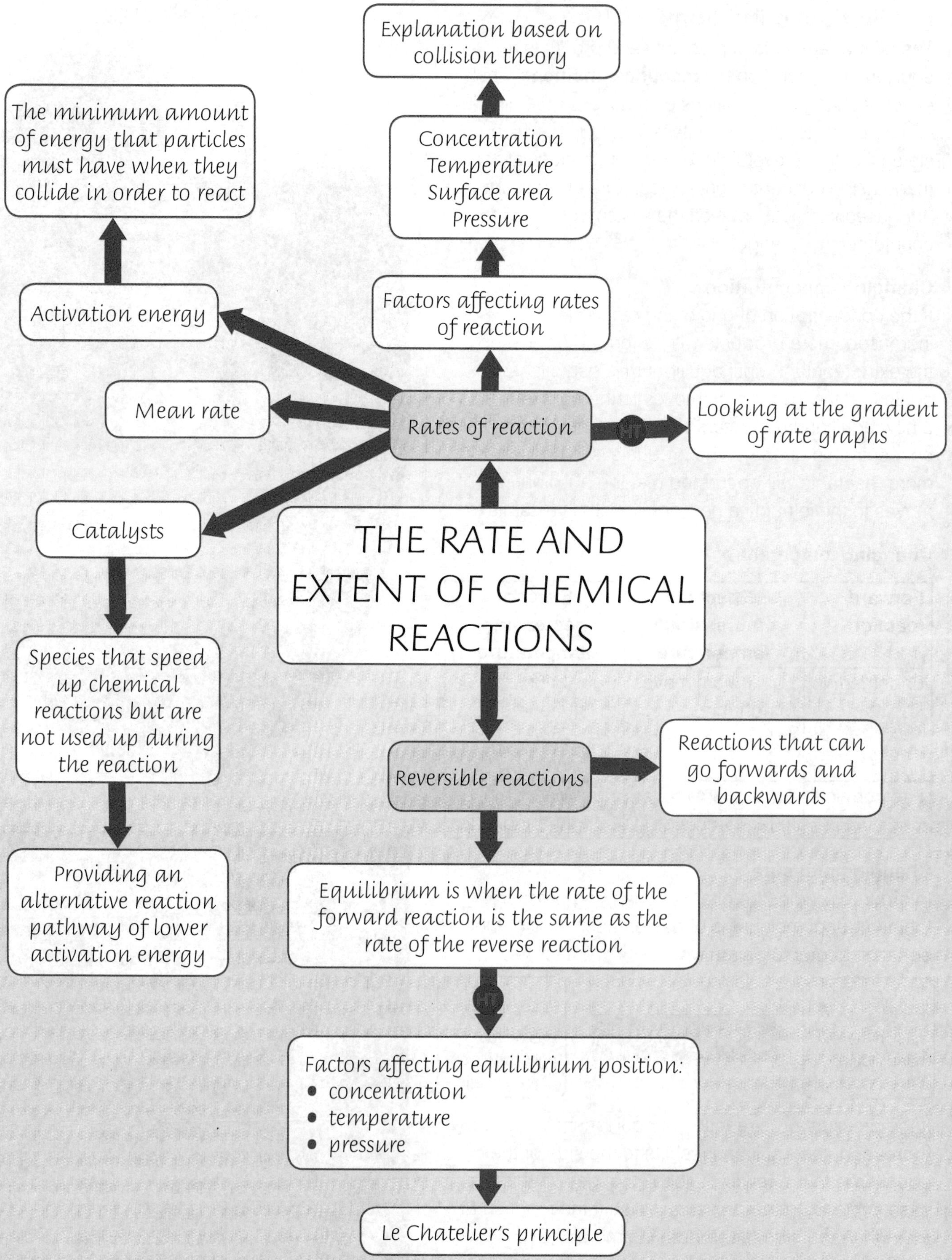
Explanation based on collision theory
Concentration
Temperature
Surface area
Pressure
Factors affecting rates of reaction
The minimum amount of energy that particles must have when they collide in order to react
Activation energy
Mean rate
Rates of reaction
HT
Looking at the gradient of rate graphs
Catalysts
THE RATE AND EXTENT OF CHEMICAL REACTIONS
Species that speed up chemical reactions but are not used up during the reaction
Providing an alternative reaction pathway of lower activation energy
Reversible reactions
Reactions that can go forwards and backwards
Equilibrium is when the rate of the forward reaction is the same as the rate of the reverse reaction
HT
Factors affecting equilibrium position:
• concentration
• temperature
• pressure
Le Chatelier's principle

Practice questions

1. A student was investigating the rate of reaction between magnesium and hydrochloric acid. He measured out a 0.25 g strip of magnesium metal and then added it to 25 cm³ of acid in a conical flask. A gas syringe was attached as shown in the diagram.

   The volume of hydrogen collected was recorded every 10 seconds. A graph of the student's results is shown below.

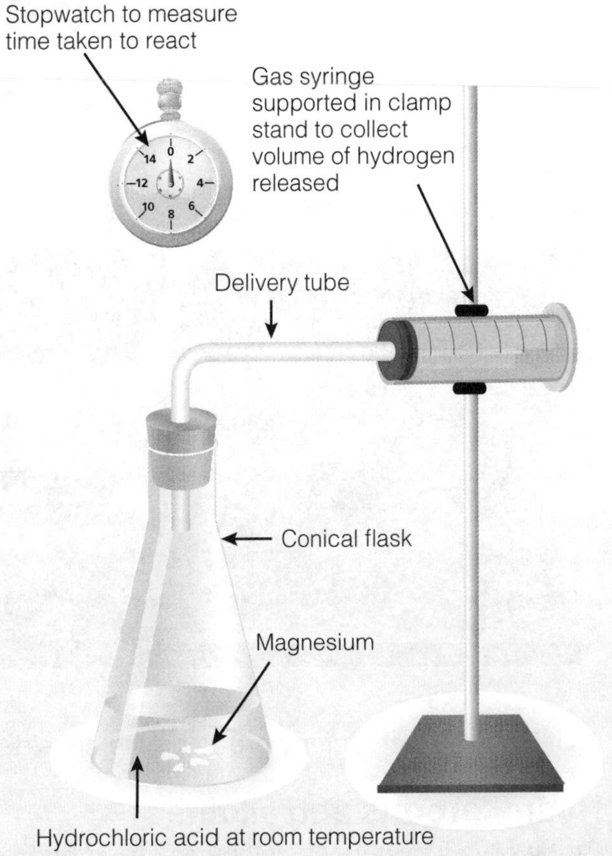
Stopwatch to measure time taken to react
Gas syringe supported in clamp stand to collect volume of hydrogen released
Delivery tube
Conical flask
Magnesium
Hydrochloric acid at room temperature

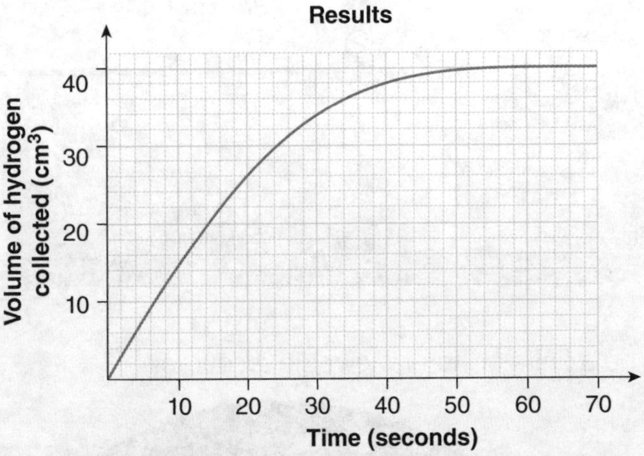
Results
Volume of hydrogen collected (cm³)
40
30
20
10
10
20
30
40
50
60
70
Time (seconds)

   a) How long did the reaction take to finish? Explain your answer. **(2 marks)**

   b) Using your answer to part **a**, calculate the mean rate of reaction. **(2 marks)**

   c) How can you tell from the graph that the rate of reaction was faster after 10 seconds than it was after 40 seconds? **(1 mark)**

   d) The student then repeated the experiment using 0.25 g of magnesium powder instead of magnesium ribbon. Everything else was kept the same. Sketch on the graph the curve that the results from this experiment would have produced. **(2 marks)**

   e) The student predicted that carrying out the experiment with a higher concentration of acid would have increased the rate of reaction. Explain why he is correct. **(2 marks)**

2. Hydrogen for use in the Haber process or in fuel cells can be produced from methane and water according to the equation below.

$$CH_{4(g)} + H_2O_{(g)} \rightleftharpoons CO_{(g)} + 3H_{2(g)}$$

   The forward reaction is endothermic.

   a) How can you tell that this process is carried out at a temperature above 100°C? **(1 mark)**

   b) What does the $\rightleftharpoons$ symbol tell you about the reaction? **(1 mark)**

   c) Explain why increasing the pressure on the equilibrium mixture will decrease the yield of hydrogen. **(1 mark)**

   d) State and explain the effect on the yield of hydrogen of increasing the temperature of the equilibrium mixture. **(2 marks)**

Crude oil, hydrocarbons and alkanes

Keywords

Hydrocarbon ➤ A molecule containing hydrogen and carbon atoms only

Fractional distillation ➤ A method used to separate mixtures of liquids

Crude oil

This process describes how crude oil is formed.

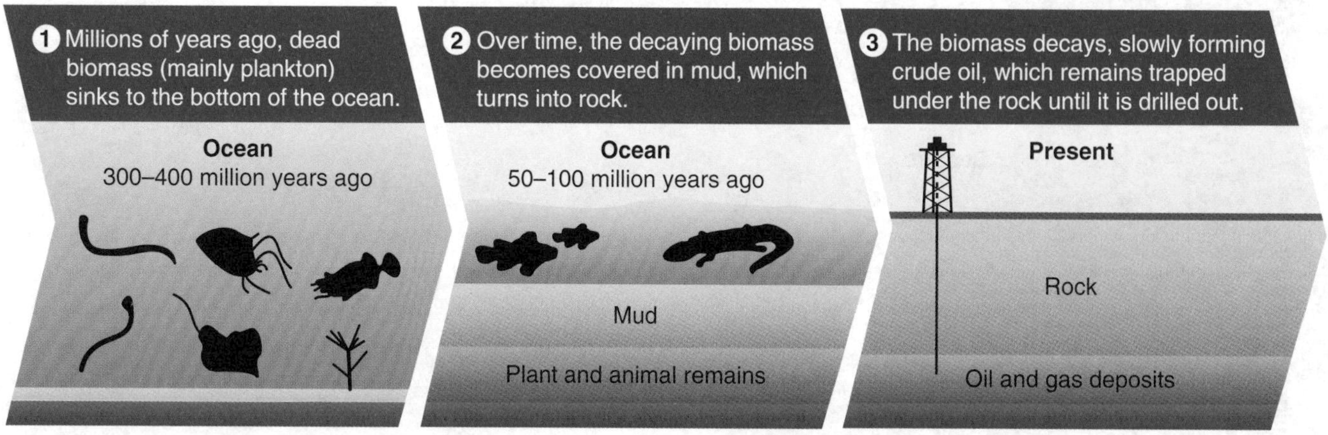

1 Millions of years ago, dead biomass (mainly plankton) sinks to the bottom of the ocean.
Ocean
300–400 million years ago
2 Over time, the decaying biomass becomes covered in mud, which turns into rock.
Ocean
50–100 million years ago
Mud
Plant and animal remains
3 The biomass decays, slowly forming crude oil, which remains trapped under the rock until it is drilled out.
Present
Rock
Oil and gas deposits

As it takes so long to form crude oil, we consider it to be a finite or non-renewable resource.

Hydrocarbons and alkanes

Crude oil is a mixture of molecules called **hydrocarbons**. Most hydrocarbons are members of a homologous series of molecules called alkanes.

Members of an homologous series…

- have the same general formula
- differ by CH_2 in their molecular formula from neighbouring compounds
- show a gradual trend in physical properties, e.g. boiling point
- have similar chemical properties.

Alkanes are hydrocarbons that have the general formula C_nH_{2n+2}.

Alkane	Methane, CH_4	Ethane, C_2H_6	Propane, C_3H_8	Butane, C_4H_{10}
Displayed formula	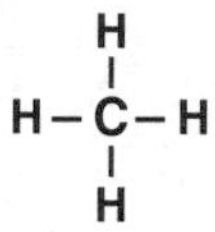	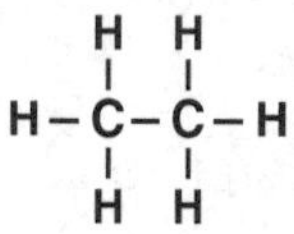	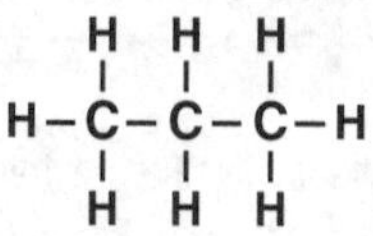	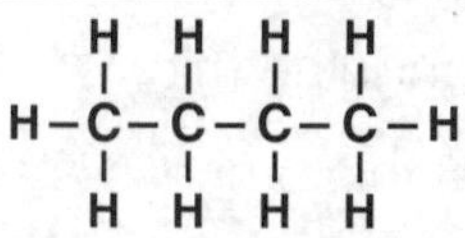

Make up your own mnemonic to remember the different fractions in a fractionating column.

Fractional distillation

Crude oil on its own is relatively useless. It is separated into more useful components (called fractions) by **fractional distillation**. The larger the molecule, the stronger the intermolecular forces and so the higher the boiling point.

- Crude oil is heated until it evaporates.
- It then enters a fractionating column which is hotter at the bottom than at the top
- where the molecules condense at different temperatures.
- Groups of molecules with similar boiling points are collected together. They are called fractions.
- The fractions are sent for processing to produce fuels and feedstock (raw materials) for the petrochemical industry
- which produces many useful materials, e.g. solvents, lubricants, detergents and polymers (plastics).

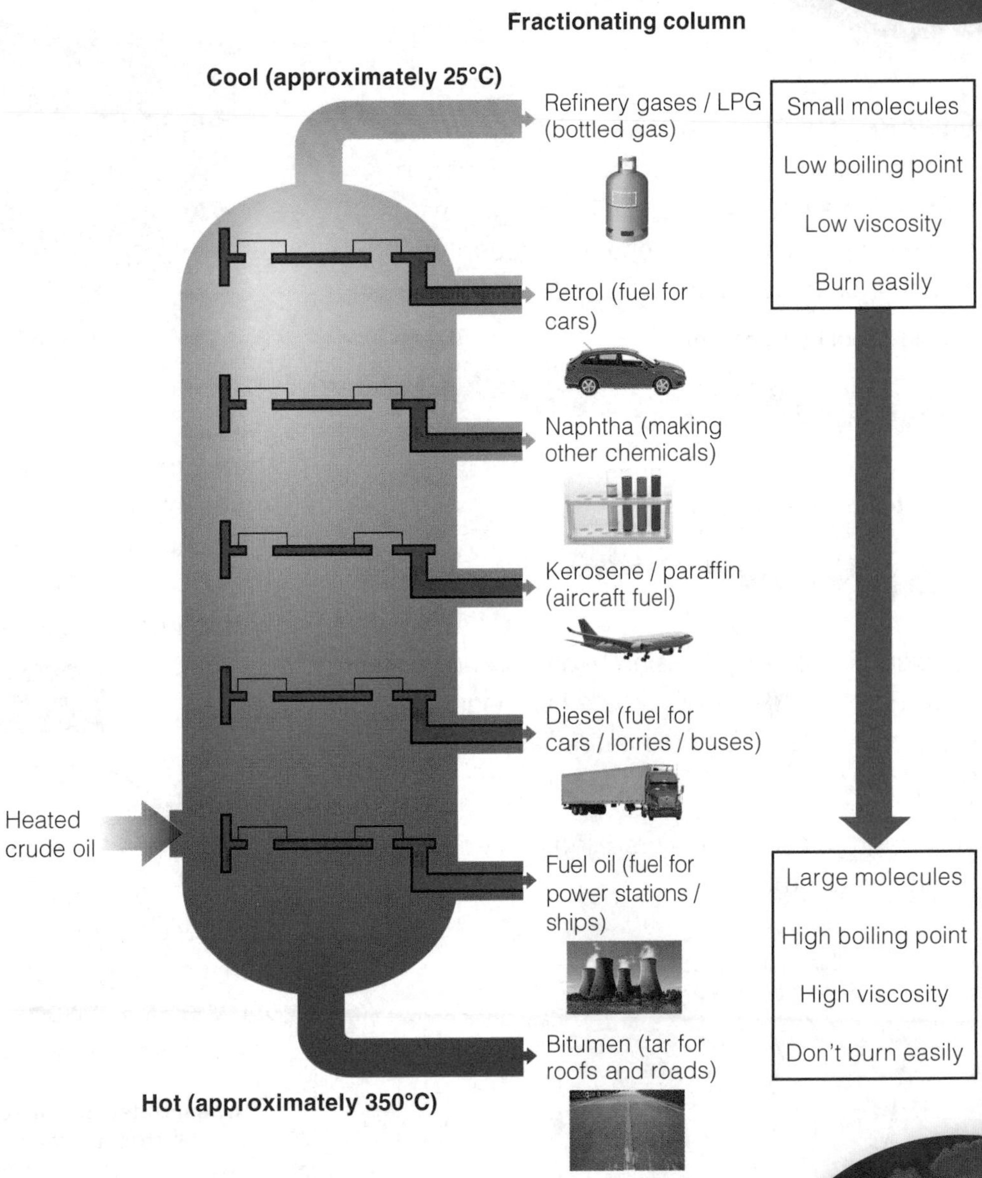

Fractionating column
Cool (approximately 25°C)
Refinery gases / LPG (bottled gas)
Petrol (fuel for cars)
Naphtha (making other chemicals)
Kerosene / paraffin (aircraft fuel)
Diesel (fuel for cars / lorries / buses)
Heated crude oil
Fuel oil (fuel for power stations / ships)
Bitumen (tar for roofs and roads)
Hot (approximately 350°C)
Small molecules
Low boiling point
Low viscosity
Burn easily
Large molecules
High boiling point
High viscosity
Don't burn easily

Combustion of hydrocarbons

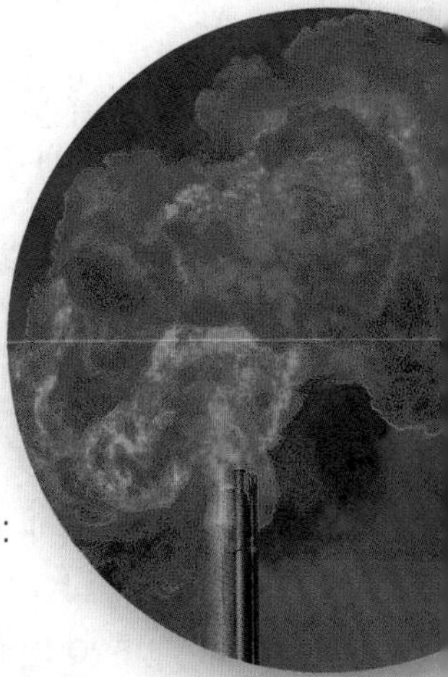

Some of the fractions of crude oil (e.g. petrol and kerosene) are used as fuels. Burning these fuels releases energy. Combustion (burning) reactions are oxidation reactions. When the fuel is fully combusted, the carbon in the hydrocarbons is oxidised to carbon dioxide and the hydrogen is oxidised to water. For example, the combustion of methane:

$$CH_{4(g)} + 2O_{2(g)} \rightarrow CO_{2(g)} + 2H_2O_{(l)}$$

1. What is crude oil formed from?
2. What are hydrocarbons?
3. By what process is crude oil separated?
4. What is the molecular formula of propane?
5. Write a balanced symbol equation for the complete combustion of ethane, C_2H_6.

26 Cracking and alkenes

Keywords

Cracking > A process used to break up large hydrocarbon molecules into smaller, more useful molecules.

Unsaturated > A molecule that contains a carbon-carbon double bond

Functional group > The group of atoms in a molecule that determines the chemical behaviour of the compound

Cracking and alkenes

Many of the long-chain hydrocarbons found in crude oil are not very useful. **Cracking** is the process of turning a long-chain hydrocarbon into shorter, more useful ones.

Long-chain hydrocarbon

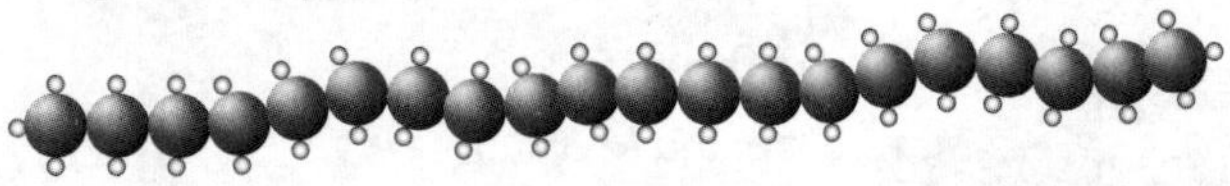

Short-chain hydrocarbons

Cracking is done by passing hydrocarbon vapour over a hot catalyst or mixing the hydrocarbon vapour with steam before heating it to a very high temperature.

The diagram shows how cracking can be carried out in the laboratory.

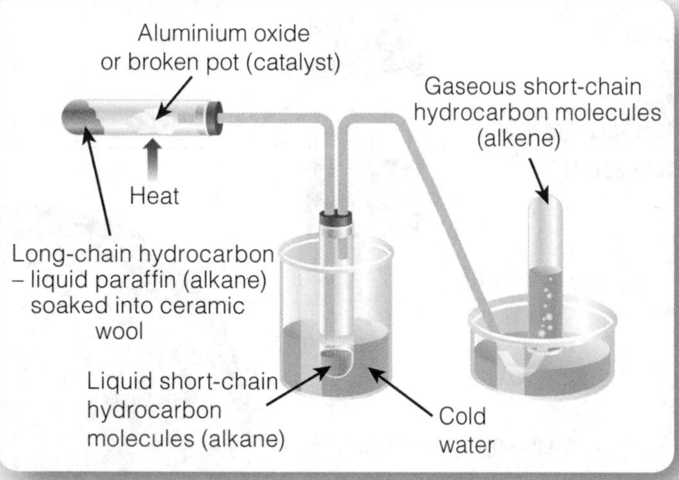
Aluminium oxide or broken pot (catalyst)
Gaseous short-chain hydrocarbon molecules (alkene)
Heat
Long-chain hydrocarbon – liquid paraffin (alkane) soaked into ceramic wool
Liquid short-chain hydrocarbon molecules (alkane)
Cold water

Cracking produces alkanes and alkenes. The small-molecule alkanes that are formed during cracking are in high demand as fuels. The alkenes are mostly used to make plastics by the process of polymerisation.

There are many different equations that can represent cracking. This is because the long hydrocarbon can break in many different places. A typical equation for the cracking of the hydrocarbon decane ($C_{10}H_{22}$) is:

$$C_{10}H_{22} \rightarrow C_8H_{18} + C_2H_4$$

Long-chain alkane | Shorter-chain alkane | Shorter-chain alkene

The presence of alkenes can be detected using bromine water. Alkenes decolourise bromine water but when it is mixed with alkanes, the bromine water stays orange.

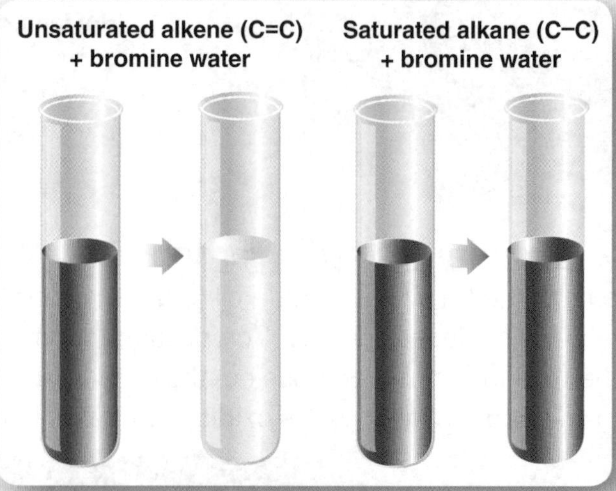
Unsaturated alkene (C=C) + bromine water
Saturated alkane (C–C) + bromine water

Produce a mind map of all of the different reactions of alkenes. Include the reactants, equation and conditions.

Alkenes

Alkenes are hydrocarbons with a carbon–carbon double bond. Molecules with carbon–carbon double bonds are called **unsaturated** molecules because there are two fewer hydrogen atoms than an alkane with the same number of carbon atoms. The general formula for the alkene homologous series is C_nH_{2n}.

Alkene	Ethene, C_2H_4	Propene, C_3H_6	Butene C_4H_8	Pentene, C_5H_{10}
Displayed Formula	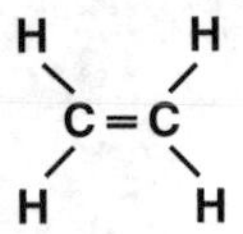	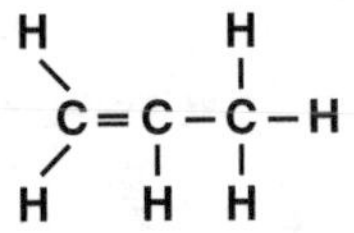	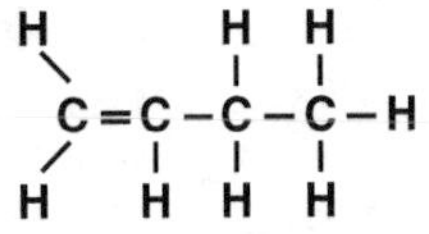	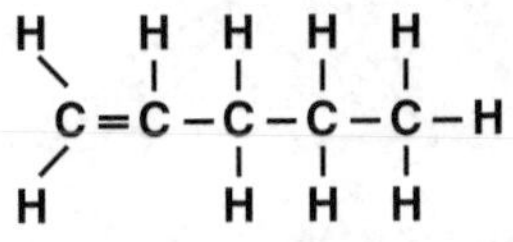

Alkenes usually **react** by atoms adding across the carbon–carbon double bond.

Reactant	Notes	Equation
Oxygen	Alkenes react with oxygen in combustion reactions. Incomplete combustion occurs when alkenes do not completely oxidise. When alkenes burn with a sooty flame incomplete combustion is taking place.	e.g. the complete combustion of ethene: $C_2H_{4(g)} + 3O_2 \rightarrow 2CO_{2(g)} + 3H_2O_{(l)}$
Hydrogen	Hydrogen atoms add across the carbon–carbon double bond so that a carbon–carbon single bond remains.	A nickel catalyst is required, e.g. when ethene reacts with hydrogen, ethane is formed: 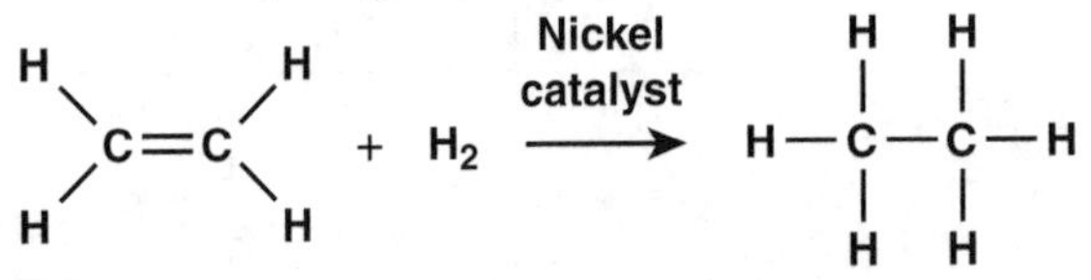
Water	One of the hydrogen atoms in water adds to one side of the carbon–carbon double bond. The remaining OH atoms add to the other carbon atom.	This reaction takes place at a high temperature so that the water is present as steam. An acid catalyst (e.g. concentrated sulfuric acid) is required: e.g. ethene reacts with steam to form the alcohol ethanol. 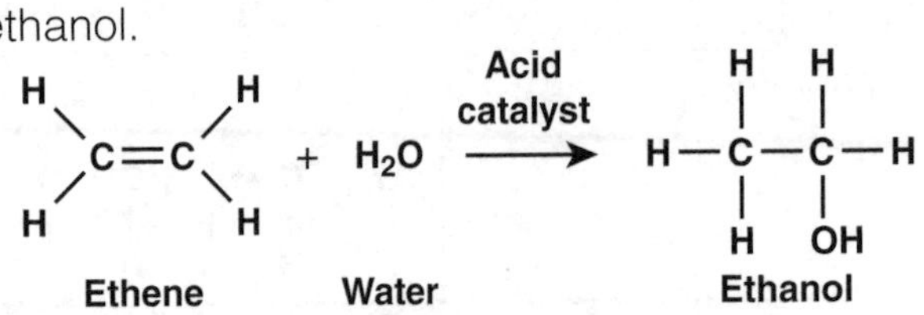
Halogens (e.g. Cl_2 / Br_2)	Halogen atoms add across the carbon–carbon double bond so that a carbon–carbon single bond remains.	Ethene reacts with bromine to form dibromoethane: 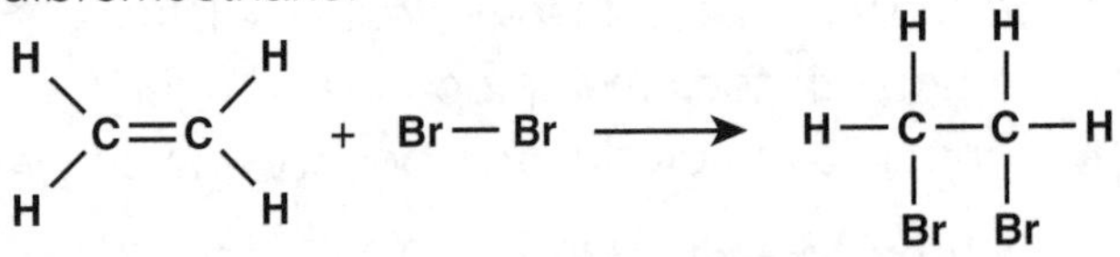

Other alkenes react in the same way as ethene. This is because all alkenes contain the same **functional group**, for example, the reaction of propene with bromine:

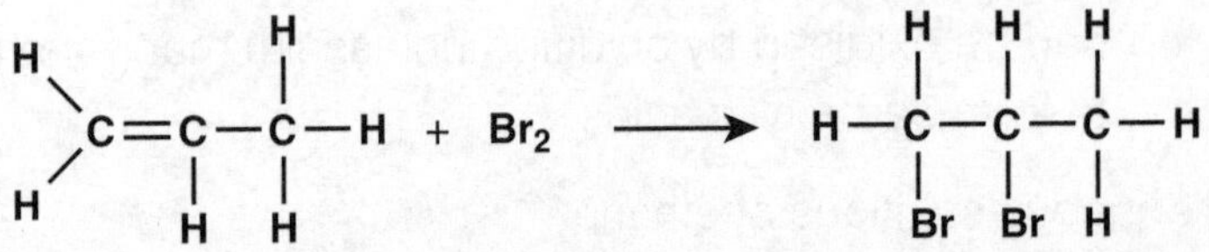

1. In this equation, give the formula for the missing hydrocarbon formed by the cracking of octane: $C_8H_{18(g)} \rightarrow 2C_2H_{4\,(g)} +$ ______________
2. What is the general formula of alkenes?
3. Draw the displayed formula of butene.
4. Write a balanced symbol equation for the reaction of ethene with bromine.
5. Name the alcohol formed when ethene reacts with steam.

Alcohols and carboxylic acids

27

Keywords

Alcohol ➤ A molecule containing the –OH functional group

Fermentation ➤ The process by which yeast converts sugars to alcohol and carbon dioxide through anaerobic respiration

Carboxylic acid ➤ A molecule containing the –COOH functional group

Alcohols

Alcohols contain the functional group –OH. The first four members of the homologous series of alcohols are shown in the table.

Alcohol (all names end in 'ol')	Displayed formula	Structural formula (always ends in –OH)
Methanol	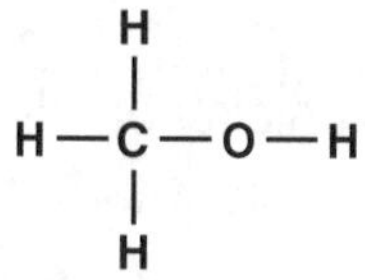	CH_3OH
Ethanol	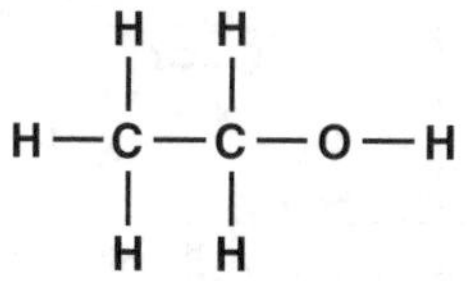	CH_3CH_2OH
Propanol	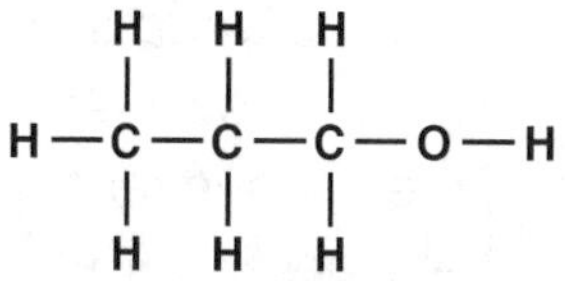	$CH_3CH_2CH_2OH$
Butanol	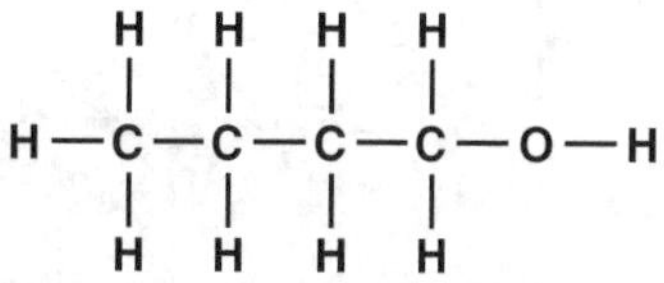	$CH_3CH_2CH_2CH_2OH$

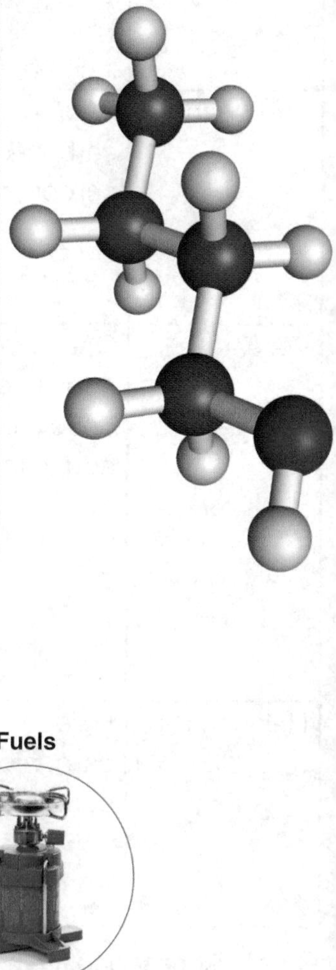

Alcohols…

- dissolve in water to form neutral solutions
- react with sodium to produce hydrogen
- burn in air to produce carbon dioxide and water

  For example: $C_2H_5OH_{(l)} + 3O_{2(g)} \rightarrow 2CO_{2(g)} + 3H_2O_{(l)}$
- can be oxidised by acidified potassium manganate(VII) to form carboxylic acids.

Aqueous solutions of ethanol are produced by the anaerobic **fermentation** of sugar solution by yeast at 30°C. The product can be distilled to produce a more concentrated solution of ethanol. Ethanol is the alcohol in alcoholic drinks.

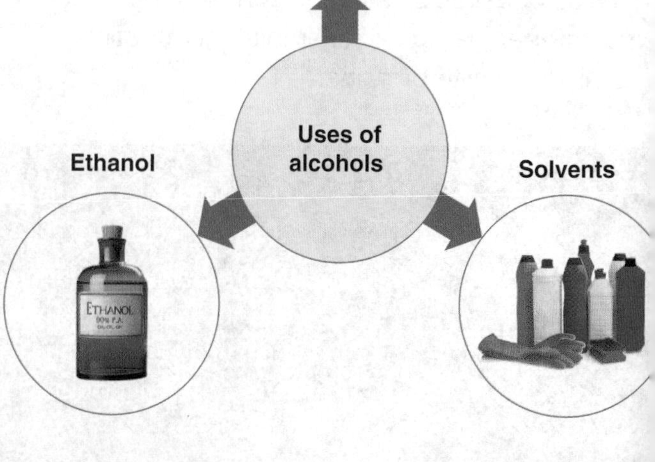
Fuels
Uses of alcohols
Ethanol
Solvents
ETHANOL

Carboxylic acids

Carboxylic acids contain the functional group –COOH. The first four members of the homologous series of carboxylic acids are shown in the table.

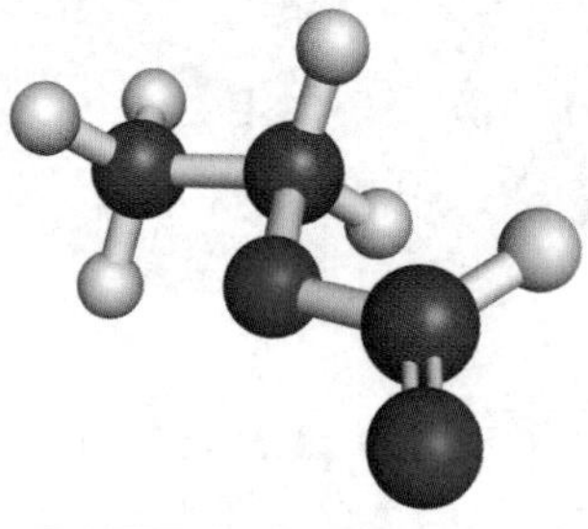

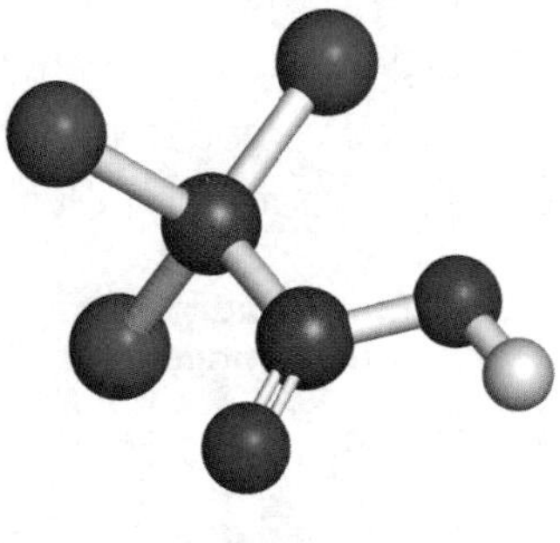

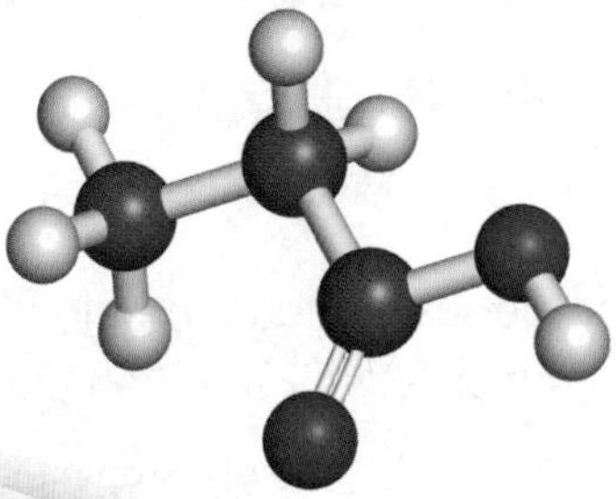

Alcohol (all names end in '…oic acid')	Displayed formula	Structural formula (always ends in COOH)
Methanoic acid	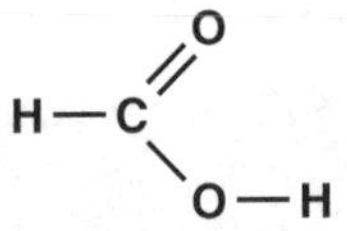	HCOOH
Ethanoic acid	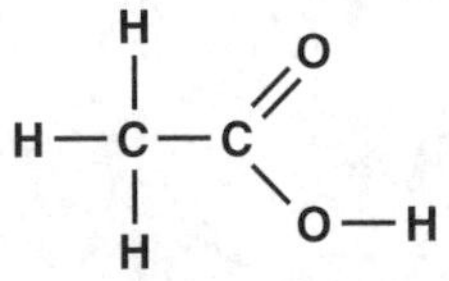	CH_3COOH
Propanoic acid	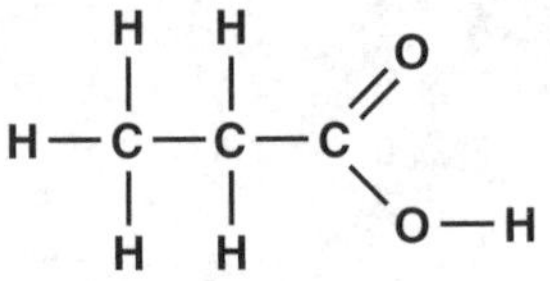	CH_3CH_2COOH
Butanoic acid	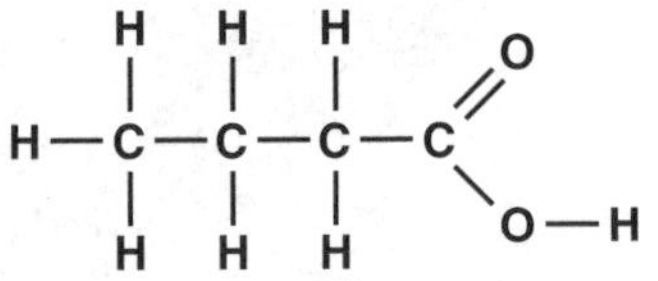	$CH_3CH_2CH_2COOH$

Carboxylic acids…

- Dissolve in water to form acidic solutions
- React with carbonates to form carbon dioxide
- Are weak acids, i.e. they do not completely ionise when dissolved in water
- React with alcohols in the presence of an acid catalyst to produce esters.

For example: ethanoic acid reacts with ethanol to produce water and the ester ethyl ethanoate.

Ethyl ethanoate

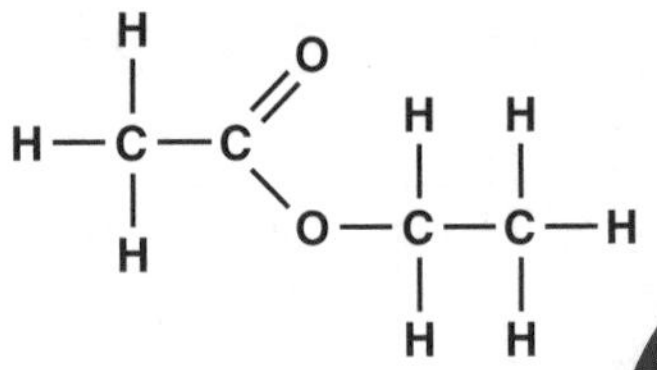

Citric acid and vitamin C

Malt vinegar

Draw the displayed formula of all of the alcohols and carboxylic acids shown on these pages and practise naming them.

1. What is the structural formula of propanol?
2. Write a balanced symbol equation for the complete combustion of butanol (C_4H_9OH).
3. Give one use for an alcohol such as methanol.
4. Draw the displayed formula of ethanoic acid.
5. Name the ester formed when ethanoic acid reacts with ethanol.

Polymerisation and natural polymers

Addition polymerisation

Addition polymerisation is the process of joining lots of small molecules (**monomers**) together to form very large molecules (**polymers**). The monomers must be alkenes because a carbon–carbon double bond is needed for addition polymerisation to occur.

Ethene monomers (unsaturated) **Poly(ethene) polymers (saturated)**

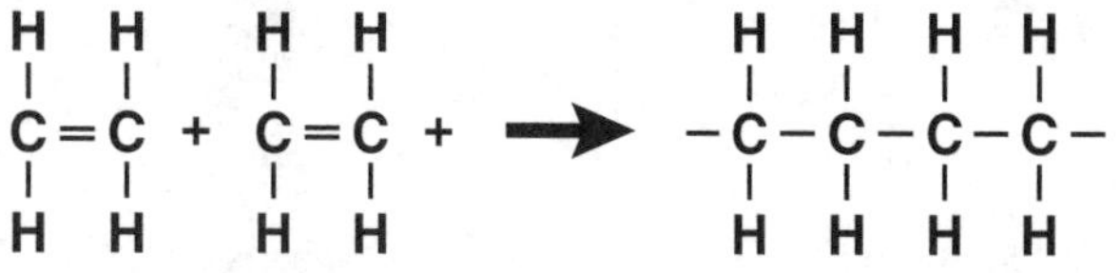

...and thousands more... ...and on and on...

The general equation below can be used to represent the formation of any addition polymer.

Poly(propene)

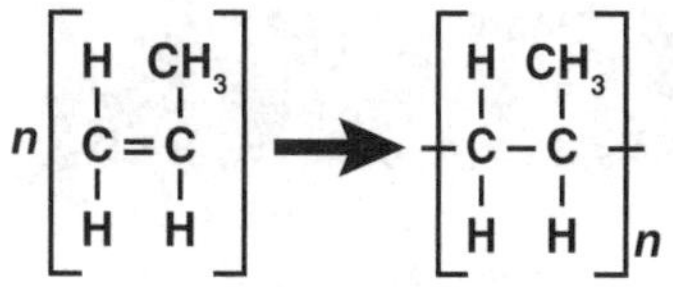

The repeat unit in an addition polymer has the same atoms as the monomer because there are no other molecules formed in the reaction.

Keywords

Addition polymerisation ➤ The process where many small unsaturated monomers join together to form a polymer

Monomer ➤ The individual molecules that join together to form a polymer

Polymer ➤ A large, long-chained molecule

HT **Condensation polymerisation** ➤ The process where many small molecules join together forming a polymer and a small molecule such as water

Find other examples of polymers in everyday life and decide whether they are natural or synthetic (manmade).

		Polymer		
Monomer	Repeat unit	Name	Uses	Properties
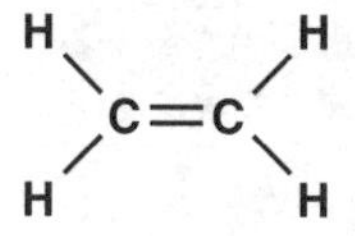	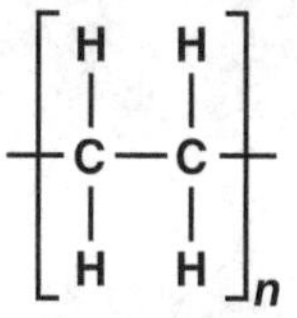	Poly(ethene)	Plastic shopping bags Water bottles	Strong and light
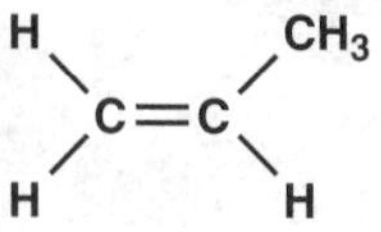	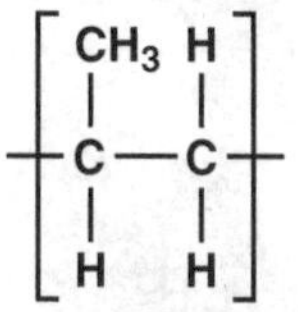	Poly(propene)	Crates and ropes	Strong and rigid
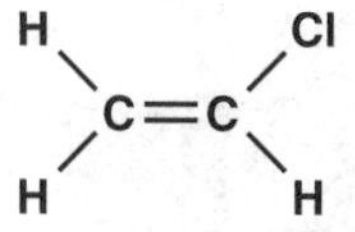	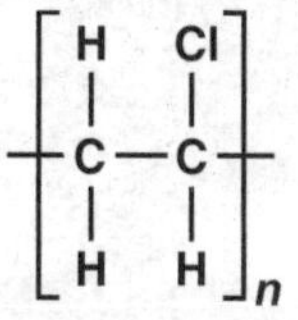	Poly(chloroethene) (PVC)	Water pipes and electrical cable insulation	Waterproof Electrical insulator Flexible
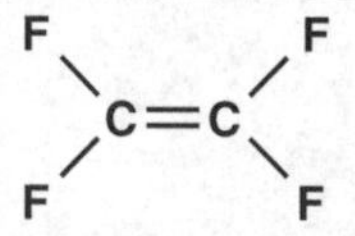	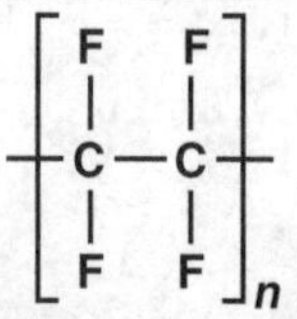	Poly(tetrafluoroethene) (PTFE)	Lining for non-stick saucepans	Slippery Chemically inert

Condensation polymerisation

Condensation polymerisation takes place when the monomer has two functional groups in the molecule, such as ethane diol, which contains an alcohol (–OH) functional group at each end of the molecule.

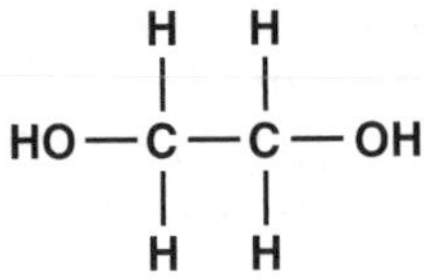

Hexanedioic acid is a molecule that contains a carboxylic acid group (–COOH) at each end of the molecule.

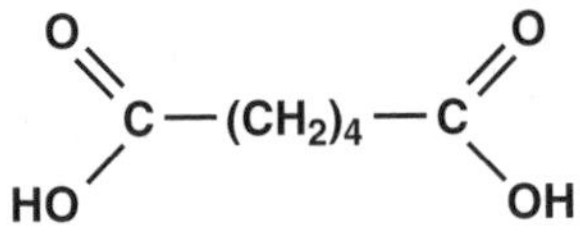

Alcohols react with carboxylic acids to form esters (see Module 27). These two molecules polymerise to form a polyester. In condensation polymerisation, a small molecule (usually water) is also produced.

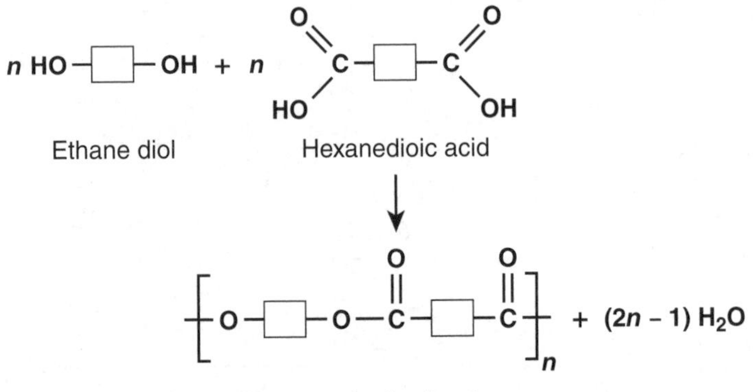

Ethane diol
Hexanedioic acid
Repeat unit of polyester

In this diagram, blocks □ are used to represent the carbon chains in each monomer molecule (i.e. CH_2CH_2 and $CH_2CH_2CH_2CH_2$), as these are not involved in the polymerisation reaction.

Amino acids

Amino acids have two different functional groups in a molecule. Amino acid molecules react with each other to form polypeptides. Different amino acids can be combined in the same chain to form proteins.

Glycine is an amino acid with the formula H_2NCH_2COOH.

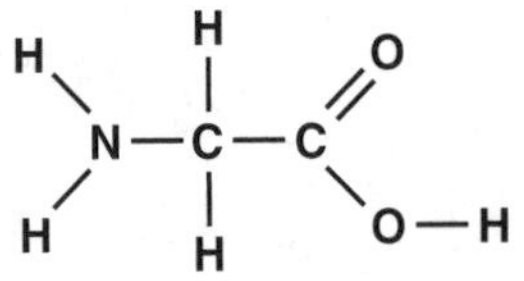

Glycine undergoes condensation polymerisation (the NH_2 functional group in one molecule reacts with the –COOH functional group in another) to form the polypeptide $(\text{–}HNCH_2COO\text{–})_n$

$$n\,H_2NCH_2COOH \rightarrow (\text{–}HNCH_2COO\text{–})_n + nH_2O$$

DNA

DNA (deoxyribonucleic acid) is a large molecule that is essential for life. DNA encodes genetic instructions for the development and functioning of living organisms and viruses.

Most DNA molecules are two polymer chains, made from four different monomers called nucleotides. These are arranged in the form of a double helix.

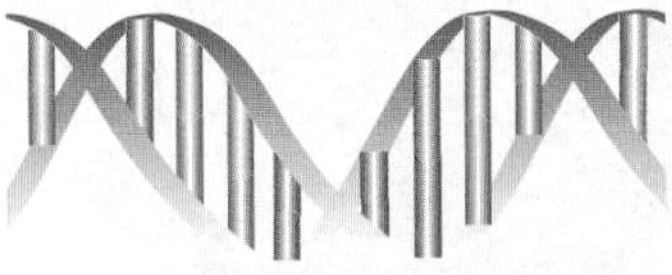

DNA double helix

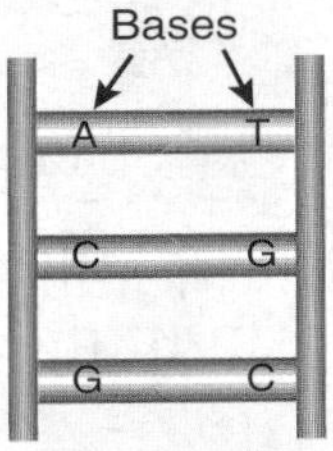

Bases
A
T
C
G
G
C

A section of the double helix

Other naturally occurring polymers

There are many polymers found in nature that are important for life. For example:

- proteins
- starch and cellulose

Starch and cellulose are polymers of sugars. Sugars, starch and cellulose are carbohydrates.

Protein-rich foods

1. What feature of alkene molecules makes them suitable for use in addition polymerisation?
2. (HT) What is formed when amino acids undergo polymerisation?
3. Why is the polymer DNA essential for life?

Mind map

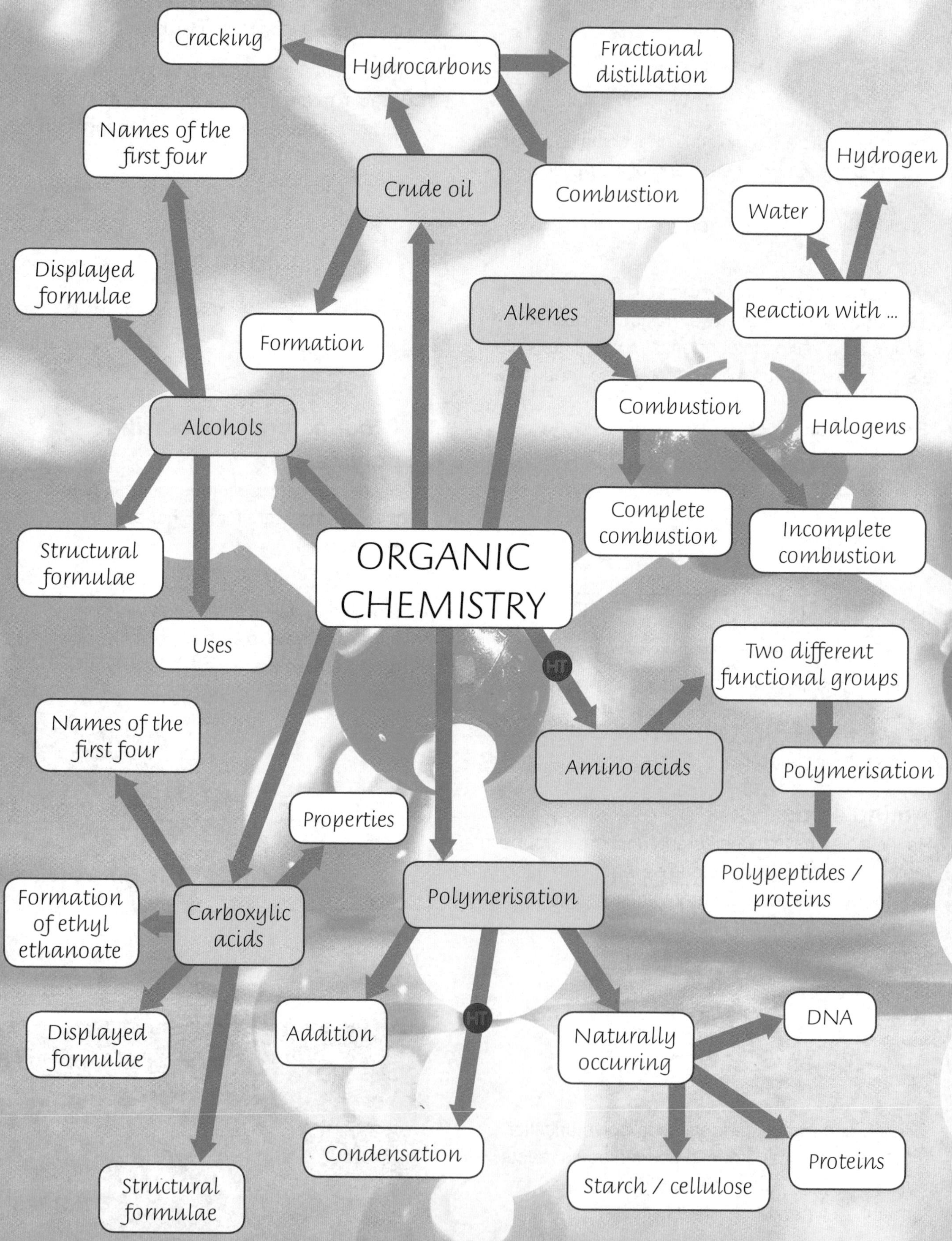

ORGANIC CHEMISTRY
Crude oil
Hydrocarbons
Cracking
Fractional distillation
Combustion
Formation
Alkenes
Reaction with …
Water
Hydrogen
Halogens
Combustion
Complete combustion
Incomplete combustion
Alcohols
Names of the first four
Displayed formulae
Structural formulae
Uses
HT
Amino acids
Two different functional groups
Polymerisation
Polypeptides / proteins
Carboxylic acids
Names of the first four
Properties
Formation of ethyl ethanoate
Displayed formulae
Structural formulae
Polymerisation
Addition
HT
Condensation
Naturally occurring
DNA
Proteins
Starch / cellulose

Practice questions

1. Crude oil is extracted from the earth by drilling and then it is separated into useful components. Some of the alkanes found in crude oil undergo further processing to make them more useful in a process called cracking.

   a) Describe the stages in the formation of crude oil. **(3 marks)**

   b) What is the name of the process by which crude oil is separated and by what property are the molecules in crude oil separated? **(2 marks)**

   c) What are alkanes? **(2 marks)**

   d) Why is cracking an important process? **(2 marks)**

   e) State one way in which cracking can be carried out. **(1 mark)**

   f) The hydrocarbon dodecane ($C_{12}H_{26}$) can be cracked to produce two molecules of ethene (C_2H_4) and one other molecule. Complete the equation below stating the formula of this other product.

   $C_{12}H_{26} \rightarrow 2C_2H_4 +$ .... **(1 mark)**

2. There are two main types of polymerisation. Poly(propene) is a polymer made from propene. Nylon is a polyester formed by polymerisation.

   a) What method of polymerisation is used to form poly(propene)? **(1 mark)**

   b) What feature of a propene molecule means that it is able to undergo this type of polymerisation? **(1 mark)**

   c) Name a naturally occurring condensation polymer. **(1 mark)**

3. The alcohol ethanol can be made by reacting ethene with steam.

   a) Write a balanced symbol equation for this reaction. **(2 marks)**

   b) Suggest a suitable catalyst for this reaction. **(1 mark)**

   c) Name the gas produced when ethanol reacts with sodium. **(1 mark)**

   d) Draw the displayed formula of the carboxylic acid formed when ethanol is oxidised by potassium manganate(VII). **(1 mark)**

   e) Name the ester formed when ethanol reacts with ethanoic acid. **(1 mark)**

Purity, formulations and chromatography

Keywords

Formulation ➤ A mixture that has been designed as a useful product

Chromatography ➤ A method of separating mixtures of dyes

Purity

In everyday language, a pure substance can mean a substance that has had nothing added to it (i.e. in its natural state), such as milk.

In chemistry, a pure substance is a single element or compound (i.e. not mixed with any other substance).

Pure elements and compounds melt and boil at specific temperatures. For example, pure water freezes at 0°C and boils at 100°C. However, if something is added to water (e.g. salt) then the freezing point decreases (i.e. goes below 0°C) and the boiling point rises above 100°C.

Formulations

A **formulation** is a mixture that has been designed as a useful product. Many formulations are complex mixtures in which each ingredient has a specific purpose.

Formulations are made by mixing the individual components in carefully measured quantities to ensure that the product has the correct properties.

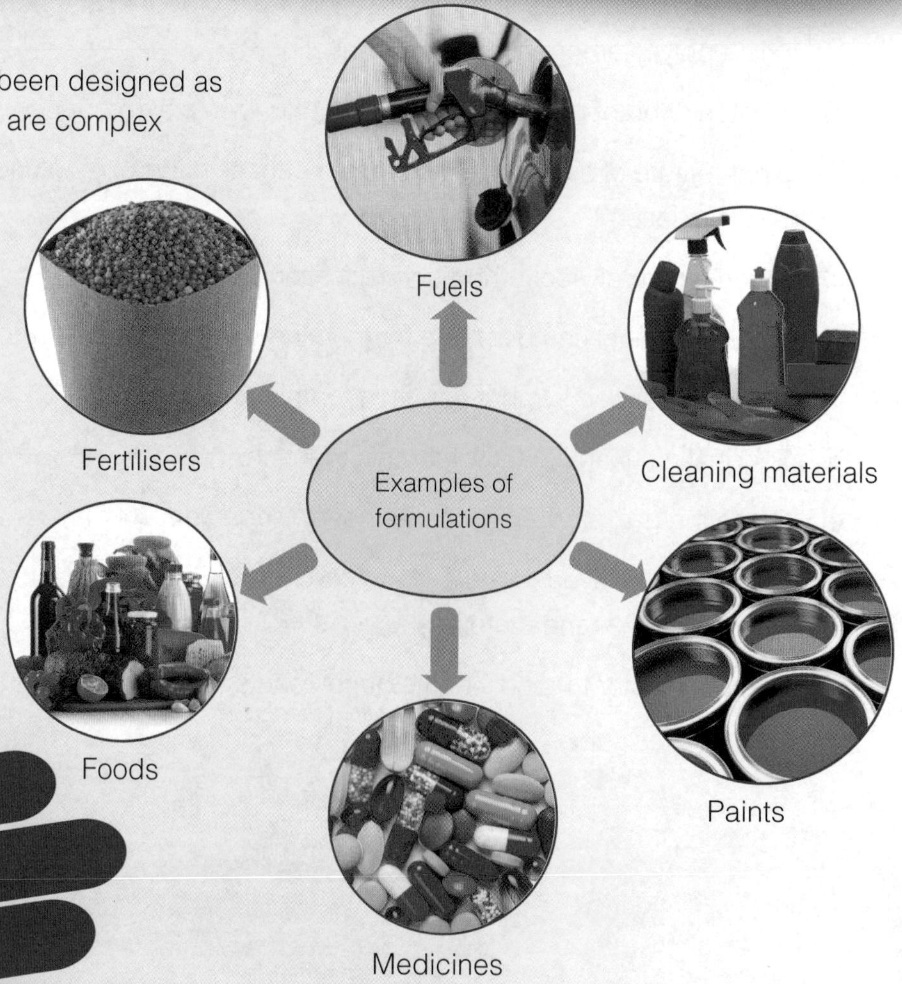
Examples of formulations
Fuels
Cleaning materials
Paints
Medicines
Foods
Fertilisers

Find five items at home or in a supermarket that are described as 'pure'. Look at their composition (e.g. from a food label) and decide whether they are chemically pure.

Chromatography

Chromatography is used to separate mixtures of dyes. It is used to help identify substances.

In paper chromatography, a solvent (the mobile phase) moves up the paper (the stationary phase) carrying different components of the mixture different distances, depending on their attraction for the paper and the solvent. In thin layer chromatography (TLC), the stationary phase is a thin layer of an inert substance (e.g. silica) supported on a flat, unreactive surface (e.g. a glass plate).

In the chromatogram on the right, substance X is being analysed and compared with samples A, B, C, D and E.

It can be seen from the chromatogram that substance X has the same pattern of spots as sample D. This means that sample X and sample D are the same substance. Pure compounds (e.g. compound A) will only produce one spot on a chromatogram.

The ratio of the distance moved by the compound to the distance moved by the solvent is known as its R_f value.

$$R_f = \frac{\text{distance moved by substance}}{\text{distance moved by solvent}}$$

Different compounds have different R_f values in different solvents. This can be used to help identify unknown compounds by comparing R_f values with known substances.

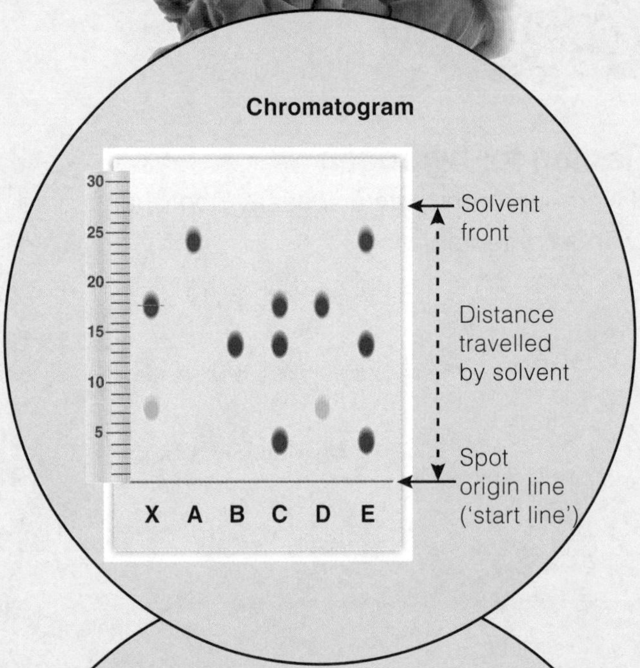
Chromatogram
30
25
20
15
10
5
X A B C D E
Solvent front
Distance travelled by solvent
Spot origin line ('start line')

In this case, the R_f value is 0.73 $\left(\frac{4.0}{5.5}\right)$

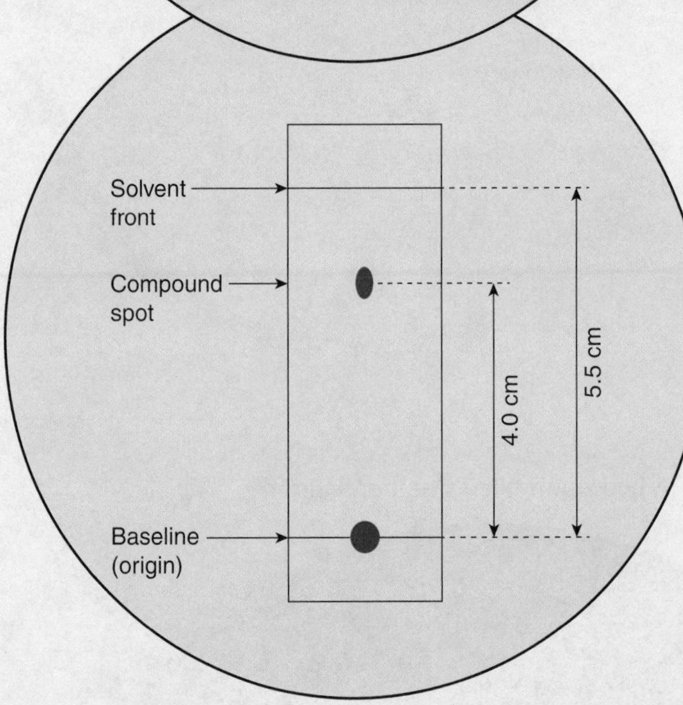
Solvent front
Compound spot
Baseline (origin)
4.0 cm
5.5 cm

1. In chemistry what is meant by the term 'pure substance'?
2. What is a formulation?
3. Give two examples of substances that are formulations.
4. In a chromatogram, the solvent travelled 6 cm and a dye travelled 3.3 cm. What is the R_f value of the dye?

Identification of gases

30

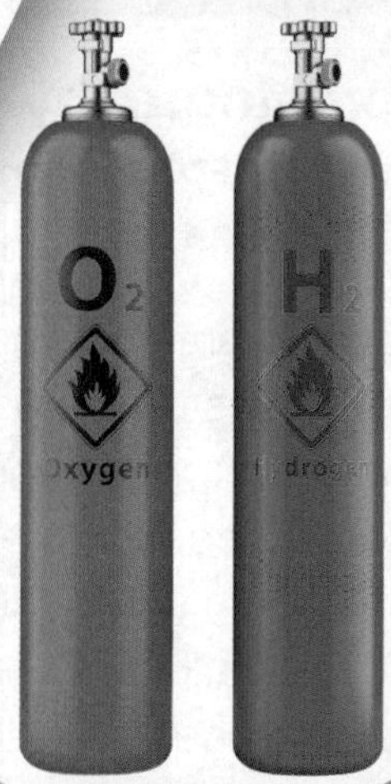
O2
Oxygen
H2

Testing for hydrogen

Hydrogen burns with a squeaky *pop* when tested with a lighted splint.

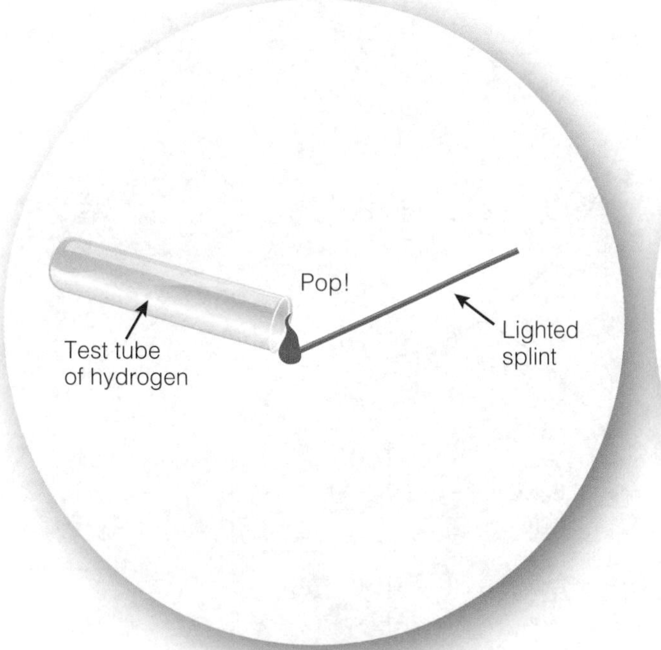
Pop!
Test tube
of hydrogen
Lighted
splint

Testing for oxygen

Oxygen relights a glowing splint.

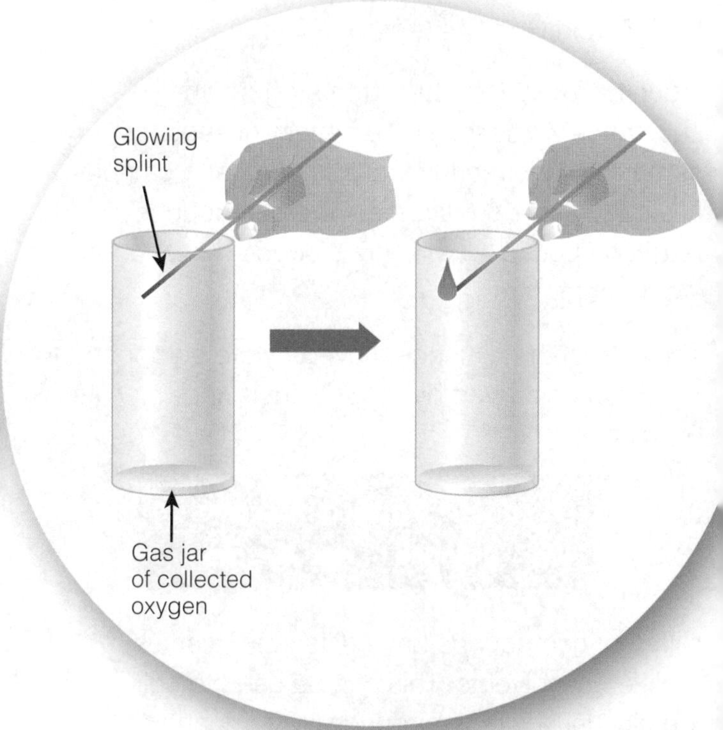
Glowing
splint
Gas jar
of collected
oxygen

A hydrogen-filled weather balloon

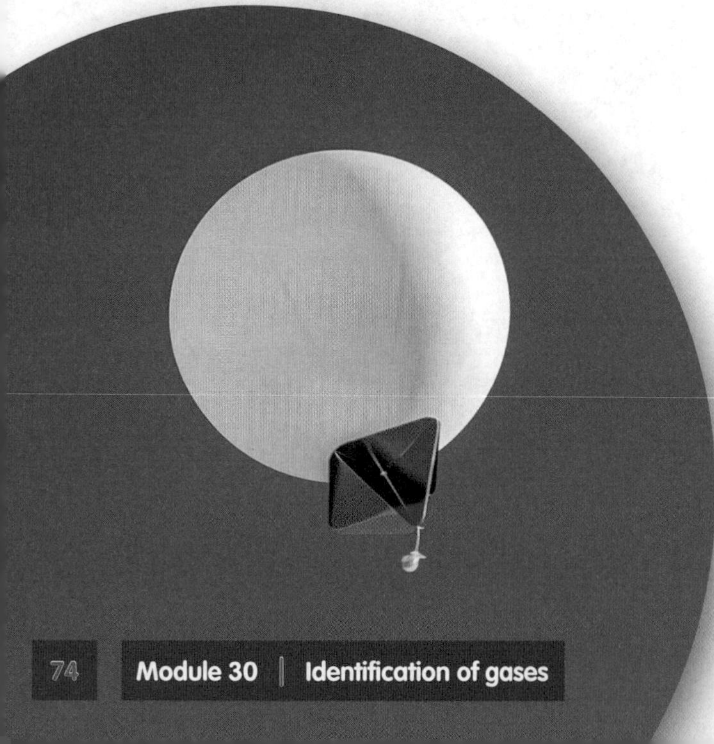

Oxygen is used in breathing masks

Carbon dioxide is released when fossil fuels are burnt

Testing for carbon dioxide

When carbon dioxide is mixed with or bubbled through limewater (calcium hydroxide solution) the limewater turns milky (cloudy).

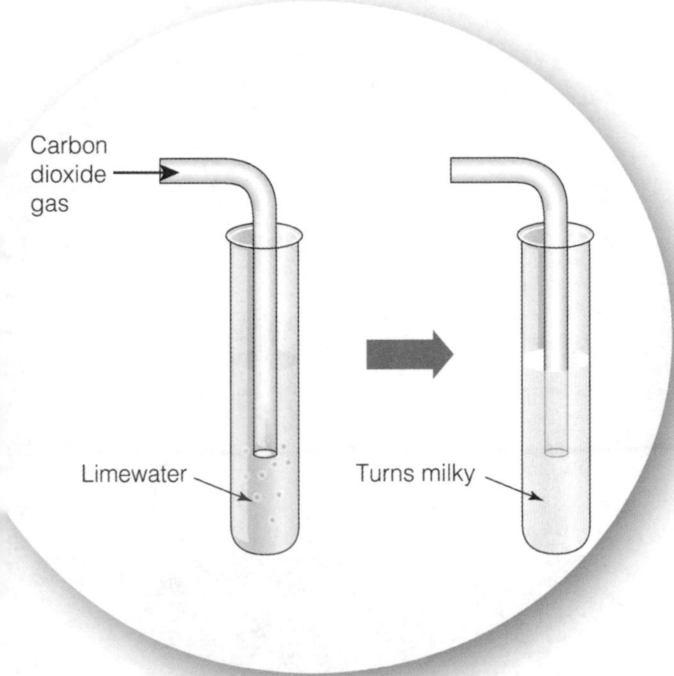

Testing for chlorine

Chlorine turns moist blue litmus paper red before bleaching it and turning it white.

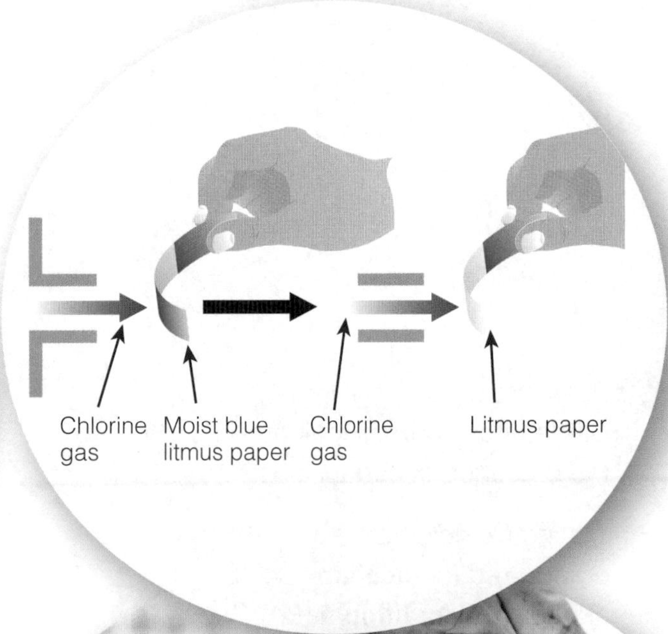

Chlorine gas is very toxic

Write the different gases and tests on separate pieces of paper. Mix up the pieces and practise correctly pairing them up.

1. Which gas relights a glowing splint?
2. What is the test for hydrogen gas?
3. What is the chemical name for limewater?
4. What happens to limewater when it is mixed with carbon dioxide gas?
5. What effect does chlorine gas have on moist blue litmus paper?

31 Identification of cations

Flame tests

Flame tests can be used to identify metal **ions**.

Lithium, sodium, potassium, calcium and copper compounds can be recognised by the distinctive colours they produce in a flame test.

To do a flame test, follow this method:

1. Heat and then dip a piece of nichrome (a nickel–chromium alloy) wire in concentrated hydrochloric acid to clean it.

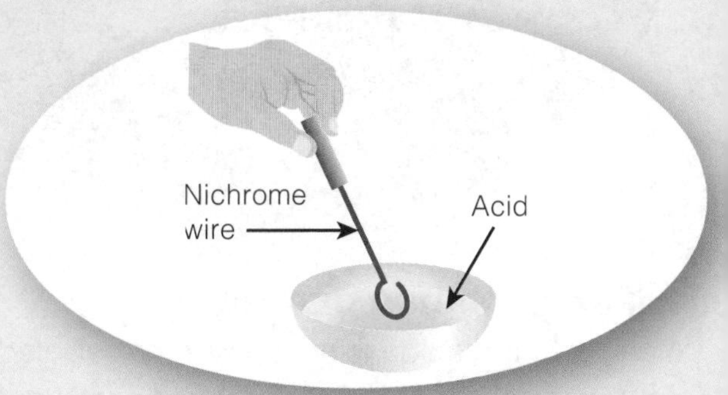
Nichrome wire
Acid

2. Dip the wire in the compound.

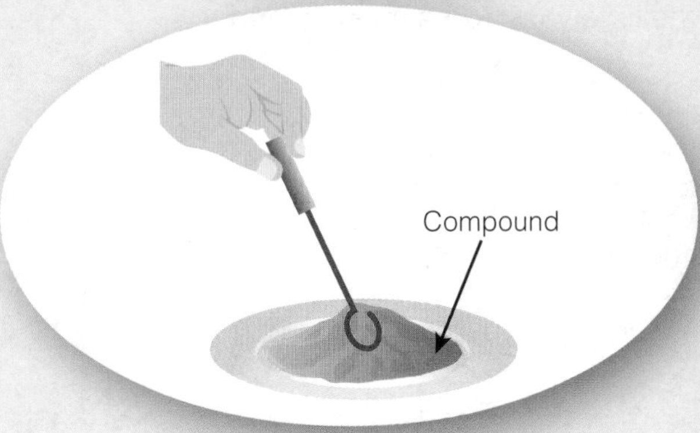
Compound

3. Put it into a Bunsen flame. Different colours will indicate the presence of certain ions.

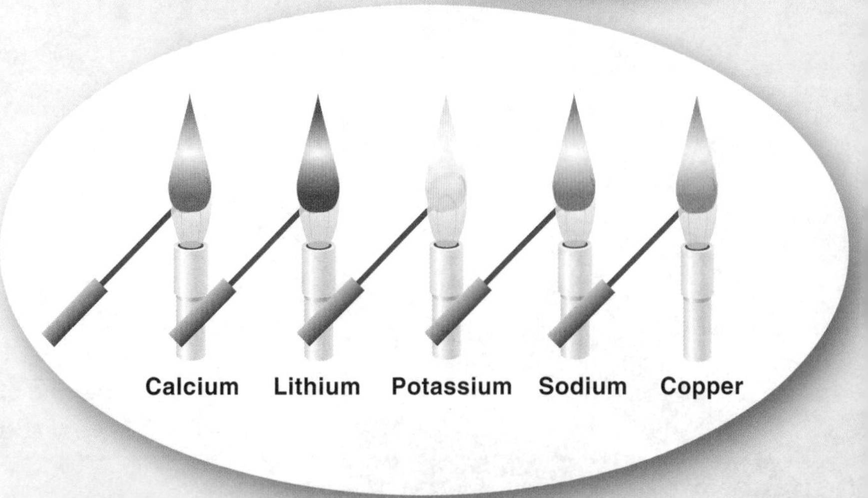
Calcium
Lithium
Potassium
Sodium
Copper

The distinctive colours are:

- orange-red for **calcium** (Ca^{2+})
- crimson red for **lithium** (Li^{+})
- lilac for **potassium** (K^{+})
- yellow for **sodium** (Na^{+})
- green for **copper** (Cu^{2+}).

If a sample containing a mixture of ions is used then some flame colours can be masked.

Keyword

Precipitate ➤ A solid formed when two solutions react together

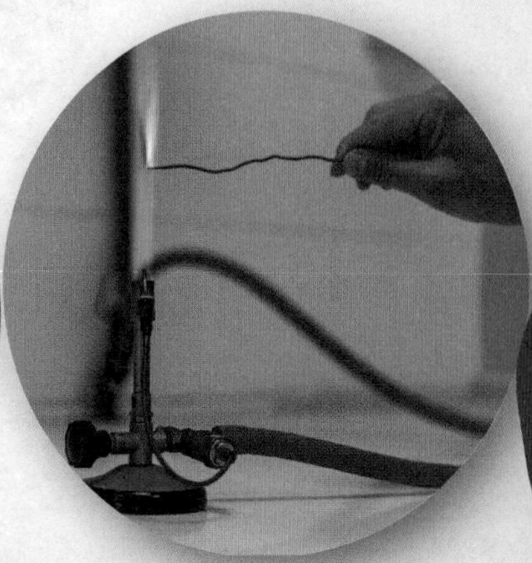

On separate cards, write the name or formula of the ions in this section. On other cards, write all the different colours of the flame tests or hydroxide precipitates – one on each card. Mix up the cards and try to pair them together.

Using sodium hydroxide

Metal compounds in solution contain **metal ions**. Some of these form **precipitates** – **insoluble** solids that come out of solution when sodium hydroxide solution is added to them.

For example, when sodium hydroxide solution is added to calcium chloride solution, a white precipitate of calcium hydroxide is formed (as well as sodium chloride solution). You can see how this precipitate is formed by considering the ions involved.

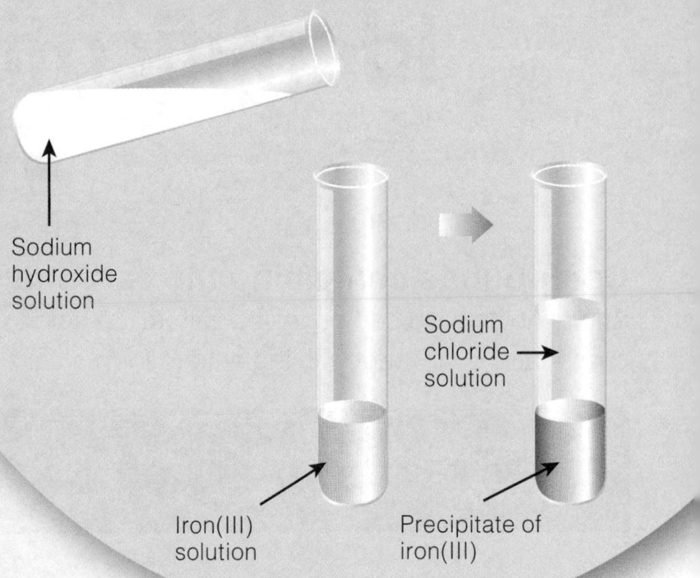

The precipitates formed when metal ions are mixed with sodium hydroxide solution			
Metal ion	**Precipitate formed**		
	Precipitate	**Precipitate colour**	**Equation for formation of precipitate**
Aluminium $Al^{3+}_{(aq)}$	Aluminium hydroxide	White (dissolves with excess sodium hydroxide)	$Al^{3+}_{(aq)} + 3OH^{-}_{(aq)} \rightarrow Al(OH)_{3(s)}$
Calcium $Ca^{2+}_{(aq)}$	Calcium hydroxide	White	$Ca^{2+}_{(aq)} + 2OH^{-}_{(aq)} \rightarrow Ca(OH)_{2(s)}$
Magnesium $Mg^{2+}_{(aq)}$	Magnesium hydroxide	White	$Mg^{2+}_{(aq)} + 2OH^{-}_{(aq)} \rightarrow Mg(OH)_{2(s)}$
Copper(II) $Cu^{2+}_{(aq)}$	Copper(II) hydroxide	Blue	$Cu^{2+}_{(aq)} + 2OH^{-}_{(aq)} \rightarrow Cu(OH)_{2(s)}$
Iron(II) $Fe^{2+}_{(aq)}$	Iron(II) hydroxide	Green	$Fe^{2+}_{(aq)} + 2OH^{-}_{(aq)} \rightarrow Fe(OH)_{2(s)}$
Iron(III) $Fe^{3+}_{(aq)}$	Iron(III) hydroxide	Brown	$Fe^{3+}_{(aq)} + 3OH^{-}_{(aq)} \rightarrow Fe(OH)_{3(s)}$

1. Which metal gives a lilac flame in a flame test?
2. What colour flame is seen when a flame test is done on a compound containing lithium?
3. What is the name of the precipitate formed when a solution containing magnesium ions reacts with sodium hydroxide solution?
4. Write an equation for the formation of the precipitate formed when a solution containing Fe^{2+} ions reacts with sodium hydroxide.
5. What is the colour of the precipitate formed in question 4?

Identification of anions

Compounds containing the carbonate (CO_3^{2-}) ion

An unknown solid can be tested with dilute acid to see if it contains carbonate ions, CO_3^{2-}. If the solid is a carbonate, it will react with the acid to form a salt, water and carbon dioxide gas, which fizzes. For example:

calcium carbonate	+	hydrochloric acid	→	calcium chloride	+	carbon dioxide	+	water
$CaCO_{3\,(s)}$	+	$2HCl_{(aq)}$	→	$CaCl_{2\,(aq)}$	+	$CO_{2\,(g)}$	+	$H_2O_{(l)}$

Limewater can be used to test for carbon dioxide. If the gas is present, the limewater will turn milky / cloudy.

Most carbonate compounds are insoluble but some (e.g. sodium carbonate and potassium carbonate) are soluble in water and produce solutions containing carbonate ions.

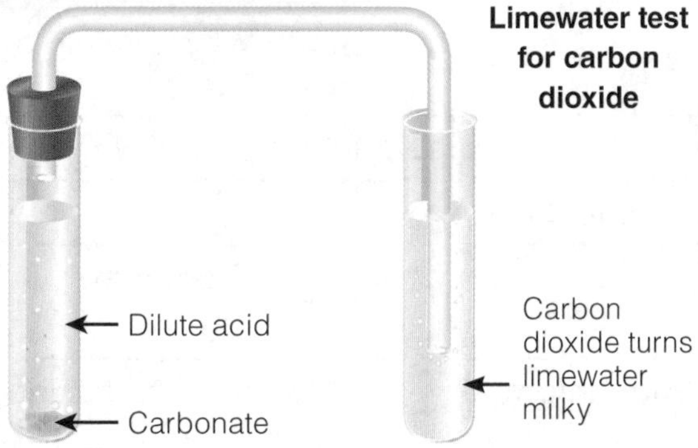
Dilute acid
Carbonate
Carbon dioxide turns limewater milky
Limewater test for carbon dioxide

Identifying dissolved ions

The **dissolved ions** of some salts are easy to identify as they will undergo **precipitation** reactions.

Sulfates (SO_4^{2-}) can be detected using dilute hydrochloric acid and barium chloride solution. A white precipitate of barium sulfate forms, as in the following example.

sodium sulfate	+	barium chloride	→	barium sulfate	+	sodium chloride
$Na_2SO_{4\,(aq)}$	+	$BaCl_{2\,(aq)}$	→	$BaSO_{4\,(s)}$ (white)	+	$2NaCl_{(aq)}$

32

Silver nitrate solution, in the presence of dilute nitric acid, is used to detect halide ions. Halides are the ions made by the halogens (group 7).

With silver nitrate:

- chlorides (Cl^-) form a white precipitate
- bromides (Br^-) form a cream precipitate
- iodides (I^-) form a yellow precipitate.

sodium chloride	+	silver nitrate	→	silver chloride	+	sodium nitrate
$NaCl_{(aq)}$	+	$AgNO_{3\,(aq)}$	→	$AgCl_{(s)}$ (white)	+	$NaNO_{3\,(aq)}$

sodium bromide	+	silver nitrate	→	silver bromide	+	sodium nitrate
$NaBr_{(aq)}$	+	$AgNO_{3\,(aq)}$	→	$AgBr_{(s)}$ (cream)	+	$NaNO_{3\,(aq)}$

sodium bromide	+	silver nitrate	→	silver iodide	+	sodium nitrate
$NaI_{(aq)}$	+	$AgNO_{3\,(aq)}$	→	$AgI_{(s)}$ (yellow)	+	$NaNO_{3\,(aq)}$

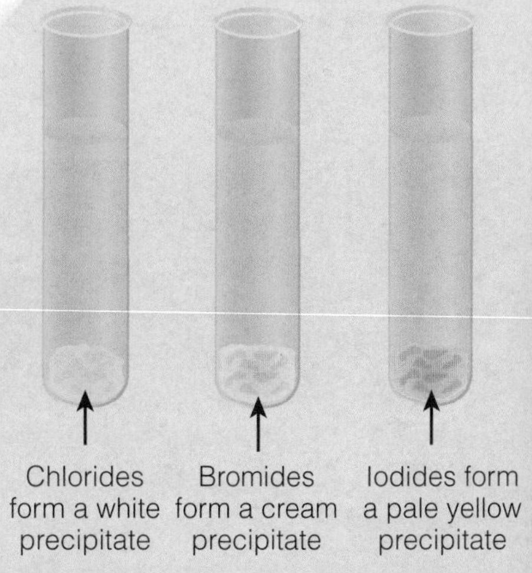
Chlorides form a white precipitate
Bromides form a cream precipitate
Iodides form a pale yellow precipitate

Instrumental methods of analysis

As well as chemical tests, elements and compounds can also be analysed and identified by instrumental methods.

Advantages of instrumental methods compared with chemical tests			
		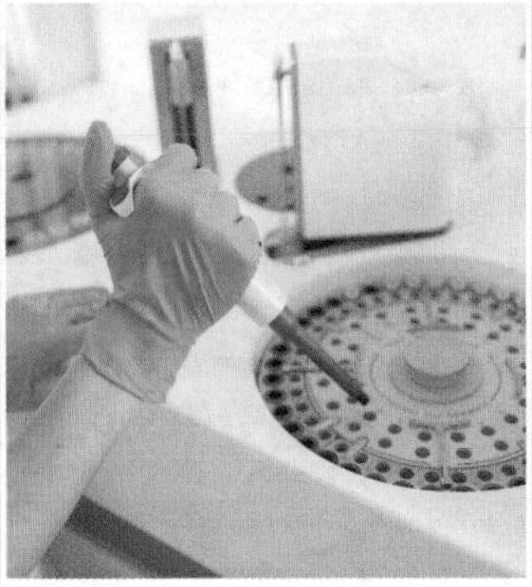	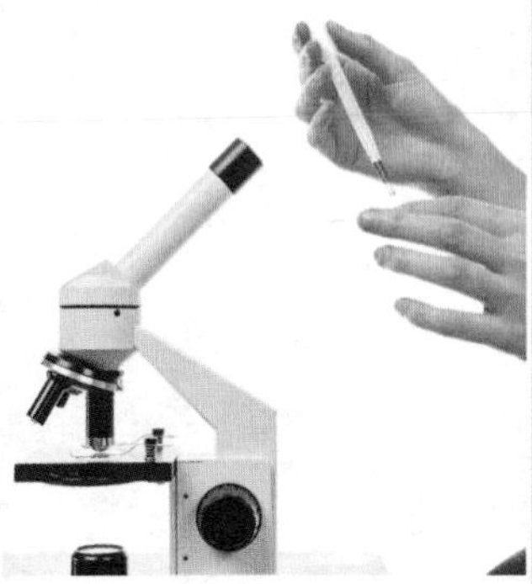
➤ Rapid	➤ More accurate	➤ More sensitive	➤ Can be used with very small samples

Flame emission spectroscopy

Flame emission spectroscopy can be used to identify metal ions present in solutions.

1. The sample is put into a flame.
2. The light given out is passed through a **spectroscope/flame photometer**.
3. A line spectrum is produced.
4. This is compared with reference spectra.
5. Metal ions present are identified.
6. The concentration of ions in solution can be determined by reference to a calibration curve.

The line spectra of some metals

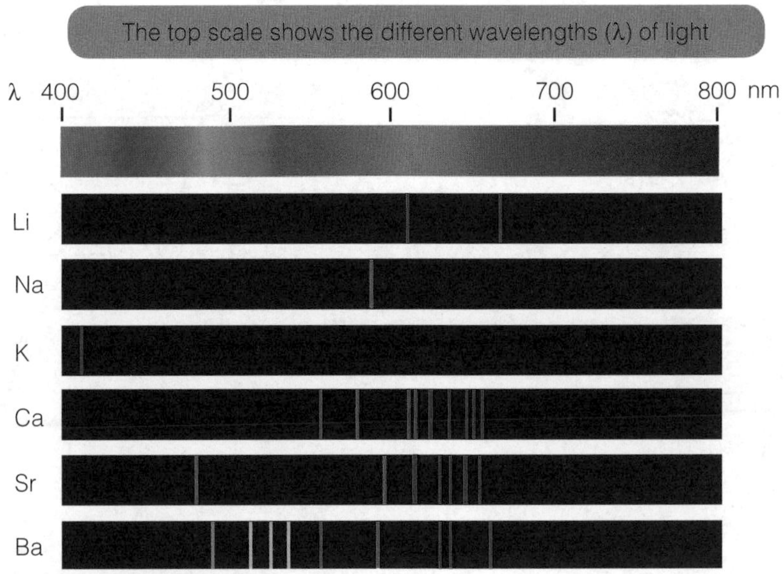
The top scale shows the different wavelengths (λ) of light
λ 400
500
600
700
800 nm
Li
Na
K
Ca
Sr
Ba

Make a table of all of the different anions on these pages and their tests and results.
Cover up the tests and results and see how many you can remember!

Keywords

Spectroscope/flame photometer ➤ A device for observing the spectrum of light produced by a source

1. Which ion reacts with acid to form CO_2 gas?
2. What colour precipitate is formed when bromide ions react with silver nitrate solution?
3. Name the solution used to test for the sulfate (SO_4^{2-}) ion after dilute hydrochloric acid has been added.
4. Give one advantage of using an instrumental method of analysis over a chemical test.

Mind map

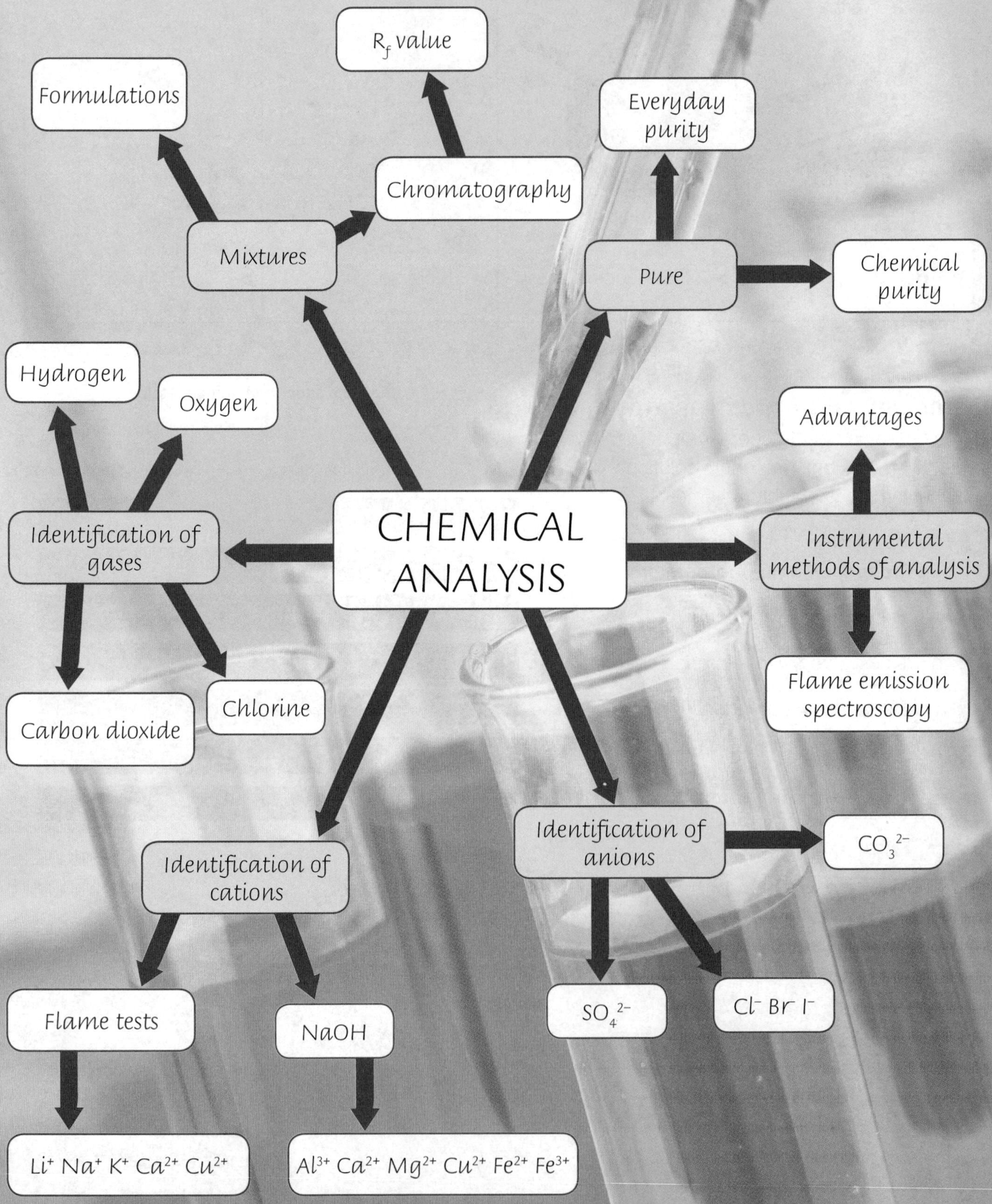
CHEMICAL ANALYSIS
Mixtures
Formulations
Chromatography
R_f value
Pure
Everyday purity
Chemical purity
Instrumental methods of analysis
Advantages
Flame emission spectroscopy
Identification of anions
CO_3^{2-}
SO_4^{2-}
Cl^- Br^- I^-
Identification of cations
Flame tests
Li^+ Na^+ K^+ Ca^{2+} Cu^{2+}
NaOH
Al^{3+} Ca^{2+} Mg^{2+} Cu^{2+} Fe^{2+} Fe^{3+}
Identification of gases
Hydrogen
Oxygen
Carbon dioxide
Chlorine

Practice questions

1. Potassium sulfate is a white solid commonly used in fertilisers.

   It contains potassium ions (K^+) and sulfate ions (SO_4^{2-}).

   A flame test can be carried out to confirm the presence of potassium in solid potassium sulfate.

   a) State the formula of potassium sulfate. **(1 mark)**

   b) Describe how to carry out a flame test. **(3 marks)**

   c) What colour flame would be observed when a flame test is carried out using potassium sulfate? **(1 mark)**

   To confirm the presence of the sulfate ion, the solid needs to be dissolved in water before adding two chemicals.

   d) Name the two chemicals that need to be added to this solution in order to test for the presence of the sulfate ion. **(2 marks)**

   e) What would be observed if the sulfate ion is present? **(2 marks)**

   f) Name an instrumental method that can be used to determine the presence of potassium ions in a sample of fertiliser. **(1 mark)**

2. Compound X produced an orange-red flame in a flame test.
   When dilute hydrochloric acid was added to compound X, a gas was produced that turned limewater milky.

   a) Give the formula of the cation present in compound X. **(1 mark)**

   b) Name the gas produced when dilute hydrochloric acid was added to X. **(1 mark)**

   c) Give the formula of the anion present in compound X. **(1 mark)**

   d) What is the formula of compound X? **(1 mark)**

   e) Describe how you would show that dilute hydrochloric acid contains the chloride ion. **(3 marks)**

Evolution of the atmosphere

The Earth's early atmosphere

Theories about the composition of Earth's early atmosphere and how the atmosphere was formed have changed over time. Evidence for the early atmosphere is limited because the Earth is approximately 4.6 billion years old.

The table below gives one theory to explain the evolution of the atmosphere.

Time scale	Condition of the atmosphere	Key factors and events that shaped the atmosphere
Formation of the Earth  **4 billion years ago** 	 Other gases CO_2 Decrease in carbon dioxide and other gases / Increase in oxygen and nitrogen	Intense volcanic activity releases…  ► mainly **carbon dioxide** (like the atmospheres of Mars and Venus today) ► **nitrogen** (which gradually built up in the atmosphere) ► **water vapour** (which condenses to form the oceans) ► small proportions of **methane** and **ammonia**
3 billion years ago 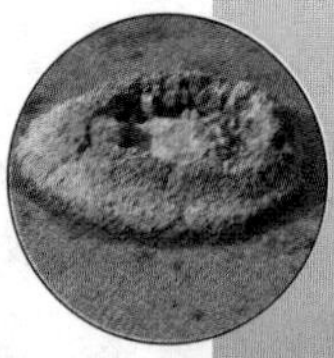 **2 billion years ago** 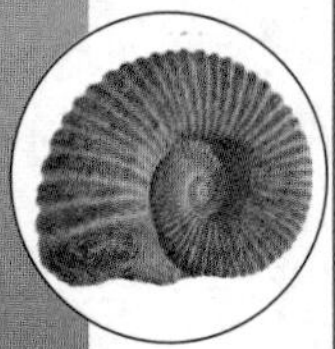	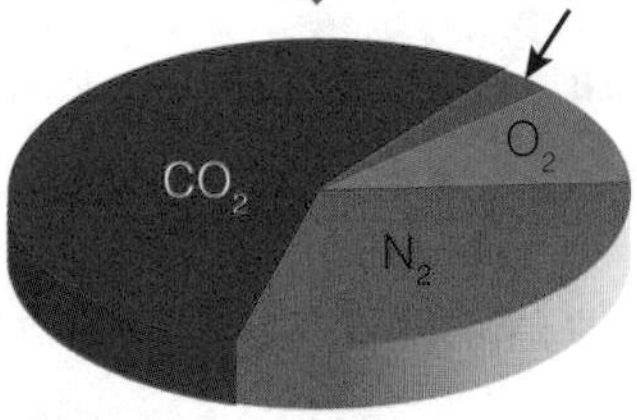 Other gases CO_2 O_2 N_2 Decrease in carbon dioxide / Increase in nitrogen and oxygen	Green plants and algae evolve and… ► **carbon dioxide** is reduced as the plants take it in and give out **oxygen** by photosynthesis: $6CO_2 + 6H_2O \longrightarrow C_6H_{12}O_6 + 6O_2$. The percentage of oxygen gradually increased to a level that enabled animals to evolve ► microorganisms that cannot tolerate oxygen are killed off ► **carbon** from carbon dioxide becomes locked up in **sedimentary rocks** formed from the shells and skeletons of marine organisms ► other gases react with oxygen to release **nitrogen** ► nitrogen is also produced by bacteria removing nitrates from decaying plant material
1 billion years ago **Now** 	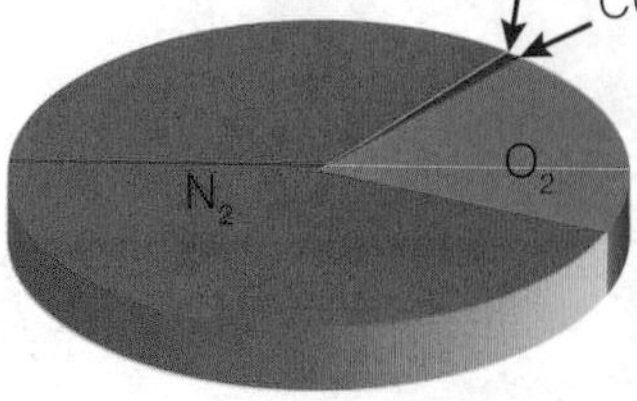 Other gases CO_2 O_2 N_2	There is now about 20% **oxygen** and about 80% **nitrogen** in the atmosphere The amount of **carbon dioxide** has decreased significantly 

Composition of the atmosphere today

The proportions of gases in the atmosphere have been more or less the same for about 200 million years. **Water vapour** may also be present in varying quantities (0–3%).

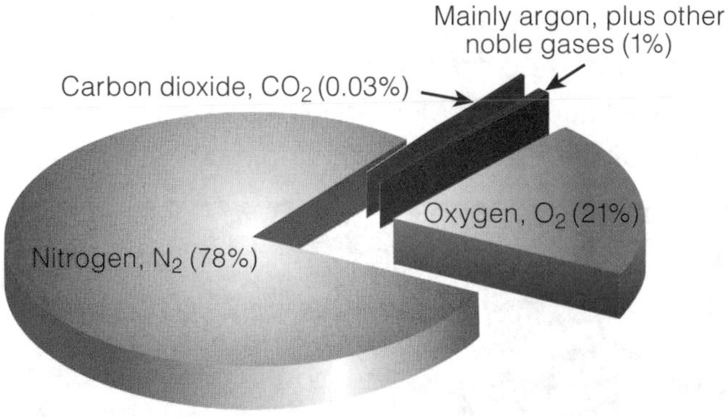
Mainly argon, plus other noble gases (1%)
Carbon dioxide, CO_2 (0.03%)
Oxygen, O_2 (21%)
Nitrogen, N_2 (78%)

Keyword

Photosynthesis ➤ The process by which green plants and algae use water and carbon dioxide to make glucose and oxygen

How carbon dioxide decreased

The amount of carbon dioxide in the atmosphere today is much less than it was when the atmosphere first formed. This is because…

- green plants and algae use carbon dioxide for **photosynthesis**

- carbon dioxide is used to form sedimentary rocks, e.g. limestone

- fossil fuels such as oil (see Module 25) and coal (a sedimentary rock made from thick plant deposits that were buried and compressed over millions of years) have captured CO_2.

Make a timeline showing the key changes in the evolution of the Earth's atmosphere.

Name two gases that volcanoes released into the early atmosphere.
How did oxygen become present in the atmosphere?
How much of the atmosphere today is nitrogen gas?
State two ways that the amount of carbon dioxide present in the early atmosphere decreased.

Climate change

Greenhouse gases

The temperature on Earth is maintained at a level to support life by the greenhouse gases in the atmosphere. These gases allow short wavelength radiation from the Sun to pass through but absorb the long wavelength radiation reflected back from the ground trapping heat and causing an increase in temperature. Common greenhouse gases are water vapour, carbon dioxide and methane.

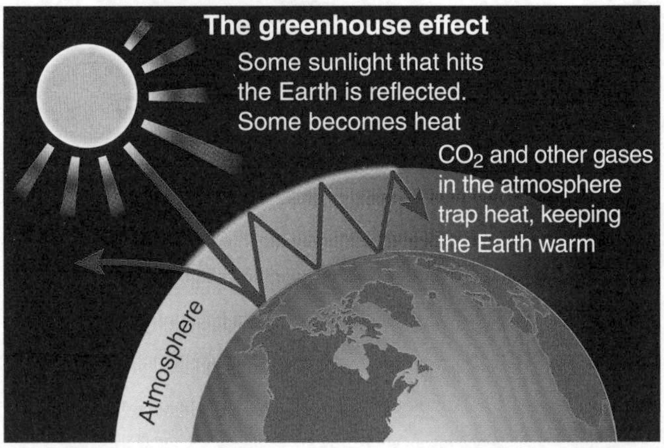

The greenhouse effect
Some sunlight that hits the Earth is reflected. Some becomes heat
CO_2 and other gases in the atmosphere trap heat, keeping the Earth warm
Atmosphere

Human activity and global warming

Some human activities increase the amounts of greenhouse gases (water vapour, carbon dioxide and methane) in the atmosphere including…

Combustion of fossil fuels releases carbon dioxide into the atmosphere

Increased animal farming releases more methane into the atmosphere, e.g. as a by-product of digestion and decomposition of waste

Deforestation reduces the amount of carbon dioxide removed from the atmosphere by photosynthesis

Decomposition of rubbish in landfill sites also releases methane into the atmosphere

The increase in carbon dioxide levels in the last century or so correlates with the increased use of fossil fuels by humans.

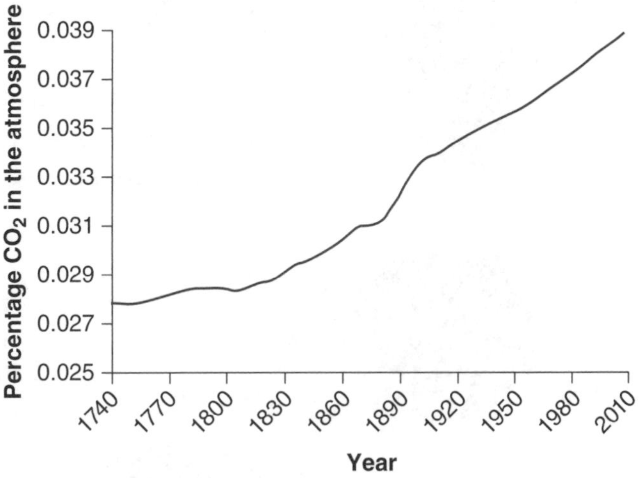

Percentage CO_2 in the atmosphere
0.039
0.037
0.035
0.033
0.031
0.029
0.027
0.025
1740
1770
1800
1830
1860
1890
1920
1950
1980
2010
Year

Based on **peer-reviewed evidence**, many scientists believe that increasing these human activities will lead to global climate change.

Predicting the impact of changes on global climate change is not easy because of the many different contributing factors involved. This can lead to simplified models and speculation often presented in the media that may not be based on all of the evidence. This means that the information could be biased.

Increased human activity resulting in more release of fossil fuels → Increased temperatures → Global climate change

Global climate change

Increasing average global temperature is a major cause of climate change. Potential effects of climate change include:

Rising sea levels, which may cause flooding and coastal erosion
More frequent and severe storms
Changes to the amount, timing and distribution of rainfall
Temperature and water stress for humans and wildlife
Changes in the food producing capacity of some regions
Changes to the distribution of wildlife species

Reducing the carbon footprint

The **carbon footprint** is a measure of the total amount of carbon dioxide (and other greenhouse gases) emitted over the life cycle of a product, service or event.

Problems of trying to reduce the carbon footprint include…

- disagreement over the causes and consequences of global climate change
- lack of public information and education
- lifestyle changes, e.g. greater use of cars / aeroplanes
- economic considerations, i.e. the financial costs of reducing the carbon footprint
- incomplete international co-operation.

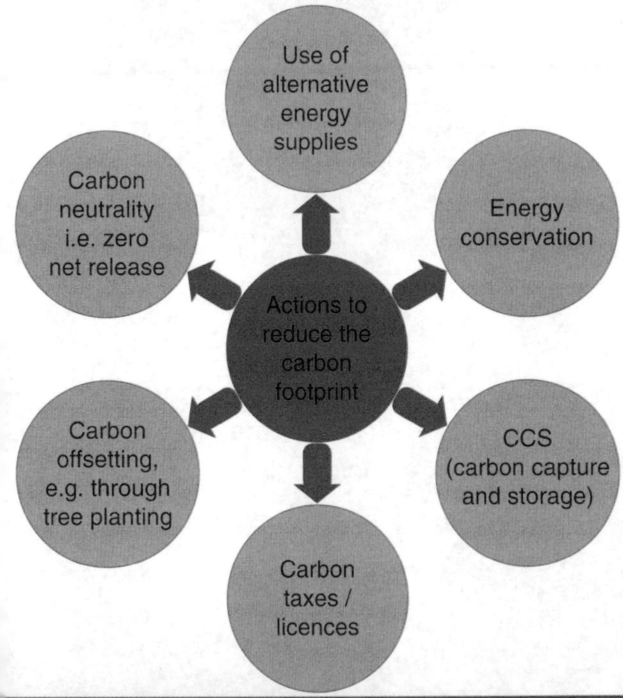

Actions to reduce the carbon footprint
Use of alternative energy supplies
Energy conservation
CCS (carbon capture and storage)
Carbon taxes / licences
Carbon offsetting, e.g. through tree planting
Carbon neutrality i.e. zero net release

Produce a leaflet informing members of the public about how they can reduce their own carbon footprint.

Keywords

Peer-reviewed evidence ➤ Work (evidence) of scientists that has been checked by other scientists to ensure that it is accurate and scientifically valid

Carbon footprint ➤ The total amount of carbon dioxide (and other greenhouse gases) emitted over the full life cycle of a product, service or event

1. Name two greenhouse gases.
2. State one way that human activity leads to an increased amount of methane in the atmosphere.
3. Give two potential effects of global climate change.
4. Give an example of one problem of trying to reduce the carbon footprint.

34

Atmospheric pollution

35

Pollutants from fuels

The combustion of **fossil fuels** is a major source of atmospheric pollutants. Most fuels contain carbon and often sulfur is present as an impurity. Many different gases are released into the atmosphere when a fuel is burned.

Solid particles and unburned hydrocarbons can also be released forming **particulates** in the air.

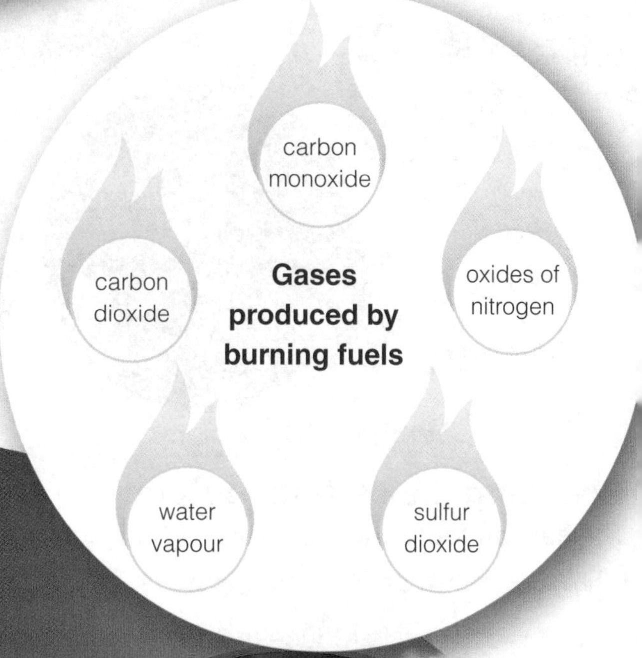

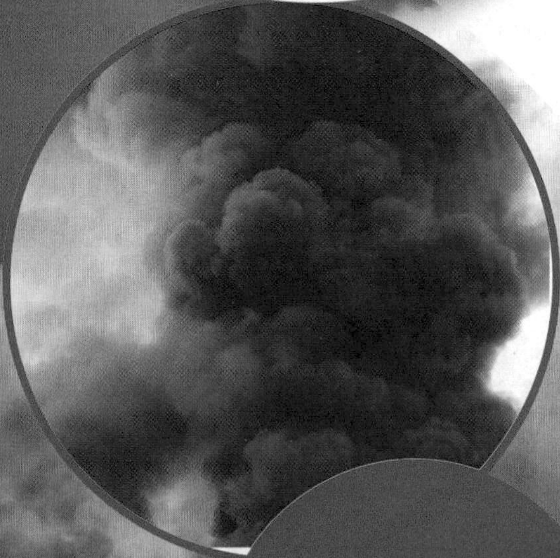

Sulfur dioxide is produced by the oxidation of sulfur present in fuels – often from coal-burning power stations

Carbon monoxide and soot (carbon) are produced by incomplete combustion of fuels

Oxides of nitrogen are formed from the reaction between nitrogen and oxygen from the air – often from the high temperatures and sparks in the engines of motor vehicles

Key words

Fossil fuel Fuel formed in the ground over millions of years from the remains of dead plants and animal

Particulates Small solid particles present in the air

Properties and effects of atmospheric pollutants

Carbon monoxide is a colourless, odourless toxic gas and so it is difficult to detect. It combines with haemoglobin in the blood, which reduces the oxygen-carrying capacity of blood.

Sulfur dioxide and **oxides of nitrogen** cause respiratory problems in humans and can form acid rain in the atmosphere. Acid rain damages plants and buildings.

Particulates in the atmosphere can cause global dimming, which reduces the amount of sunlight that reaches the Earth's surface. Breathing in particulates can also damage lungs, which can cause health problems.

Make a list of all of the ways in one day that you see waste gases being released into the atmosphere.

1. Name two gases produced by burning fuels.
2. How is carbon monoxide formed?
3. What problems do atmospheric sulfur dioxide and oxides of nitrogen cause?

Using the Earth's resources and obtaining potable water

Keywords

Sustainable development > Living in a way that meets the needs of the current generation without compromising the potential of future generations to meet their own needs

Potable water > Water that is safe to drink

Earth's resources

We use the Earth's **resources** to provide us with warmth, shelter, food and transport. These needs are met from natural resources which, supplemented by agriculture, provide food, timber, clothing and fuels. Resources from the earth, atmosphere and oceans are processed to provide energy and materials.

Industrial chemical processes can be used to make new materials, reducing the demand for natural resources

Chemistry plays a role in providing **sustainable development**. This means that the needs of the current generation are met without compromising the potential of future generations to meet their own needs. For example…

Chemistry plays an important role in improving agricultural processes, e.g. by developing fertilisers

Drinking water

Water that is safe to drink is called **potable water**. It is not pure in the chemical sense (see Module 29) because it contains dissolved minerals and ions.

Water of appropriate quality is essential for life. This means that it contains sufficiently low levels of dissolved salts and microbes.

In the UK, most potable water comes from rainwater. To turn rainwater into potable water, water companies carry out a number of processes.

1. An appropriate source of fresh water is selected

2. It is then passed through filter beds to remove any solid impurities

3. Finally it is sterilised (suitable sterilising agents include chlorine, ozone and ultraviolet light) to kill microbes, making it safe to drink

Waste water

Urban lifestyles and industrial processes generate large quantities of waste water, which requires treatment before being released into the environment. Sewage and agricultural waste water require removal of organic matter and harmful microbes. Industrial waste water may require removal of organic matter and harmful chemicals.

Sewage treatment includes…

- screening and grit removal
- sedimentation to produce sewage sludge and effluent
- anaerobic digestion of sewage sludge
- aerobic biological treatment of effluent.

When supplies of fresh water are limited, removal of salt (desalination) of salty water / seawater can be used.

This is done in two ways:

- By distillation.

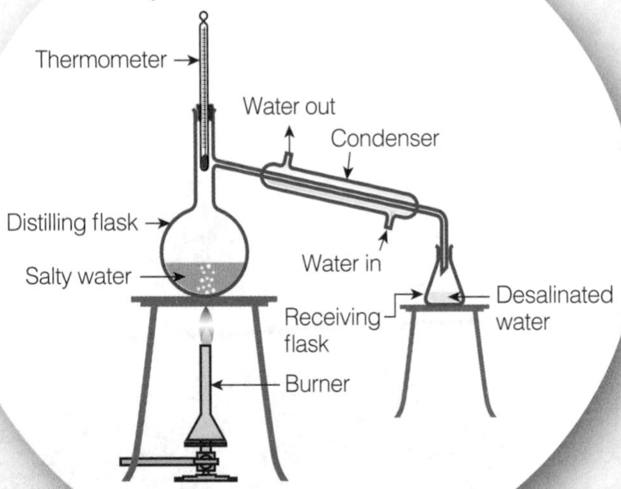

Thermometer
Water out
Condenser
Distilling flask
Salty water
Water in
Desalinated water
Receiving flask
Burner

- By processes that use membranes, such as reverse osmosis.

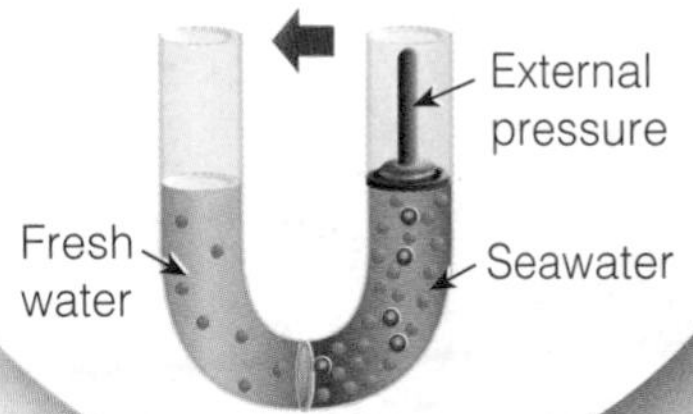

External pressure
Fresh water
Seawater

However, these processes require large amounts of energy.

Find out different ways of making water potable.

36

What is sustainable development?
State the difference between pure water and potable water.
What are the two main stages in turning rainwater into potable water?
Name one way of desalinating salty water.

Alternative methods of extracting metals

HT

copper ore

Extracting copper

Copper is an important metal with lots of uses. It is used in electrical wiring because it is an excellent conductor of electricity. It is also used in water pipes because it conducts heat and does not corrode or react with the water.

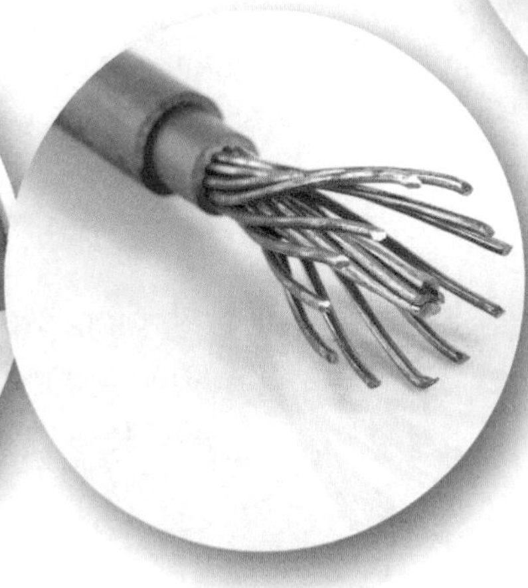

The Earth's resources of metal **ores** are limited and copper ores are becoming scarce.

New ways of extracting copper from **low-grade ores** include...

- **phytomining**
  Phytomining uses plants to absorb metal compounds. This means that the plants accumulate metal within them. Harvesting and then burning the plants leaves ash that is rich in the metal compounds.

- **bioleaching**
  Bioleaching uses bacteria to extract metals from low-grade ores. A solution containing bacteria is mixed with a low-grade ore. The bacteria release the metals into solution (known as a leachate) where they can be easily extracted.

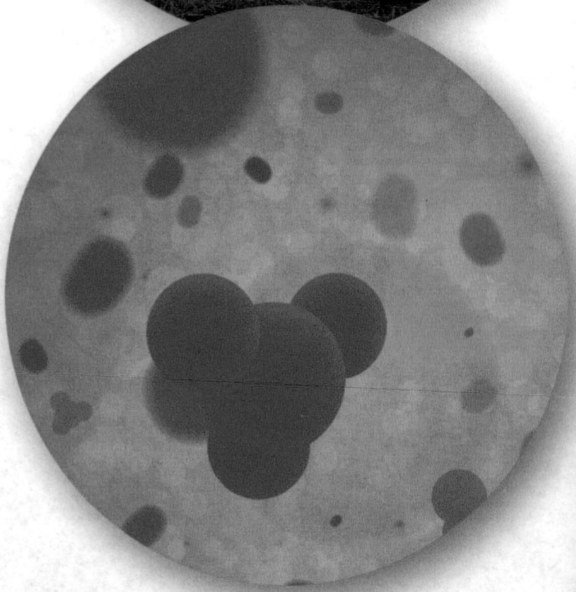

These new extraction methods reduce the impact on the Earth of mining, moving and disposing of large amounts of rock.

Processing metal compounds

The metal compounds from phytomining and bioleaching are processed to obtain the metal. Copper can be obtained from solutions of copper compounds by…

- **displacement** using scrap iron – iron is more reactive than copper, so placing iron into a solution of copper will result in copper metal being displaced.

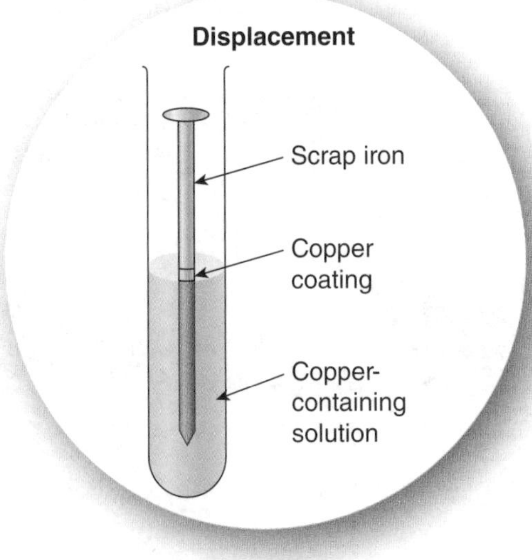
Displacement
Scrap iron
Copper coating
Copper-containing solution

- **electrolysis**.

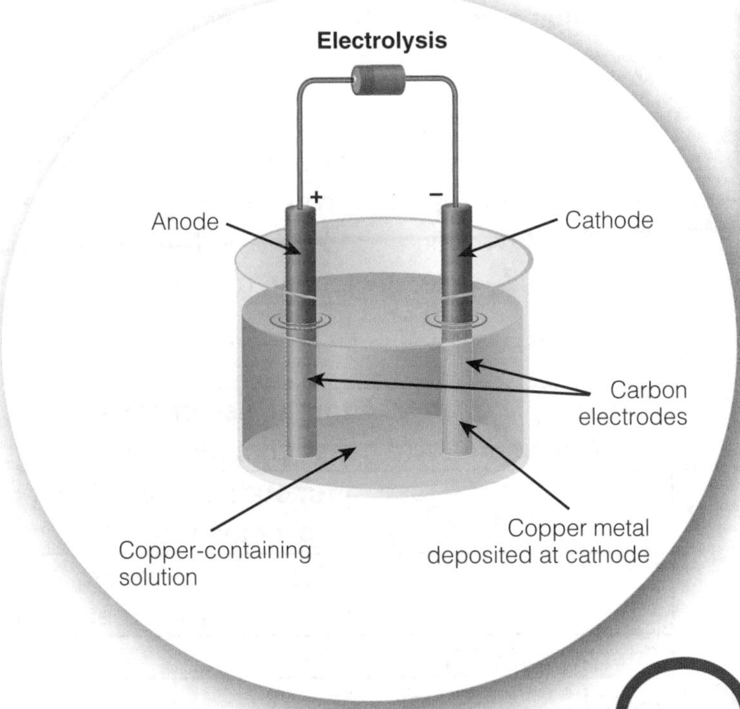
Electrolysis
+
–
Anode
Cathode
Carbon electrodes
Copper-containing solution
Copper metal deposited at cathode

Keywords

Ore ➤ A naturally occurring mineral from which it is economically viable to extract a metal

Low-grade ores ➤ Ores that contain small amounts of metal

Phytomining ➤ A method of metal extraction that involves growing plants in metal solutions so that they accumulate metal; the plants are then burnt and the metal extracted from the ash

Bioleaching ➤ An extraction method that uses bacteria to extract metals from low-grade ores

Find examples of copper being used in your home.
Think what properties of copper make it suitable for that use.

37

State one use of copper.
Why is it important to develop new ways of extracting metals?
Which biological method of extracting metals involves bacteria?
Give one way that metal can be extracted from a metal containing solution.

Life-cycle assessment and recycling

Life-cycle assessments

Life-cycle assessments (LCAs) are carried out to evaluate the environmental impact of products in each of the following stages.

Extracting and processing raw materials

Manufacturing and packaging

Disposal at the end of useful life

Transport and distribution at each of the previous stages

The following steps are considered when carrying out an LCA.

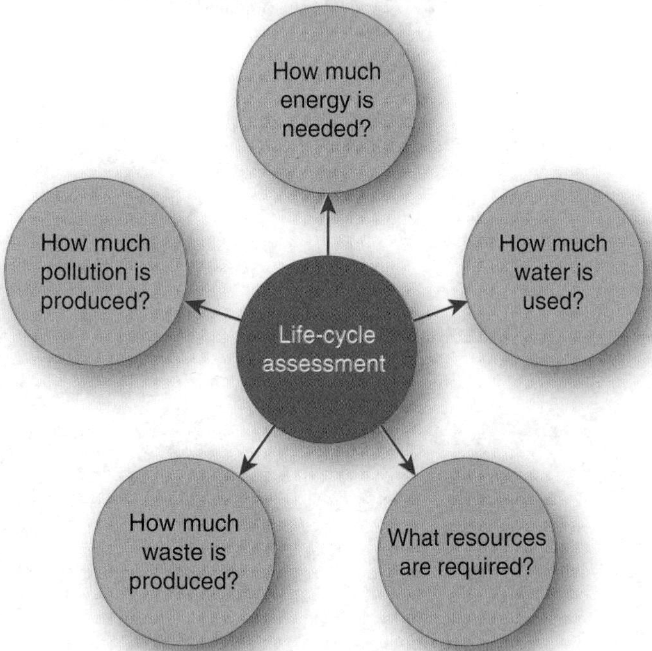
Life-cycle assessment
How much energy is needed?
How much water is used?
What resources are required?
How much waste is produced?
How much pollution is produced?

Many of these values are relatively easy to quantify. However, some values, such as the amount of pollution, are often difficult to measure and so value judgements have to be made. This means that carrying out an LCA is not a purely objective process.

It is not always easy to obtain accurate figures. This means that selective or abbreviated LCAs, which are open to bias or misuse, can be devised to evaluate a product, to reinforce predetermined conclusions or to support claims for advertising purposes.

For example, look at the LCA below.

Example of an LCA for the use of plastic (polythene) and paper shopping bags

	Amount per 1000 bags over the whole LCA	
	Paper	**Plastic (polythene)**
Energy use (MJ)	2590	713
Fossil fuel use (Kg)	28	13
Solid waste (Kg)	34	6
Greenhouse gas emissions (kg CO_2)	72	36
Freshwater use (litres)	3387	198

This LCA provides evidence supporting the argument that using polythene bags is better for the environment than paper bags!

Ways of reducing the use of resources

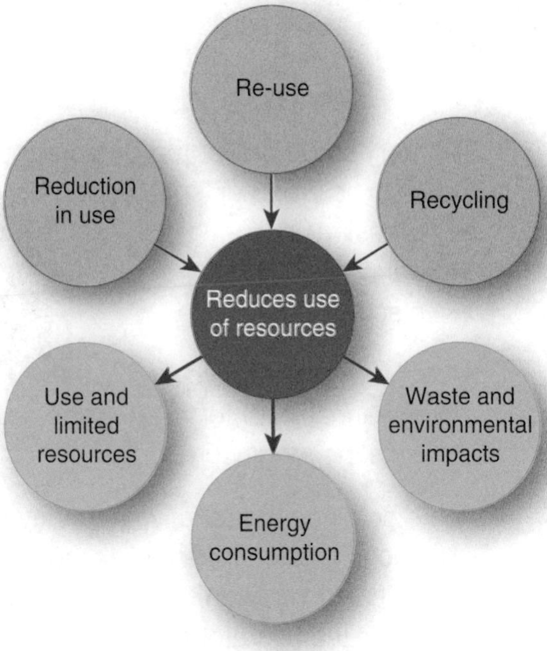

Re-use
Reduction in use
Recycling
Reduces use of resources
Use and limited resources
Waste and environmental impacts
Energy consumption

Keywords

Life-cycle assessment >> An evaluation of the environmental impact of a product over the whole of its lifespan

Blast furnace >> Industrial method of extracting iron from iron ore

Many materials such as glass, metals, building materials, plastics and clay ceramics are produced from limited raw materials. Most of the energy used in their production comes from limited resources, such as fossil fuels. Obtaining raw materials from the earth by quarrying and mining has a detrimental environmental impact.

Some products, like glass, can be **reused** (e.g. washing and then using again for the same purpose). Recycled glass is crushed, melted and remade into glass products.

Other products cannot be reused and so they are **recycled** for a different use.

Metals are recycled by sorting them, followed by melting them and recasting / reforming them into different products. The amount of separation required for recycling depends on the material (e.g. whether they are magnetic or not) and the properties required of the final product. For example, some scrap steel can be added to iron from a **blast furnace** to reduce the amount of iron that needs to be extracted from iron ore.

Quarrying

Blast furnace

Recycling

GLASS

Try to identify the environmental impact of this book by considering the effects of all of the stages of its life cycle.

1. What does a life-cycle assessment measure?
2. State two factors that a life-cycle assessment tries to evaluate.
3. Why are life-cycle assessments not always totally objective?
4. State one way in which we can reduce the use of resources.

Using materials

Corrosion and its prevention

Corrosion is the destruction of materials (e.g. metals) by chemical reactions by chemicals in the environment. Rusting is a common form of corrosion. It involves iron reacting with oxygen and water.

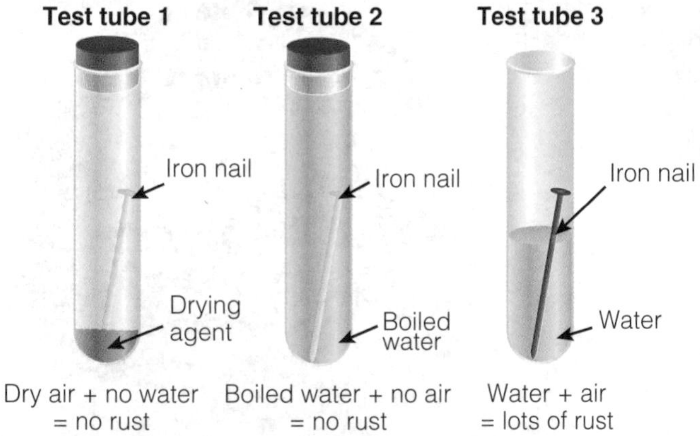
Test tube 1
Test tube 2
Test tube 3
Iron nail
Drying agent
Iron nail
Boiled water
Iron nail
Water
Dry air + no water = no rust
Boiled water + no air = no rust
Water + air = lots of rust

Rusting can be prevented by applying a coating that acts as a barrier, such as…

- greasing
- painting
- electroplating.

Aluminium is a reactive metal that naturally forms an oxide coating which prevents the metal from further corrosion.

Some coatings are reactive and may contain corrosion inhibitors or a more reactive metal. For example, zinc is often used to **galvanise** iron. If the coating is then scratched, the zinc reacts instead of the iron. This is called **sacrificial protection**.

Magnesium blocks can be attached to a ship's hull to provide sacrificial protection.

Alloys as useful materials

Many of the metals we use every day are **alloys**. Pure metals such as gold, copper, iron and aluminium are too soft for many uses. Alloys are made by mixing metals together. This makes them harder and more suitable for everyday use.

100% pure **gold** (known as 24-carat gold) is often mixed with other metals. The proportion of gold in the alloy gives the carat rating (e.g. 18 carat contains 75% gold).	
Bronze (an alloy of copper and tin) is used to make statues and other decorative objects.	
Brass is an alloy of copper and zinc that is used to make water taps and door fittings.	
Steel is an alloy of iron, carbon and other metals such as chromium or nickel.	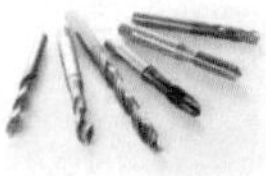
High-carbon steel is strong but brittle – it is used to make cutting tools.	
Low-carbon steel is softer, so it can be more easily shaped. It is used to make car body panels.	
Steels containing nickel and chromium are known as **stainless steels** because of their resistance to corrosion. They are hard and are used to make cutlery and railway tracks.	
Aluminium alloys are strong and low in density. They are used in aerospace manufacturing, for example to make the bodies of aeroplanes.	

Ceramics

Everyday glass is soda-lime glass.

sand + sodium carbonate + limestone → soda-lime glass

Borosilicate glass, made from sand and boron trioxide, melts at a higher temperature than soda-lime glass.

Clay ceramics, including pottery and bricks, are made by shaping wet clay and then heating it in a furnace.

Polymers

The properties of **polymers** depend on the monomer used to make the polymer and the conditions under which they are made. Low-density and high-density poly(ethene) are made from ethene, but using different catalysts and reaction conditions.

Thermosoftening polymers consist of individual polymer chains all tangled together which melt when heated. Thermosetting polymers consist of cross-links between the polymer chains and so they have a more rigid structure which means that they do not melt easily when they are heated.

Thermosoftening polymer (no cross-links)

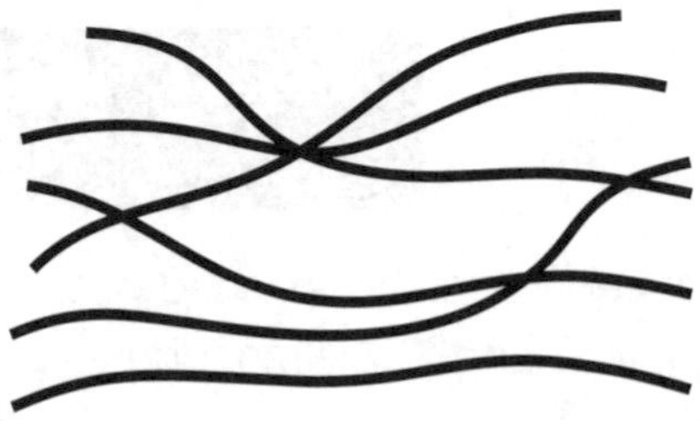

Thermosetting polymer

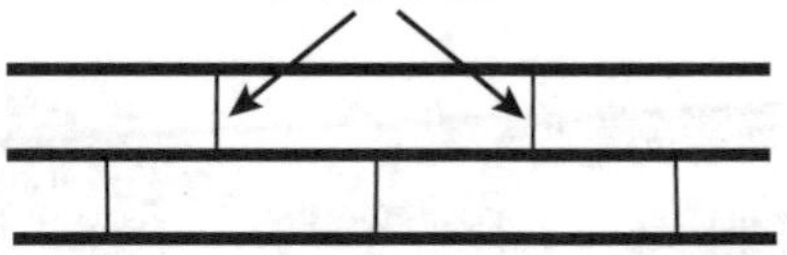

Find examples of ceramics, polymers and composite materials in your home.

Composites

Most **composite materials**, such as reinforced concrete, wood and fibreglass, consist of two materials: a matrix or binder and a reinforcement substance.

Some advanced composites are made from carbon fibres or carbon nanotubes instead of glass fibres.

Reinforced concrete column

Keywords

Galvanise Protect a metal by coating it with zinc
Alloy A mixture of metals
Polymer A large, long-chained molecule
Composite material Two (or more) different materials combined together

39

1. State two ways of preventing corrosion.
2. What is an alloy?
3. What property does stainless steel have compared with ordinary steel?
4. Name the three raw materials used to make soda-lime glass.
5. What is the difference between the structures in thermosoftening and thermosetting polymers?
6. What is a composite material?

The Haber process and the use of NPK fertilisers

40

The Haber process

Fertiliser

Ammonia (NH_3) is produced by the Haber process. The ammonia is used to make nitrogen-based **fertilisers**.

Ammonia is made by combining nitrogen (obtained by fractional distillation of liquid air) and hydrogen (from natural gas).

$$\text{nitrogen} + \text{hydrogen} \rightleftharpoons \text{ammonia}$$
$$N_{2(g)} + 3H_{2(g)} \rightleftharpoons 2NH_{3(g)}$$

The purified gases are passed over an iron catalyst. The reaction is carried out at 450°C and 200 atmospheres pressure.

The reaction is reversible, so some of the ammonia produced will break down into nitrogen and hydrogen.

Upon cooling the ammonia liquefies and is removed. The unreacted nitrogen and hydrogen are recycled back into the reaction chamber.

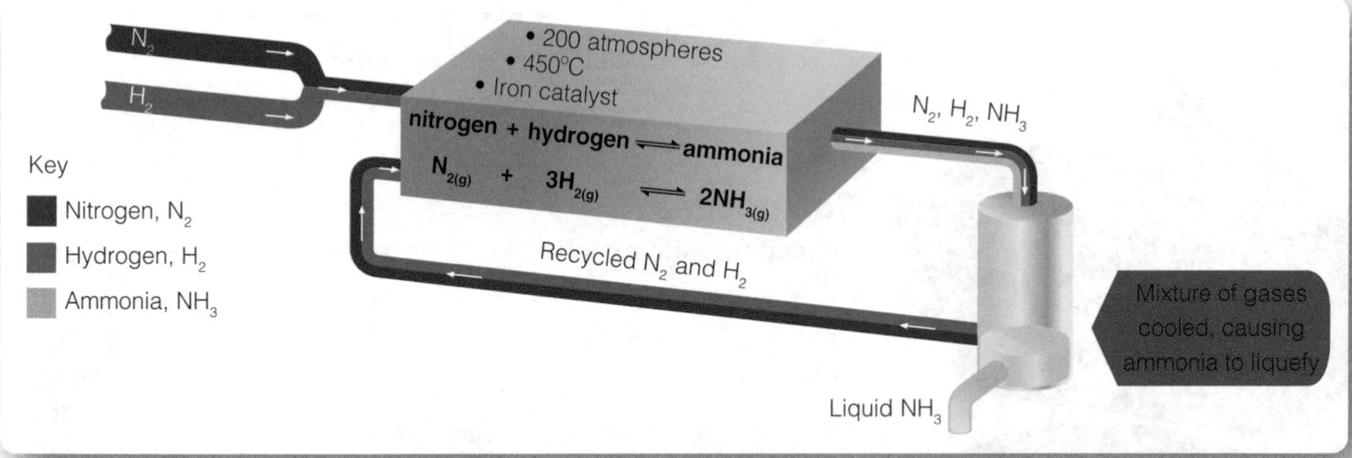
N2
H2
• 200 atmospheres
• 450°C
• Iron catalyst
nitrogen + hydrogen ⇌ ammonia
N2(g) + 3H2(g) ⇌ 2NH3(g)
N2, H2, NH3
Key
Nitrogen, N2
Hydrogen, H2
Ammonia, NH3
Recycled N2 and H2
Mixture of gases cooled, causing ammonia to liquefy
Liquid NH3

Produce a flow chart outlining each different stage involved in the production of ammonia.

Keyword

Fertiliser ► Any material added to the soil or applied to a plant to improve the supply of minerals and increase crop yield

Production and uses of NPK fertilisers

NPK fertilisers contain the elements nitrogen (chemical symbol **N**), phosphorus (**P**) and potassium (**K**). NPK fertilisers supply three important chemical elements that plants need and so the addition of NPK fertilisers improves agricultural productivity.

NPK fertilisers are formulations (see Module 29) of various salts containing appropriate percentages of N, P and K. Production of fertilisers can be achieved by using a variety of raw materials in several integrated processes.

Ammonia can be used to manufacture ammonium salts, such as ammonium sulfate $(NH_4)_2SO_4$ and nitric acid HNO_3.

Potassium chloride, potassium sulfate and phosphate rock are obtained by mining. Phosphate rock requires further processing as it is insoluble and so cannot be used directly as a fertiliser.

Phosphate rock is treated with nitric acid to make phosphoric acid (H_3PO_4) and calcium nitrate, $Ca(NO_3)_2$. Phosphoric acid is neutralised with ammonia to make ammonium phosphate.

$$H_3PO_4 + 3NH_3 \rightarrow (NH_4)_3PO_4$$

When phosphate rock is reacted with sulfuric acid, 'single super phosphate' is produced. This is a mixture of calcium phosphate and calcium sulfate.

If phosphate rock is reacted with phosphoric acid then 'triple superphosphate' calcium phosphate is produced.

Explaining the conditions used in the Haber process

The reaction to produce ammonia is exothermic:

$$N_{2(g)} + 3H_{2(g)} \rightleftharpoons 2NH_{3(g)} \qquad \Delta H = -92\ \text{kJmol}^{-1}$$

High temperatures favour endothermic reactions (see Module 24) so if the temperature is too high then the yield (amount produced) of ammonia will be low. If the temperature is too low then the yield of ammonia will be higher but the rate will be too slow. 450°C is a compromise temperature between rate and yield.

High pressure favours the reaction that produces fewer molecules of gas (in this case, high pressure favours the forward reaction, i.e. the production of ammonia). If the pressure is increased, the yield of ammonia and the rate of production will both increase but so will the cost of production. The increased revenue from the sale of the extra ammonia does not compensate for the additional costs. 200 atmospheres pressure is a compromise between yield, rate and cost.

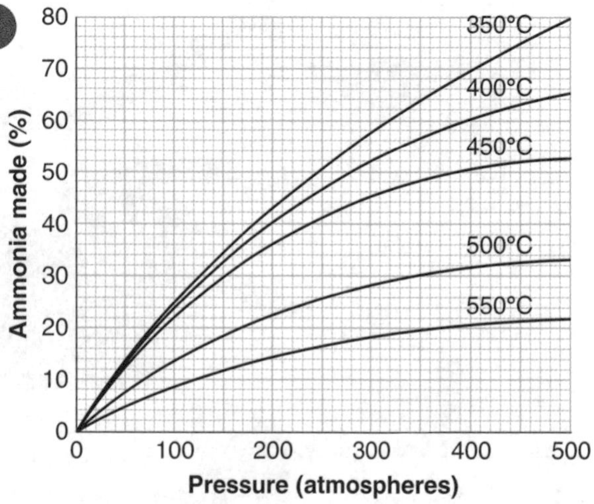

Different Haber process plants operate at slightly different conditions based upon...

- the availability and cost of raw materials and energy
- the demand for ammonia.

What are the raw materials needed to make ammonia?
Name the three chemical elements present in NPK fertiliers.
Name the compound formed when ammonia is reacted with phosphoric acid.

Mind map

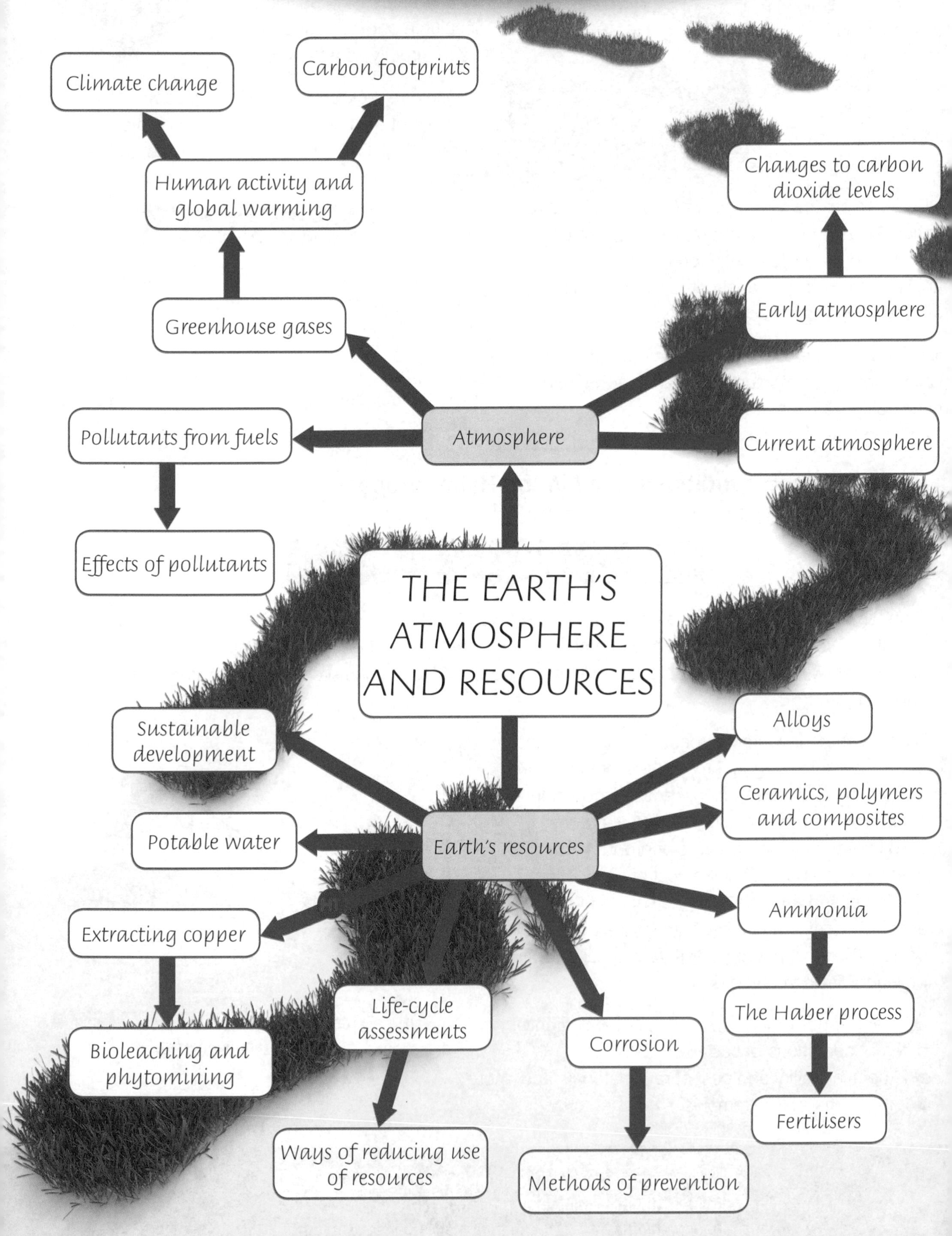

THE EARTH'S ATMOSPHERE AND RESOURCES
Atmosphere
Greenhouse gases
Human activity and global warming
Climate change
Carbon footprints
Pollutants from fuels
Effects of pollutants
Early atmosphere
Changes to carbon dioxide levels
Current atmosphere
Earth's resources
Sustainable development
Potable water
Extracting copper
Bioleaching and phytomining
Life-cycle assessments
Ways of reducing use of resources
Corrosion
Methods of prevention
Alloys
Ceramics, polymers and composites
Ammonia
The Haber process
Fertilisers

Practice questions

1. The composition of the Earth's atmosphere today is very different from how it was 4.6 million years ago. The pie charts below show the composition of the atmosphere today compared with millions of years ago.

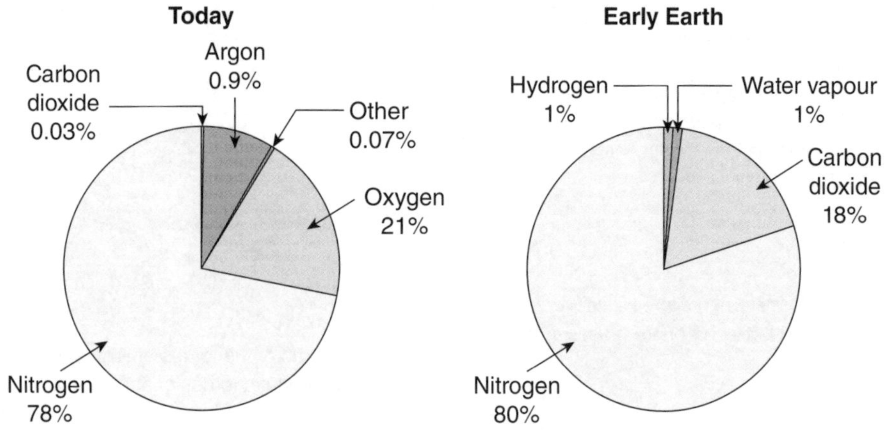

a) When the Earth was formed, where did many of the gases in the early atmosphere come from? **(1 mark)**

b) Name one gas whose composition has remained fairly constant over time. **(1 mark)**

c) Explain why oxygen is now present in the atmosphere and why it has not always been there. **(2 marks)**

d) Why is the amount of carbon dioxide in the atmosphere much lower today than in the early atmosphere? **(2 marks)**

e) Explain why the level of carbon dioxide in the atmosphere has been steadily increasing over the last couple of centuries. **(2 marks)**

2. Ammonia (NH_3) is an important gas used in the production of NPK fertilisers. The equation for the production of ammonia is shown below.

$$N_{2(g)} + 3H_{2(g)} \rightleftharpoons 2NH_{3(g)}$$

a) Where are the raw materials for the production of ammonia obtained from? **(2 marks)**

b) What conditions are typically used to manufacture ammonia? **(3 marks)**

c) Ammonia can be reacted with phosphoric acid (H_3PO_4) to make ammonium phosphate. Write a balanced symbol equation for this reaction. **(2 marks)**

Answers

Page 5

1. A compound.
2. Simple distillation.

Page 7

1. The plum pudding model suggests that the electrons are embedded within the positive charge in an atom. The nuclear model suggested that the positive charge was confined in a small volume (the nucleus) of an atom.
2. Because most of the positive charge passed straight through the atom. As only a few alpha particles were deflected, this suggested that the positive part of the atom was very small.
3. 6 protons, 6 electrons and 7 neutrons.
4. Isotopes.

Page 9

1. 2, 8, 1
2. He predicted that there were more elements to be discovered. He predicted their properties and left appropriate places in the periodic table based on his predictions.
3. A metal.

Page 11

1. Because they have full outer shells of electrons.
2. Lithium hydroxide and hydrogen.
3. The reactivity decreases.
4. Potassium bromide and iodine.

Page 13

1. **Any two from**: Transition metals have higher melting points (except for mercury); are more dense; are less reactive with water and oxygen.
2. **Any suitable example**: e.g. potassium manganite(VII): purple; copper(II) sulfate: blue.
3. Iron

Page 15

1. **a)** protons = 17 (**1 mark**), electrons = 17 (**1 mark**), neutrons = 18 (**1 mark**).
   b) 2, 8, 7 (**1 mark**).
   c) Similarity: same number of protons in each atom, same number of electrons in each atom, same chemical properties (**1 mark**). Difference: different number of neutrons in each atom (**1 mark**).
   d) **One from**: does not conduct heat/electricity; gas at room temperature (**1 mark**).
   e) $Cl_2 + 2NaI \rightarrow 2NaCl + I_2$ (**1 mark for correct formula**, **1 mark for correct balancing**).
   f) Chlorine is less reactive than fluorine (**1 mark**), so it is unable to displace fluorine from a compound (**1 mark**).
2. **a)** Filtration (**1 mark**).
   b) Flask connected to condenser with bung/thermometer in place (**1 mark**).
   Water flowing in at the bottom and leaving at the top (**1 mark**).
   Salt water and pure water labelled (**1 mark**).

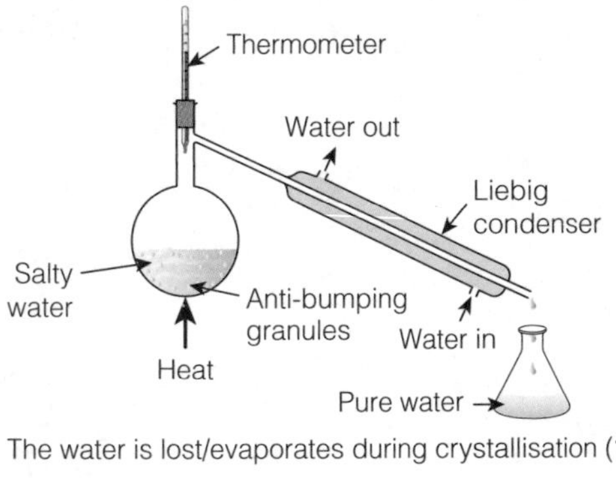

Thermometer
Water out
Liebig condenser
Salty water
Anti-bumping granules
Water in
Heat
Pure water

   c) The water is lost/evaporates during crystallisation (**1 mark**).

3. $\frac{(10 \times 20) + (11 \times 80)}{100}$ (**1 mark**)
   = 10.8 (**1 mark**)
   Answer to 3 significant figures. (**1 mark**)

Page 17

1. Ionic.
2. Two.
3. A lattice (regular arrangement) of cations surrounded by a sea of (delocalised) electrons.

Page 19

1. Electrostatic forces/strong forces between cations and anions
2. Simple molecular, polymers, giant covalent
3.

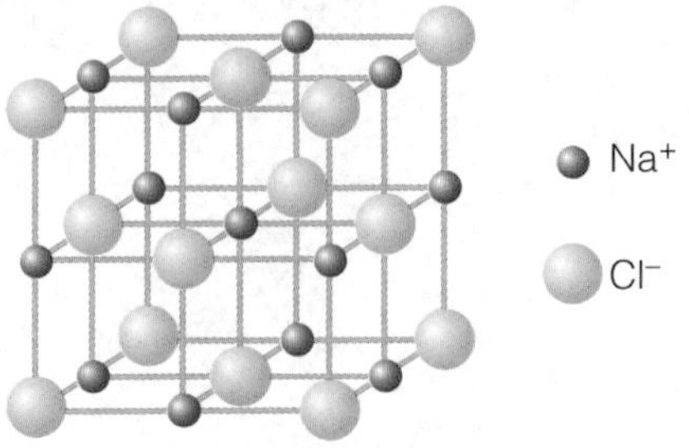

Na+
Cl−

Page 21

1. The strength of the forces acting between the particles present.
2. The electrostatic forces of attraction between the ions are strong.
3. The intermolecular forces/forces between the molecules.
4. Polymers have larger molecules therefore there are more forces between the molecules.
5. There are lots of strong covalent bonds that need lots of energy to break them all.

Page 23

1. Because there are strong forces of attraction between the metal cations and delocalised electrons.
2. In alloys, the layers of metal ions are not able to slide over each other.
3. Each carbon atom has a spare electron that allows it to conduct electricity.
4. **Two from**: high tensile strength; high electrical conductivity; high thermal conductivity.
5. **Two from**: drug delivery into the body; lubricants; reinforcing materials.

Page 25

1. Less than 100 nm (1×10^{-7} m).
2. It increases by a factor of 10.
3. **Two from**: controlled drug delivery; synthetic skin; electronics; cosmetics and sun creams; development of new catalysts for fuel cell materials; in deodorants and fabrics to prevent the growth of bacteria.
4. **One advantage**: better skin coverage; more effective protection from the sun's UV rays. **One disadvantage**: potential cell damage in the body; harmful effects on the environment.

Page 27

1. **a)** Ionic (**1 mark**)
   b)

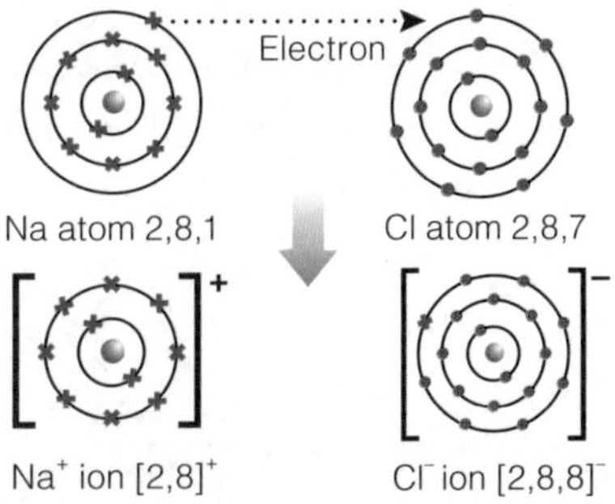

Electron
Na atom 2,8,1
Cl atom 2,8,7
+
−
Na+ ion [2,8]+
Cl− ion [2,8,8]−

(**Correct electronic structure of atoms, 1 mark**; **correct electronic structure of ions, 1 mark**; **correct charges on ions, 1 mark**.)

c) There are strong electrostatic forces of attraction (**1 mark**) between the ions (**1 mark**).

d) High (**1 mark**). Lots of energy is needed to overcome the forces holding the ions together (**1 mark**).

e)

(**1 mark**)

2. a) Covalent (**1 mark**).
   b) i) Two (**1 mark**).
   ii) Simple molecular (**1 mark**).
   c) i) Giant covalent (macromolecular) (**1 mark**).
   ii) Simple molecular structures consist of many individual molecules held together by weak intermolecular forces (**1 mark**). Giant covalent structures are lots of atoms all held together by covalent bonds (**1 mark**).
   d) Silicon dioxide will have a higher boiling point (**1 mark**). The covalent bonds in silicon dioxide that need to be broken in order to boil it are much stronger than the intermolecular forces that need to be broken in order to boil carbon dioxide (**1 mark**).

Page 29

1. The same.
2. a) 80 b) 58
3. Lower.

Page 31

1. 100 g
2. 124 g
3. 0.05 cm^3
4. sodium

Page 33

1. 72%
2. **One from**: the reaction may not go to completion because it is reversible; some of the products may be lost when it is separated from the reaction mixture; some of the reactants may react in ways that are different to the expected reaction.
3. 45.9%.

Page 35

1. 2.3 g
2. 0.2 mol/dm^3
3. 0.72 mol/dm^3

Page 37

1. 0.0625
2. 9600 cm^3 (9.6 dm^3)
3. $Si + 2Cl_2 \rightarrow SiCl_4$

Page 39

1. a) Lower (**1 mark**), because the $CaCO_3$/calcium carbonate will have thermally decomposed meaning that some of the $CaCO_3$ will have decomposed into carbon dioxide, which will have gone into the air (**1 mark**).
   b) 100 (**1 mark**).
   c) 100 g of $CaCO_3$ forms 44 g of CO_2; therefore 10 g of $CaCO_3$ will have formed 4.4 g of CO_2 (**1 mark for working, 1 mark for the correct answer based on working; correct answer on its own scores 2 marks. The final answer must include the units**).
   d) moles of Mg: 0.15 ÷ 24 = 0.00625 (**1 mark**); number of atoms: $0.00625 \times 6 \times 10^{23} = 3.75 \times 10^{21}$ (**1 mark**).
   e) (0.2 ÷ 0.25) × 100 = 80% (**1 mark**).
2. a) (22.50 × 0.2) ÷ 1000 = 0.0045 (**1 mark**).
   b) 0.0045 (**1 mark**); the ratio of moles of hydrochloric acid to sodium hydroxide in the equation is 1:1. This means that the number of moles of sodium hydroxide reacting is the same as the number of moles of hydrochloric acid (**1 mark**).
   c) (0.0045 × 1000) ÷ 25 = 0.18 mol/dm^3 (**1 mark for working, 1 mark for the correct answer based on the working; the correct answer on its own scores 2 marks. The final answer must include the units**).
   d) 0.18 × 40 = 7.2 g/dm^3 (**1 mark for correct M_r of sodium hydroxide (40), 1 mark for the correct answer**).

Page 41

1. magnesium + oxygen → magnesium oxide
2. Sodium (because it is more reactive).
3. **Two from**: zinc, iron, copper.
4. Magnesium is being oxidised (because it loses electrons) and Zn^{2+} is being reduced (because it gains electrons).

Page 43

1. zinc + sulfuric acid → zinc sulfate + hydrogen.
2. Fe
3. A metal, metal oxide or metal carbonate.
4. Lithium nitrate.
5. Add solid until no more reacts, filter off the excess solid, crystallise the remaining solution.

Page 45

1. An acid.
2. OH^-
3. $H^+_{(aq)} + OH^-_{(aq)} \rightarrow H_2O_{(l)}$
4. A strong acid fully ionises/dissociates in solution. A weak acid only partially ionises/dissociates in solution.
5. So that the ions are able to move.

Page 47

1. Potassium will be formed at the cathode; iodine will be formed at the anode.
2. Hydrogen will be formed at the cathode; iodine will be formed at the anode.
3. $4OH^- \rightarrow O_2 + 2H_2O + 4e^-$ (or $4OH^- - 4e^- \rightarrow O_2 + 2H_2O$).

Page 49

1. It cools down.
2.

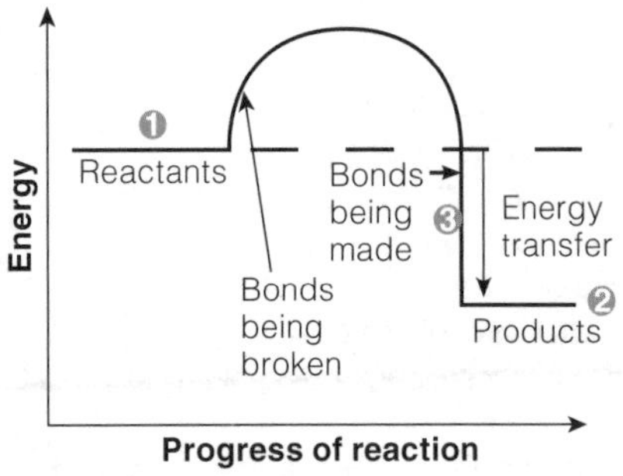

3. −1299 kJ (allow 1299 kJ).
4. Exothermic – more energy is released when bonds are made than is used up in breaking the bonds in the reactants/ΔH is negative.

Page 51

1. A system containing chemicals that react together to produce electricity.
2. A fuel cell has a constant supply of fuel; a chemical cell has the fuel contained within it and it is not replaced.
3. Water.
4. $4H^+_{(aq)} + O_{2(g)} + 4e^- \rightarrow 2H_2O_{(g)}$

Page 53

1. a) $2\ Zn_{(s)} + O_{2(g)} \rightarrow 2\ ZnO_{(s)}$ (state symbols are not required. **1 mark awarded for the correct symbols/formulae and for the equation being correctly balanced**).
   b) ZnO/zinc oxide (**1 mark**), because it loses oxygen (**1 mark**).
   c) Less reactive (**1 mark**); magnesium is able to displace zinc from zinc oxide, meaning that magnesium is more reactive than zinc (**1 mark**).
   d) By reduction with carbon (**1 mark**), because it is below carbon in the reactivity series (**1 mark**).
   e) Zinc (**1 mark**), because it loses electrons (**1 mark**).
2. a) A chemical cell where the source of fuel is supplied externally (**1 mark**).
   b) There is a constant supply of fuel in a fuel cell but not in a chemical cell (**1 mark**).

c)

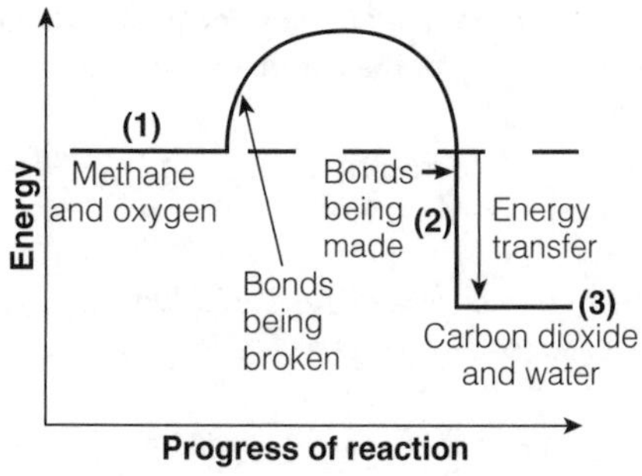

(**1 mark for each label numbered on the graph**.)

d) Bonds broken:
4 C–H: 4 × 413 = 1652 kJ
2 O=O: 2 × 498 = 996 kJ
Total = 2648 kJ (**1 mark**)
Bonds formed:
2 C=O: 2 × 803 = 1606 kJ
4 O–H: 4 × 464 = 1856 kJ
Total = 3462 kJ (**1 mark**)
ΔH = Bonds broken – bonds formed = 2648 – 3462
= – 814 kJ/mol (**1 mark for correct calculation, including correct sign**).

Page 55

1. 0.75 g/s
2. **Two from**: the concentrations of the reactants in solution; the pressure of reacting gases; the surface area of any solid reactants; temperature; presence of a catalyst.
3. By attaching a gas syringe and recording the volume of gas collected in a certain amount of time, e.g. volume collected every 10 seconds.
4. The rate increases.

Page 57

1. The idea that, for a chemical reaction to occur, the reacting particles must collide with sufficient energy.
2. The minimum amount of energy that the particles must have when they collide in order to react.
3. There are more particles in the same volume of liquid and so there are more chances of reactant particles colliding.
4. A species that speeds up a chemical reaction but is not used up during the reaction.
5. They provide an alternative pathway of lower activation energy.

Page 59

1. $\rightleftharpoons$
2. Endothermic.
3. **a)** The amount of nitrogen will decrease.
   b) The amount of nitrogen will decrease.

Page 61

1. **a)** 50 seconds (**1 mark**), as after this time no more gas was collected/the volume of gas did not change (**1 mark**).
   b) 40 ÷ 50 = 0.8 cm³/s (working **1 mark**: allow 40 ÷ answer to part a; answer with units, **1 mark**).
   c) The gradient was steeper after 10 seconds than after 40 seconds. (**1 mark**)
   d)

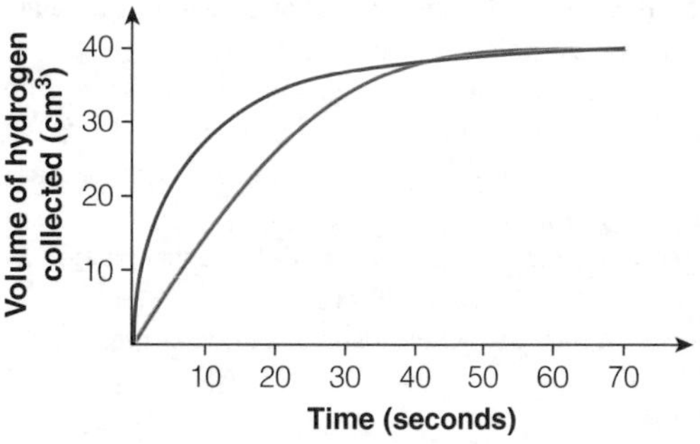

(**Curve is steeper than in original graph**, **1 mark**; **final volume is 40 cm³**, **1 mark**.)

e) At a higher concentration there will be more particles of acid in the same volume of solution (**1 mark**), and so there will be more/an increased probability/more likelihood of/collisions (**1 mark**).

2. **a)** The water in the equation appears as a gas (**1 mark**).
   b) That the reaction is reversible (**1 mark**).
   c) High pressure favours the reaction that produces the smaller number of molecules of gas; i.e. the reverse reaction will be favoured, which uses up hydrogen (**1 mark**).
   d) The yield of hydrogen will increase (**1 mark**); increasing temperature favours the endothermic (in this case forward) reaction (**1 mark**).

Page 63

1. Dead biomass.
2. Molecules that contain carbon and hydrogen atoms only.
3. Fractional distillation.
4. C_3H_8
5. $C_2H_6 + 3.5\ O_2 \rightarrow 2CO_2 + 3H_2O$ **or** $2C_2H_6 + 7\ O_2 \rightarrow 4CO_2 + 6H_2O$

Page 65

1. C_4H_{10}
2. C_nH_{2n}
3. 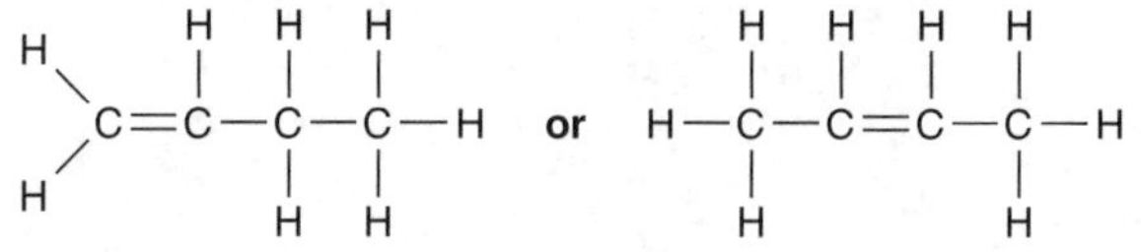
4. $C_2H_4 + Br_2 \rightarrow C_2H_4Br_2$
5. Ethanol.

Page 67

1. $CH_3CH_2CH_2OH$
2. $C_4H_9OH + 6O_2 \rightarrow 4CO_2 + 5H_2O$
3. As a fuel/solvent.
4. 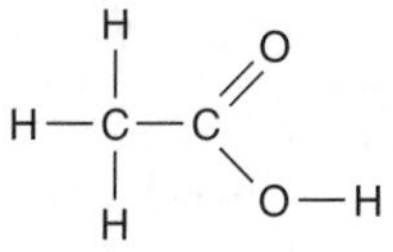
5. Ethyl ethanoate.

Page 69

1. They contain a carbon–carbon double bond.
2. Polypeptides/proteins.
3. It encodes genetic instructions for the development and functioning of living organisms and viruses.

Page 71

1. **a)** Dead biomass sinks to ocean bottom (**1 mark**); decaying biomass is covered in mud, which turns to rock (**1 mark**); biomass decays, slowly forming crude oil under the rock (**1 mark**).
   b) Fractional distillation (**1 mark**); the molecules in crude oil are separated according to their boiling points (**1 mark**).
   c) Saturated (**1 mark**); hydrocarbons/molecules with the general formula C_nH_{2n+2} (**1 mark**).
   d) Cracking turns relatively useless long-chain molecules (**1 mark**) into more useful products (**1 mark**).
   e) By passing the hydrocarbon vapour over a hot catalyst/mixing the hydrocarbon with steam at high temperatures (**1 mark**).
   f) C_4H_{10} (**1 mark**).
2. **a)** Addition polymerisation (**1 mark**).
   b) The carbon–carbon double bond (**1 mark**).
   c) **One from**: proteins; DNA; starch; cellulose (**1 mark**).
3. **a)** $C_2H_4 + H_2O \rightarrow C_2H_5OH$ (**1 mark for reactants**; **1 mark for correct formula of ethanol – allow** C_2H_6O)
   b) Any acid, e.g. concentrated sulfuric acid (**1 mark**)
   c) Hydrogen (**1 mark**)

d) 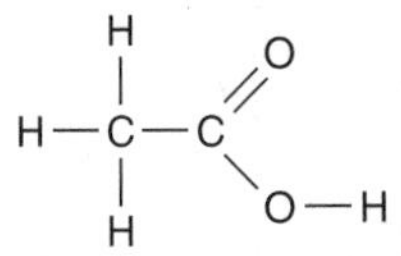 (**1 mark**)

e) Ethyl ethanoate (**1 mark**)

Page 73

1. A single element or compound.
2. A mixture that has been designed as a useful product.
3. **Two from**: fuels; cleaning materials; paints; medicines; foods; fertilisers.
4. 0.55

Page 75

1. Oxygen.
2. Add a lit splint and there will be a squeaky pop.
3. Calcium hydroxide solution.
4. It turns milky.
5. It turns it red before bleaching it.

Page 77

1. Potassium.
2. Crimson red.
3. Magnesium hydroxide.
4. $Fe^{2+}(aq) + 2OH^{-}(aq) \rightarrow Fe(OH)_2(s)$
5. Green.

Page 79

1. The carbonate (CO_3^{2-}) ion.
2. Cream/off white.
3. Barium chloride solution.
4. **One from**: more accurate; more sensitive; can be used with very small sample sizes.

Page 81

1. a) K_2SO_4 (**1 mark**).
   b) Heat and then dip a piece of nichrome wire in concentrated hydrochloric acid to clean it (**1 mark**); dip the wire in the compound (**1 mark**); put the wire into a Bunsen burner and observe the colour of the flame (**1 mark**).
   c) Lilac (**1 mark**).
   d) Dilute hydrochloric acid (**1 mark**); barium chloride solution (**1 mark**).
   e) A white (**1 mark**) precipitate (**1 mark**).
   f) Flame emission spectrometer (**1 mark**).
2. a) Ca^{2+} (**1 mark**).
   b) Carbon dioxide (**1 mark**).
   c) CO_3^{2-} (**1 mark**).
   d) $CaCO_3$ (**1 mark**).
   e) Add dilute nitric acid (**1 mark**) followed by silver nitrate solution/aqueous silver nitrate (**1 mark**) and a white precipitate/solid (**1 mark**) will be observed.

Page 83

1. **Two from**: carbon dioxide; water vapour; methane; ammonia; nitrogen.
2. As a product of photosynthesis.
3. Approximately $\frac{4}{5}$ or 80%.
4. Because it was used in photosynthesis and to form sedimentary rocks.

Page 85

1. **Two from**: water vapour; carbon dioxide; methane.
2. Increased animal farming/rubbish in landfill sites.
3. **Two from**: rising sea levels leading to flooding/coastal erosion; more frequent/severe storms; changes to the amount, timing and distribution of rainfall; temperature and water stress for humans and wildlife; changes in the food producing capacity of some regions; changes to the distribution of wildlife species.
4. **One from**: disagreement over the causes and consequences of climate change; lack of public information and education; lifestyle changes, e.g. greater use of cars and aeroplanes; economic considerations, i.e. the financial costs of reducing the carbon footprint; incomplete international cooperation.

Page 87

1. **Two from**: carbon dioxide; carbon monoxide; water vapour; sulfur dioxide; nitrogen oxides.
2. From the incomplete combustion of fossil fuels.
3. They cause respiratory problems and can form acid rain.

Page 89

1. Living such that the needs of the current generation are met without compromising the ability of future generations to meet their own needs.
2. Pure water has no chemicals added to it. Potable water may have other substances in it but it is safe to drink.
3. Filtered and then sterilised.
4. Distillation or reverse osmosis.

Page 91

1. **One from**: electrical wiring; water pipes.
2. We are running out of metal ores.
3. Bioleaching.
4. **One from**: displacement using scrap iron; electrolysis.

Page 93

1. The environmental impact of a product over the whole of its life.
2. **Two from**: how much energy is needed; how much water is used; what resources are required; how much waste is produced; how much pollution is produced.
3. Some of the values are difficult to quantify, meaning that value judgements have to be made which could be biased/based on opinion.
4. **One from**: using fewer items that come from the earth; reusing items; recycling more of what we use.

Page 95

1. **One from**: greasing; painting; electroplating; attaching a more reactive metal.
2. A mixture of metals.
3. It is more resistant to corrosion/rusting.
4. Sand, sodium carbonate and limestone.
5. Thermosetting polymers have cross-links between the polymer chains; thermoplastic polymers are just tangles of polymer chains.
6. Two (or more) different materials combined.

Page 97

1. Nitrogen and hydrogen.
2. Nitrogen, phosphorus, potassium.
3. Ammonium phosphate.

Page 99

1. a) Volcanoes (**1 mark**).
   b) Nitrogen (**1 mark**).
   c) Oxygen is formed by photosynthesis (**1 mark**); oxygen has not always been present in the atmosphere because green plants/algae have not always existed (**1 mark**).
   d) Carbon dioxide is absorbed into the oceans/forms carbonate rocks (**1 mark**), and is used in photosynthesis (**1 mark**).
   e) There has been increased consumption of fossil fuels (**1 mark**), e.g. since the Industrial Revolution/greater use of transport such as cars which produce carbon dioxide when they burn fuel (**1 mark**).
2. a) Nitrogen is obtained from the fractional distillation of liquefied air (**1 mark**); hydrogen is obtained from natural gas (**1 mark**).
   b) 450 °C **(1 mark)**, 200 atmospheres **(1 mark)**, an iron catalyst (**1 mark**).
   c) $3NH_3 + H_3PO_4 \rightarrow (NH_4)_3PO_4$ (**1 mark for correct formula of the three species in the equation**, **1 mark for a correctly balanced equation**).

The Periodic Table

Key

- Metals
- Non-metals

Relative atomic mass → 1
Atomic symbol → **H**
Name → hydrogen
Atomic number → 1

1	2											3	4	5	6	7	0 or 8
																	4 **He** helium 2
7 **Li** lithium 3	9 **Be** beryllium 4											11 **B** boron 5	12 **C** carbon 6	14 **N** nitrogen 7	16 **O** oxygen 8	19 **F** fluorine 9	20 **Ne** neon 10
23 **Na** sodium 11	24 **Mg** magnesium 12											27 **Al** aluminium 13	28 **Si** silicon 14	31 **P** phosphorus 15	32 **S** sulfur 16	35.5 **Cl** chlorine 17	40 **Ar** argon 18
39 **K** potassium 19	40 **Ca** calcium 20	45 **Sc** scandium 21	48 **Ti** titanium 22	51 **V** vanadium 23	52 **Cr** chromium 24	55 **Mn** manganese 25	56 **Fe** iron 26	59 **Co** cobalt 27	59 **Ni** nickel 28	63.5 **Cu** copper 29	65 **Zn** zinc 30	70 **Ga** gallium 31	73 **Ge** germanium 32	75 **As** arsenic 33	79 **Se** selenium 34	80 **Br** bromine 35	84 **Kr** krypton 36
85 **Rb** rubidium 37	88 **Sr** strontium 38	89 **Y** yttrium 39	91 **Zr** zirconium 40	93 **Nb** niobium 41	96 **Mo** molybdenum 42	[98] **Tc** technetium 43	101 **Ru** ruthenium 44	103 **Rh** rhodium 45	106 **Pd** palladium 46	108 **Ag** silver 47	112 **Cd** cadmium 48	115 **In** indium 49	119 **Sn** tin 50	122 **Sb** antimony 51	128 **Te** tellurium 52	127 **I** iodine 53	131 **Xe** xenon 54
133 **Cs** caesium 55	137 **Ba** barium 56	139 **La*** lanthanum 57	178 **Hf** hafnium 72	181 **Ta** tantalum 73	184 **W** tungsten 74	186 **Re** rhenium 75	190 **Os** osmium 76	192 **Ir** iridium 77	195 **Pt** platinum 78	197 **Au** gold 79	201 **Hg** mercury 80	204 **Tl** thallium 81	207 **Pb** lead 82	209 **Bi** bismuth 83	[209] **Po** polonium 84	[210] **At** astatine 85	[222] **Rn** radon 86
[223] **Fr** francium 87	[226] **Ra** radium 88	[227] **Ac*** actinium 89	[261] **Rf** rutherfordium 104	[262] **Db** dubnium 105	[266] **Sg** seaborgium 106	[264] **Bh** bohrium 107	[277] **Hs** hassium 108	[268] **Mt** meitnerium 109	[271] **Ds** darmstadtium 110	[272] **Rg** roentgenium 111	Elements with atomic numbers 112–116 have been reported but not fully authenticated						

*The lanthanoids (atomic numbers 58–71) and the actinoids (atomic numbers 90–103) have been omitted.

The relative atomic masses of copper and chlorine have not been rounded to the nearest whole number.

Letts

GCSE Success

Complete Revision & Practice

AQA

Chemistry

Dan Evans,
Steven Langfield,
Dorothy Warren

Exam Practice Workbook

Chemistry

Atomic Structure and the Periodic Table

Structure, Bonding and the Properties of Matter

Quantitative Chemistry

Chemical and Energy Changes

Contents

The Rate and Extent of Chemical Reactions

Organic Chemistry

Chemical Analysis

The Earth's Atmosphere and Resources

Practice Exam Papers

Atoms and the periodic table

Module 1

1 The chemical sodium chloride is more commonly known as 'salt' (i.e. the food flavouring).

Sodium chloride can be made in the laboratory by reacting sodium with chlorine gas. Salt is very soluble in water.

(a) Give the chemical symbols for the two elements present in sodium chloride. Use the periodic table on page 88 to help you. (2)

....

(b) Write a word equation to show the reaction between sodium and chlorine to produce sodium chloride. (2)

....

....

(c) Is sodium chloride a mixture or a compound? Explain your answer. (2)

....

....

(d) When salt dissolves in water, does it form a mixture or a compound? Explain your answer. (2)

....

....

(e) A student wants to separate salt and water from salty water. Which two methods of separation listed below would be appropriate for the student to use? Tick the relevant box or boxes. (2)

Filtration	☐	Simple distillation	☐
Crystallisation	☐	Chromatography	☐

For more help on this topic, see Letts GCSE Chemistry Revision Guide pages 4–5

1 One of the early representations of the atom, the 'plum pudding' model, was further developed in light of Rutherford, Geiger and Marsden's scattering experiment. This led to the conclusion that the positive charge of an atom is contained within a small volume known as the nucleus. Niels Bohr improved this model and it is this model that forms the basis of the way in which we represent the structure of atoms today.

The plum pudding model

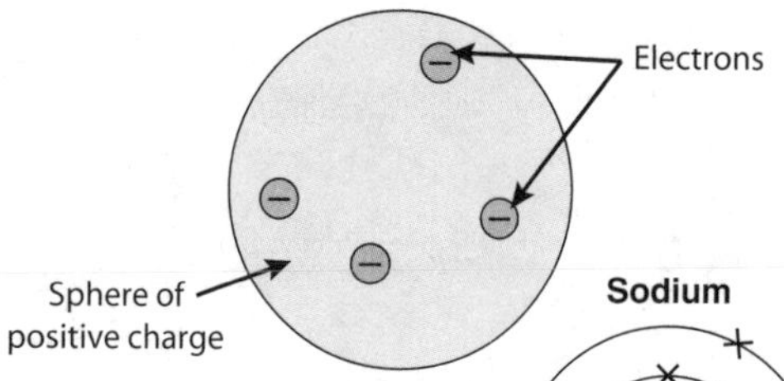

Sodium

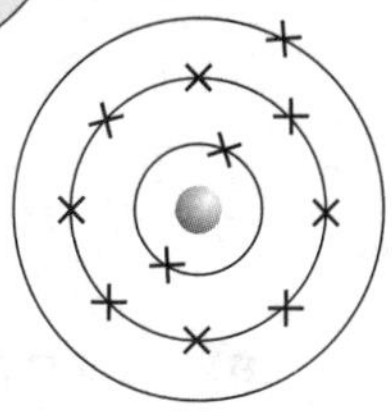

The plum pudding version of an atom is shown above.

Today, an atom such as sodium is represented by a diagram like the one above.

(a) Give two differences between the 'plum pudding' model of an atom and today's model. (2)

....

....

(b) What observation in Rutherford, Geiger and Marsden's scattering experiment led them to conclude that the positive charge of an atom was contained in a small volume? (1)

....

(c) What improvements did Niels Bohr make to the nuclear model and what evidence did he have to support these changes? (2)

....

....

(d) James Chadwick developed the idea that the nucleus of an atom contains protons and neutrons.

Complete the table below showing the properties of the sub-atomic particles. (4)

Particle	Relative charge	Relative mass
Proton	+ 1	
Neutron		1
Electron		

(e) An atom of sodium contains 11 protons, 12 neutrons and 11 electrons.

(i) What is the atomic number of sodium? .... (1)

(ii) What is the mass number of sodium? .... (1)

For more help on this topic, see Letts GCSE Chemistry Revision Guide pages 6–7

1 The diagrams below represent an atom of magnesium and an atom of fluorine:

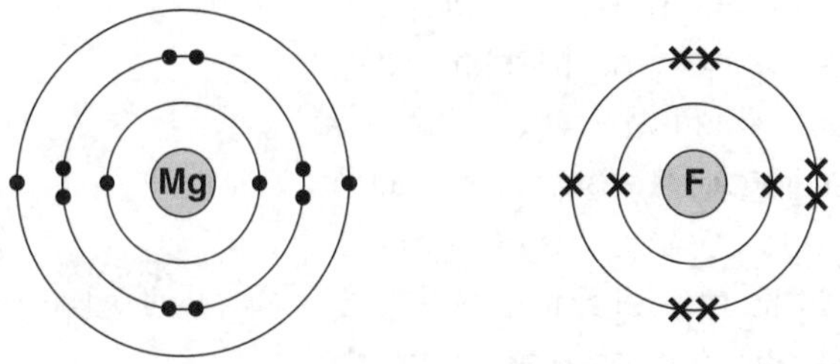

The electronic structure of magnesium can also be written as 2,8,2

(a) How many shells of electrons does a magnesium atom have? (1)

....

(b) What is the electronic structure of fluorine? (1)

....

(c) In which group of the periodic table would you expect to find fluorine? Explain your answer. (2)

....

....

2 Dmitri Mendeleev is often referred to as the father of the periodic table, as he was instrumental in its construction.

Mendeleev placed the metals lithium and sodium in the same group of the periodic table.

(a) How are the elements arranged in the periodic table? (1)

....

(b) Explain why Mendeleev placed sodium and lithium in the same group of the periodic table. (1)

....

(c) Give two characteristic properties of metals. (2)

....

....

For more help on this topic, see Letts GCSE Chemistry Revision Guide pages 8–9

1 **(a)** Explain why the noble gases are chemically inert. (2)

....

....

(b) What is the trend in boiling point as the relative atomic mass of the noble gases increases? .... (1)

2 The element sodium reacts vigorously with water. When universal indicator solution is added to the resulting solution a colour change is observed.

(a) Write a balanced symbol equation for the reaction between sodium and water. (2)

....

(b) What colour would universal indicator solution turn when it is added to the resulting solution? Explain your answer. (2)

....

....

(c) The element potassium reacts more vigorously with water than sodium. Explain why. (2)

....

....

3 Sodium reacts with bromine gas as shown by the equation below:

$.........Na_{(s)} + ...Cl_{2(g)} \longrightarrow ....NaCl_{(s)}$

(a) Balance the above equation. (2)

(b) What type of bonding is present in sodium chloride (NaCl)? (1)

....

(c) When chlorine gas is bubbled through sodium bromide solution a chemical reaction occurs. Write a word equation for this reaction. (2)

....

(d) What name is given to the type of reaction that occurs when chlorine gas reacts with sodium bromide solution? Explain why the reaction occurs. (2)

....

....

For more help on this topic, see Letts GCSE Chemistry Revision Guide pages 10–11

1 The table below shows information about two metals, L and M.

One of the metals is a transition metal and the other is in group 1.

	Metal L	Metal M
Melting point (°C)	181	1538
Density (g cm^{-3})	0.53	7.9

(a) Which of the two metals is the transition metal? Explain your answer. (2)

....

....

(b) Complete the sentence below by inserting the correct word.

Transition metals are .... reactive than group 1 metals. (1)

(c) Name the only transition metal that has a melting point below room temperature. (1)

....

2 Iron(II) chloride and iron(III) chloride are both soluble in water.

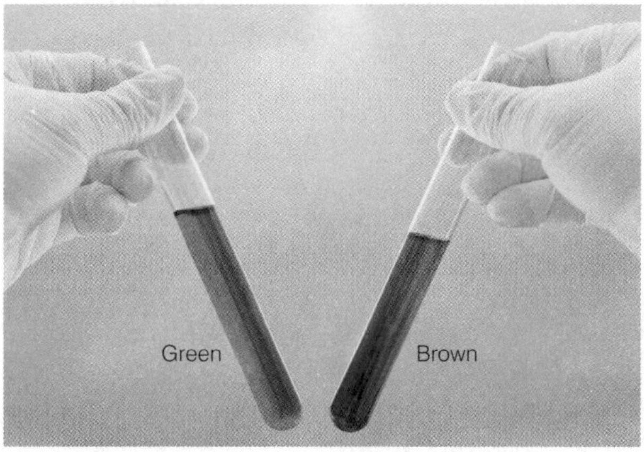

(a) State the property of transition metals that is demonstrated by the above image. (1)

....

(b) Iron is added to the reaction vessel that produces ammonia (NH_3) from nitrogen (N_2) and hydrogen (H_2).

Explain why this is done. (2)

....

....

For more help on this topic, see Letts GCSE Chemistry Revision Guide pages 12–13

1 Consider the structures of sodium (Na), chlorine (Cl_2) and sodium chloride (NaCl).

Draw arrows from each substance to its correct structure. One structure will not have an arrow drawn to it. (3)

Substance	Structure
	Ionic
Sodium	Simple molecular
Chlorine	Giant molecular
Sodium chloride	Metallic

2 Calcium reacts with oxygen to form calcium oxide. The bonding in calcium oxide is ionic.

(a) Complete the diagrams below to show the electronic configurations and charges of the calcium and oxygen ions. (2)

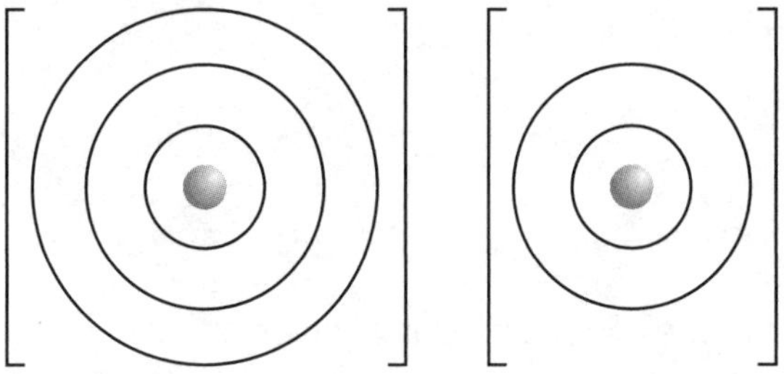

(b) State the charges on each ion. (2)

....

....

3 **(a)** Draw a dot-and-cross diagram to show the bonding in HCl. (1)

(b) The dot-and-cross diagram for a molecule of oxygen is shown below.

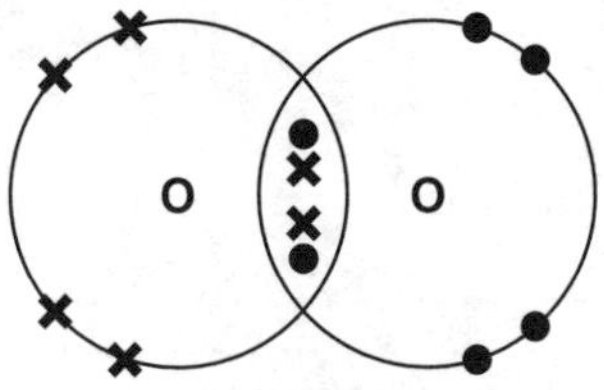

How many covalent bonds are there between the two oxygen atoms? (1)

....

For more help on this topic, see Letts GCSE Chemistry Revision Guide pages 16–17

1 The structure of calcium oxide is shown below.

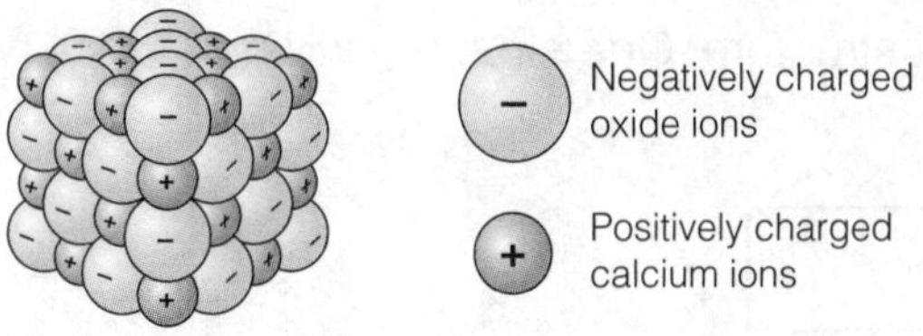
Negatively charged oxide ions
Positively charged calcium ions

(a) What force holds the ions in place in calcium oxide? (1)

....

(b) What is the empirical formula of calcium oxide? Explain your answer. (2)

....

....

2 The structure of a covalent compound is shown below.

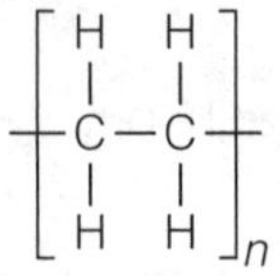

(a) Name this type of structure. .... (1)

(b) What is the empirical formula of this structure? Explain your answer. (2)

....

....

3 Part of the structure of boron nitride is shown below.

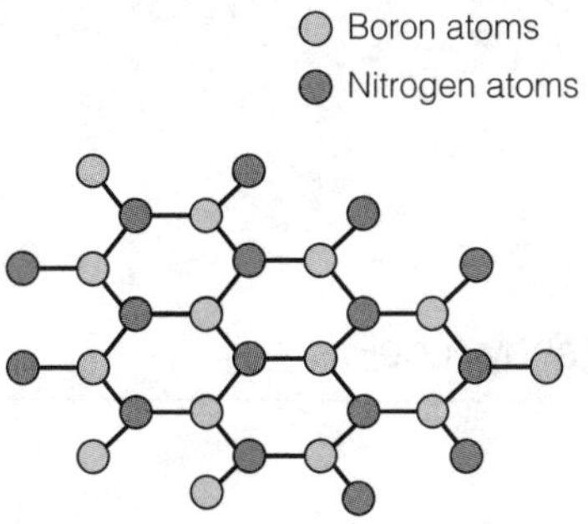
Boron atoms
Nitrogen atoms

What type of structure does boron nitride have? Explain your answer. (2)

....

....

For more help on this topic, see Letts GCSE Chemistry Revision Guide pages 18–19

1 Solids, liquids and gases are the three main states of matter. The three physical states of matter can be easily interconverted.

(a) Draw a diagram to show the arrangement of particles in a solid. (2)

(b) What forces are broken when a solid turns into a liquid? (1)

....

2 Consider the table below, which provides information about the physical properties of two materials.

	Material A	Material B
Melting point/°C	801	3730
Electrical conductivity of solid	Poor	Poor
Electrical conductivity of liquid	Good	Poor

(a) Material A has a giant ionic structure. Explain how this can be deduced from the table. (1)

....

(b) Explain why material A is a poor conductor of electricity in the solid state. (2)

....

....

(c) Deduce the structure of material B. Explain your answer. (2)

....

....

(d) Explain why material B is a poor conductor of electricity in both the solid and liquid states. (2)

....

....

For more help on this topic, see Letts GCSE Chemistry Revision Guide pages 20–21

1 The diagram shows the structure of a metal such as magnesium.

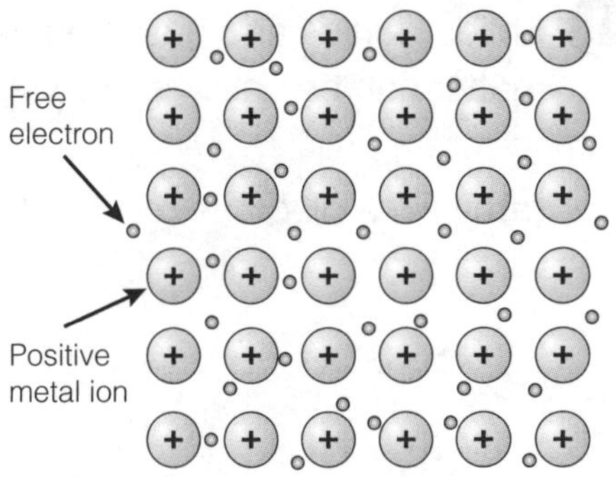
Free electron
Positive metal ion

With reference to the diagram, explain the following:

(a) Why metals are malleable (i.e. able to be bent and shaped). (2)

....

....

(b) Why metals usually have high melting points. (2)

....

....

(c) Why metals are good conductors of electricity. (2)

....

....

2 Most metals in everyday use are alloys, such as steel.

(a) What is an alloy? (1)

....

(b) With reference to its structure, explain why most alloys are harder than pure metals. (2)

....

....

3 This question is about different structures of carbon.

(a) Give two uses of fullerenes. (2)

....

....

(b) State two properties of fullerenes. (2)

....

....

(c) What is the difference between a fullerene and a carbon nanotube? (1)

....

For more help on this topic, see Letts GCSE Chemistry Revision Guide pages 22–23

1 Draw lines to match the particles below to their size. (3)

Name of particle	Diameter of particle
Nanoparticles	Between 1×10^{-5} and 2.5×10^{-6} m
Fine particles ($PM_{2.5}$)	Between 1×10^{-7} and 2.5×10^{-6} m
Coarse particles/dust (PM_{10})	Less than 1×10^{-7} m (100 nm)

2 Nanoparticles sometimes have properties that are different from larger amounts of the same material.

(a) Explain why this is true. (1)

....

(b) Outline the main advantage of this. (1)

....

....

3 Nanoparticles typically have properties that differ from larger quantities of the same material. One explanation for this is the different surface area to volume ratios.

(a) What effect on the surface area to volume ratio does decreasing particle size have? (1)

....

(b) Other than use in sun creams, give two uses of nanoparticles. (2)

....

....

(c) Outline the advantages and potential disadvantages of using nanoparticles in sun creams. (4)

....

....

....

....

....

For more help on this topic, see Letts GCSE Chemistry Revision Guide pages 24–25

1 Consider the equation below.

$2Al_{(s)} + Fe_2O_{3(l)} \longrightarrow Al_2O_{3(s)} + 2Fe_{(l)}$

(a) With reference to the above equation, what do you understand by the term 'conservation of mass'? (1)

....

(b) Complete the table below by filling in the relative atomic (A_r) or formula (M_r) mass of each substance in the equation. (4)

Substance	A_r / M_r
Al	
Fe_2O_3	
Al_2O_3	
Fe	

2 Magnesium oxide can be made by heating magnesium in air or by the thermal decomposition of magnesium carbonate.

(a) Explain why the mass of magnesium increases when it is burnt in air. (2)

....

....

(b) Write a balanced symbol equation for the reaction that occurs when magnesium is heated in air. (2)

....

(c) Explain why the mass of magnesium carbonate decreases when it is heated in air. (2)

....

....

(d) Write a balanced symbol equation for the thermal decomposition of magnesium carbonate. (2)

....

For more help on this topic, see Letts GCSE Chemistry Revision Guide pages 28–29

HT **1** Consider the equation below.

$4Na_{(s)} + O_{2(g)} \longrightarrow 2Na_2O_{(s)}$

(a) How many atoms are present in 4 moles of sodium? (1)

....

(b) What is the mass of 4 moles of Na? (1)

....

(c) How many moles are present in 11.5 g of sodium? (1)

....

(d) What mass of sodium oxide is formed when 11.5 g of sodium reacts with oxygen? (2)

....

2 A student weighed out a 3 cm piece of magnesium on a balance that reads to 0.01g. He then added the magnesium to 25 cm^3 of hydrochloric acid that was measured out using a measuring cylinder that has graduations at every 1 cm^3.

(a) What is the uncertainty of the mass reading? .... (1)

(b) What values does the true volume of hydrochloric acid used lie between? Explain your answer. (2)

....

....

HT **3** During an experiment, 0.48g of magnesium was added to a solution containing 0.025 moles of sulfuric acid. The equation for the reaction is shown below:

$Mg_{(s)} + H_2SO_{4\,(aq)} \longrightarrow MgSO_{4\,(aq)} + H_{2\,(g)}$

(a) Calculate the number of moles of magnesium reacting. (2)

....

(b) Which reactant is the limiting reactant? Explain your answer. (2)

....

....

(c) How many moles of hydrogen gas will be formed? Explain your answer. (2)

....

....

For more help on this topic, see Letts GCSE Chemistry Revision Guide pages 30–31

Module 13 Percentage yield and atom economy

1 Ethanol is a chemical present in alcoholic drinks. In its pure form, it is also a solvent.

Ethanol can be made…

- by the fermentation of sugars, e.g. glucose ($C_6H_{12}O_6$)

$$C_6H_{12}O_{6(aq)} \longrightarrow 2C_2H_5OH_{(aq)} + 2CO_{2(g)}$$

or

- by reacting ethene (C_2H_4) with steam

$$C_2H_{4(g)} + H_2O_{(g)} \longrightarrow C_2H_5OH_{(g)}$$

The relative formula mass (M_r) of ethene is 28 and of ethanol is 46.

(a) Calculate the percentage yield when, during a fermentation experiment, the mass of ethanol obtained was 11.5 g and the expected mass was 15.0 g. (2)

....

....

(b) In an experiment, 7 g of ethene reacted with an excess of steam to form 11 g of ethanol.

HT **(i)** Calculate the number of moles of ethene reacting. (2)

....

....

(ii) How many moles of ethanol would be expected to be formed? Explain your answer. (2)

....

....

(iii) What mass of ethanol would be expected to be formed? (2)

....

(iv) Calculate the percentage yield. (2)

....

....

(c) Calculate the atom economy for both methods of producing ethanol. (2)

....

....

For more help on this topic, see Letts GCSE Chemistry Revision Guide pages 32–33

1 During a titration, a student adds acid to a known volume of alkali until neutralisation occurs. The alkali has an indicator added to it.

(a) Name the piece of apparatus used to measure out the known volume of alkali. (1)

....

(b) Name the piece of apparatus used to add the acid to the alkali. (1)

....

(c) How will the student know when the alkali has been neutralised? (1)

....

HT **2** In a titration, 23.80 cm^3 of 0.2 mol/dm^3 lithium hydroxide (LiOH) solution reacted with 25.0 cm^3 of hydrochloric acid (HCl) of unknown concentration.

The equation for the reaction is shown here: $LiOH_{(aq)} + HCl_{(aq)} \longrightarrow LiCl_{(aq)} + H_2O_{(l)}$

(a) Calculate the number of moles of lithium hydroxide (LiOH) used in each titration. (2)

....

....

(b) How many moles of hydrochloric acid (HCl) were present in the 25.0 cm^3 portion? Explain your answer. (2)

....

....

(c) Using your answer to part **b**, calculate the concentration of the hydrochloric acid solution in mol/dm^3. (2)

....

....

(d) Use your answer to part **c** to work out the concentration of the hydrochloric acid solution in g/dm^3. (2)

....

(e) What mass of hydrochloric acid was present in the 25.0 cm^3 portion? (2)

....

....

For more help on this topic, see Letts GCSE Chemistry Revision Guide pages 34–35

HT 1 Magnesium reacts with oxygen according to the equation below:

$$2Mg_{(s)} + O_{2(g)} \longrightarrow 2MgO_{(s)}$$

(a) A scientist reacted 120 cm^3 of oxygen (at room temperature and pressure) with magnesium. How many moles of oxygen did the scientist use? (2)

....

....

(b) Another scientist reacted 6 g of magnesium with oxygen. Calculate the volume of oxygen required (at room temperature and pressure) to react with this amount of magnesium. (3)

....

....

....

HT 2 Lead forms the following oxides: PbO, PbO_2 and Pb_3O_4. In an experiment, 41.4 g of lead reacts with 3.2 g of oxygen to form 44.6 g of PbO.

Complete the table below to work out the equation for the reaction of lead with oxygen to form lead oxide. (4)

Chemical	Pb	O_2	PbO
Mass from question/g	41.4	3.2	44.6
A_r or M_r	207		223
Moles = $\frac{\text{mass}}{M_r}$	$\frac{41.4}{207}$ = 0.2		
÷ smallest			

Balanced equation: .... Pb + O_2 $\longrightarrow$ .... PbO

For more help on this topic, see Letts GCSE Chemistry Revision Guide pages 36–37

1 Calcium reacts with oxygen present in the air to form calcium oxide.

(a) Write a word equation for this reaction. (2)

....

(b) Explain why this is an oxidation reaction. (2)

....

....

(c) Name a metal that could be used to displace calcium from calcium oxide.
Explain your choice of metal. (2)

....

....

(d) Write a word equation for this reaction. (2)

....

(e) In your equation from part **d**, give the name of the substance that has been reduced. (1)

....

2 Many metals are found in the Earth's crust as ores. For example, haematite is an ore containing iron(III) oxide (Fe_2O_3); bauxite is an ore containing aluminium oxide (Al_2O_3). Both metals can be extracted from their ores by reduction.

(a) What process is used to extract metals above carbon in the reactivity series from their ores? .... (1)

(b) When iron(III) oxide is reduced by carbon, iron and carbon dioxide are formed.
Write a balanced symbol equation for this reaction. (2)

....

HT **(c)** In the extraction of aluminium the following equation occurs: $Al^{3+} + 3e^- \longrightarrow Al$

Is this an oxidation or reduction reaction? Explain your answer. (3)

....

....

HT **(d)** Aluminium can also be formed by reacting a reactive metal such as potassium.
An ionic equation for this reaction would be: $3K + Al^{3+} \longrightarrow Al + 3K^+$
Which substance is oxidised in this reaction? Explain your answer. (2)

....

....

For more help on this topic, see Letts GCSE Chemistry Revision Guide pages 40–41

1 Zinc, zinc oxide and zinc carbonate all react with acids.

(a) Name the salt formed when zinc, zinc oxide and zinc carbonate react with sulfuric acid. (1)

....

(b) Write a word equation for the reaction between zinc oxide and hydrochloric acid. (2)

....

(c) Name and give the formula of the gas formed when zinc carbonate reacts with nitric acid. (2)

....

HT **(d)** The ionic equation for the reaction between calcium and acid is:

$$Ca_{(s)} + 2H^{+}_{(aq)} \longrightarrow Ca^{2+}_{(aq)} + H_{2(g)}$$

(i) Which substance is oxidised in the above reaction? (1)

....

(ii) Which substance is reduced? (1)

....

HT **(e)** In terms of electrons, what is meant by an oxidation reaction? (2)

....

2 Copper(II) oxide (CuO) reacts with sulfuric acid to make the soluble salt copper(II) sulfate according to the equation below.

$$CuO_{(s)} + H_2SO_{4(aq)} \longrightarrow CuSO_{4(aq)} + H_2O_{(l)}$$

(a) Describe the steps you would take to prepare a sample of solid copper(II) sulfate, starting from copper(II) oxide and sulfuric acid solution. (3)

....

....

....

(b) The salt sodium nitrate can be formed by the reaction of sodium carbonate with an acid. Name this acid. (1)

....

For more help on this topic, see Letts GCSE Chemistry Revision Guide pages 42–43

1 Hydrogen chloride (HCl) and ethanoic acid (CH_3COOH) both dissolve in water to form acidic solutions.

(a) What is the pH range of acids? (1)

....

(b) Give the name and formula for the ion present in solutions of hydrogen chloride and ethanoic acid. (2)

....

(c) What is the common name for hydrogen chloride solution? (1)

....

(d) Acids can be neutralised by reaction with an alkali such as sodium hydroxide.

Write an ionic equation for the reaction that occurs when an acid is neutralised by an alkali. Include state symbols in your equation. (2)

....

HT **2** Ethanoic acid is a key ingredient in vinegar. It is a weak acid. Nitric acid is a strong acid.

(a) What is the difference between a weak acid and a strong acid? (2)

....

....

(b) Write a balanced symbol equation for the dissociation of ethanoic acid in water. (2)

....

(c) Will a solution of nitric acid of the same concentration as a solution of ethanoic acid have a higher or lower pH?

Explain your answer. (2)

....

....

(d) What happens to the pH value of an acid when it is diluted by a factor of 10? (2)

....

....

For more help on this topic, see Letts GCSE Chemistry Revision Guide pages 44–45

1 The diagram shows how a molten salt such as lead(II) bromide ($PbBr_2$) can be electrolysed. Lead(II) bromide consists of Pb^{2+} and Br^- ions.

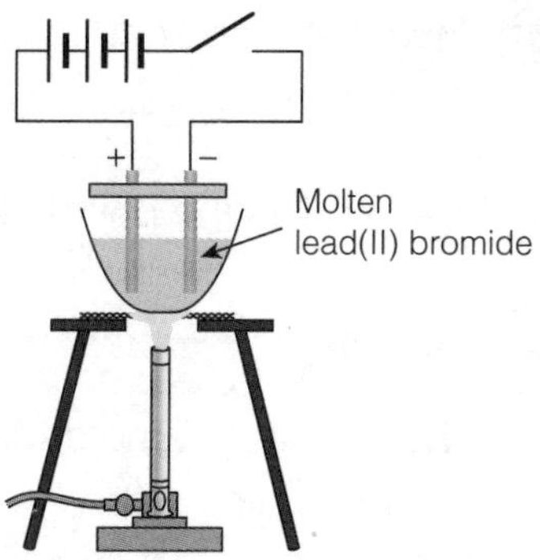

(a) What general name is given to positive ions? (1)

....

(b) What general name is given to negative ions?

.... (1)

(c) Explain why the lead(II) bromide needs to be molten. (2)

....

....

HT **(d)** At the anode, the following reaction occurs: $2Br^- \longrightarrow Br_2 + 2e^-$

Is this an oxidation or a reduction reaction? Explain your answer. (2)

....

....

2 **(a)** The table below shows the products at each electrode when the following solutions are electrolysed. Some answers have already been filled in. Complete the table. (6)

Solution	Product at anode	Product at cathode
NaCl	H_2	
KNO_3		
$CuSO_4$		
Water diluted with sulfuric acid		O_2

(b) Explain why sodium is not formed at the cathode when aqueous sodium chloride is electrolysed. (2)

....

....

HT **(c)** Write a half-equation for the formation of oxygen at the anode in the electrolysis of water diluted with sulfuric acid. (2)

....

For more help on this topic, see Letts GCSE Chemistry Revision Guide pages 46–47

Module 19 Applications of electrolysis

1 When methane burns in air an exothermic reaction takes place. The equation for the reaction is shown here:

$$CH_{4(g)} + 2O_{2(g)} \longrightarrow CO_{2(g)} + 2H_2O_{(l)}$$

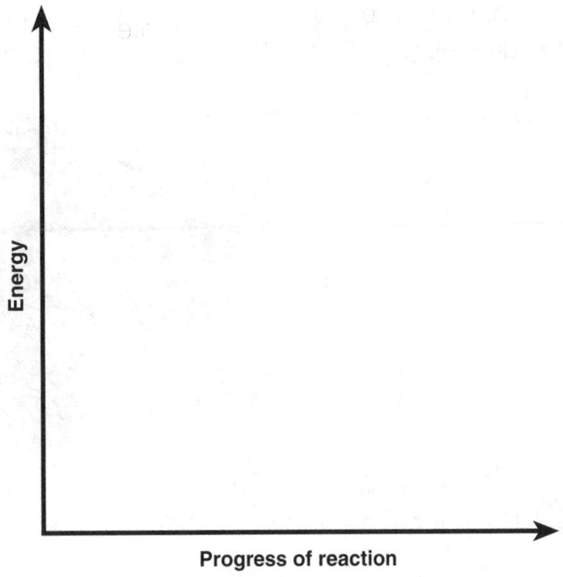

(a) On the axes, draw and label a reaction profile for an exothermic reaction. Label the reactants, products, activation energy and the overall energy change. (5)

(b) In terms of bond energies, explain why this reaction is exothermic. (2)

....

....

(c) Give an example of an endothermic chemical reaction. (1)

....

HT 2 Hydrogen peroxide (H_2O_2) decomposes in air to form water and oxygen. The diagram below shows this reaction by displaying all of the bonds present in the reactants and products.

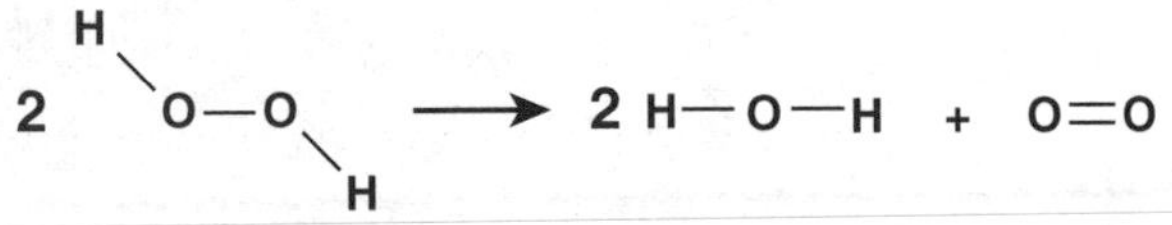

The table states the bond energy values of the bonds present in hydrogen peroxide, water and oxygen.

For the decomposition of hydrogen peroxide:

Bond	Bond energy kJ/mol
H–O	463
O–O	146
O=O	496

(a) Calculate the energy change for the reaction. (3)

....

....

(b) Is this reaction exothermic or endothermic? Explain your answer. (2)

....

....

For more help on this topic, see Letts GCSE Chemistry Revision Guide pages 48–49

Everyday batteries, like the ones shown below, are actually chemical 'cells' used to provide electrical energy. Fuel cells are also sources of energy and were used in the space shuttle.

1. Describe the internal structure of a chemical cell. (2)

   ....

   ....

2. What causes a current to flow in a chemical cell? (2)

   ....

   ....

3. Outline two ways in which the voltage produced by a chemical cell can be varied. (2)

   ....

   ....

4. Why do alkaline 'batteries' eventually stop producing an electric current? (1)

   ....

   ....

5. What is the main difference between a fuel cell and a chemical cell? (1)

   ....

6. Write the overall equation for the reaction occurring in a hydrogen fuel cell. (2)

   ....

For more help on this topic, see Letts GCSE Chemistry Revision Guide pages 50–51

1 A pupil was investigating the effect of temperature on the rate of reaction between aqueous sodium thiosulfate with dilute hydrochloric acid. When the acid is added to the sodium thiosulfate solution, a precipitate of sulfur gradually forms. The pupil recorded the time taken for a cross written on a piece of paper to disappear from view.

The experiment was repeated at different temperatures. The results are shown in the table below.

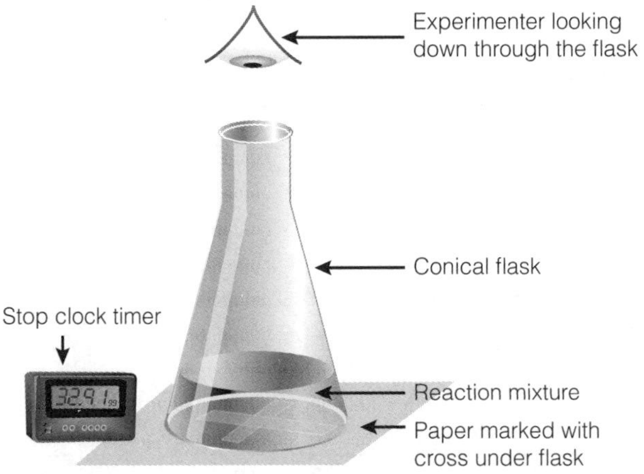

Experimenter looking down through the flask
Conical flask
Stop clock timer
32.9 1
Reaction mixture
Paper marked with cross under flask

Temperature (°C)	Time taken for cross to disappear from view (s)
15	70
25	44
40	30
55	22
70	14

(a) At which temperature was the reaction the fastest? .... (1)

(b) Suggest how the rate of this reaction at 30°C will change when the concentration of hydrochloric acid is increased. Explain your answer. (2)

....

....

2 A student investigating the rate of reaction between magnesium and hydrochloric acid carried out two experiments: one using magnesium ribbon and the other using magnesium powder.

The equation for the reaction is shown here: $Mg_{(s)} + 2HCl_{(aq)} \longrightarrow MgCl_{2(aq)} + H_{2(g)}$

In the first experiment, 69 cm^3 of hydrogen gas was collected in 46 seconds. In the second experiment, 18 cm^3 of hydrogen gas was collected in 10 seconds.

(a) Calculate the rate of reaction in both experiments. (3)

....

....

(b) Which experiment was carried out using magnesium powder? Explain your answer. (2)

....

Rates of reaction

Module 22

For more help on this topic, see Letts GCSE Chemistry Revision Guide pages 54–55

1 One aspect of collision theory states that, for a chemical reaction to occur, the reacting particles must first collide with each other.

(a) What else must occur in order for the collision to be successful? (1)

....

(b) Explain how:

(i) Increasing the pressure of a gas increases the rate of a reaction. (2)

....

....

(ii) Increasing the temperature of a solution increases the rate of a reaction. (3)

....

....

....

(c) Adding a catalyst to a reaction increases the rate of reaction. Draw, on the diagram below, the reaction profile for the reaction when a catalyst is added. (1)

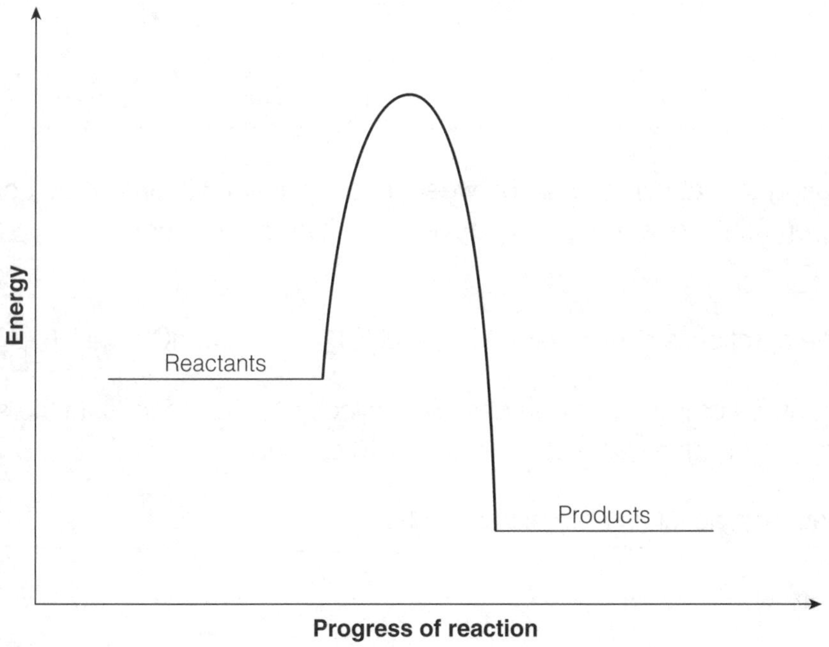
Energy
Reactants
Products
Progress of reaction

(d) Explain how a catalyst is able to increase the rate of a reaction. (2)

....

....

For more help on this topic, see Letts GCSE Chemistry Revision Guide pages 56–57

1 In an experiment, a student heated some blue crystals of hydrated copper(II) sulfate in an evaporating dish.

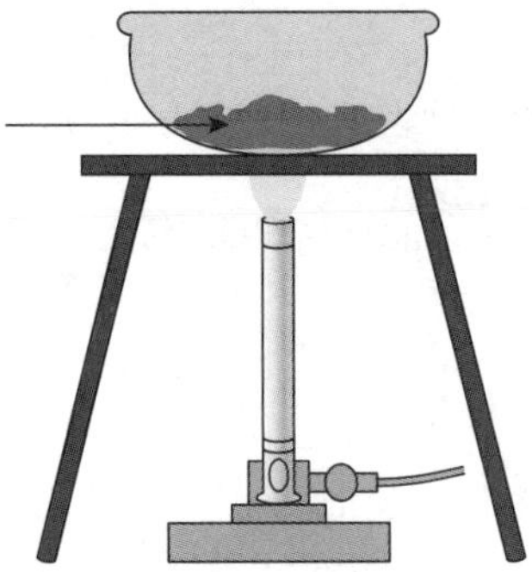

(a) State what colour change will be observed during the reaction. (1)

....

(b) Write a word equation for the change that occurs to the hydrated copper(II) sulfate during this experiment. (2)

....

(c) Describe what will be observed when water is added to the solid remaining at the end of the experiment. (1)

....

(d) Is the addition of water an exothermic or endothermic reaction? (1)

....

2 Consider the reaction given here: $2SO_{2(g)} + O_{2(g)} \rightleftharpoons 2SO_{3(g)}$

(a) What does the $\rightleftharpoons$ symbol represent? .... (1)

HT **(b)** What would be the effect on the yield of SO_3 if the above reaction was carried out at a higher pressure? Explain your answer. (3)

....

....

....

HT **(c)** The forward reaction is exothermic. What would be the effect on the yield of SO_3 if the above reaction was carried out at a higher temperature? Explain your answer. (3)

....

....

....

For more help on this topic, see Letts GCSE Chemistry Revision Guide pages 58–59

1 Crude oil is separated into its constituent components by fractional distillation. A fractionating column is used to carry out fractional distillation.

A diagram of a fractionating column is shown here.

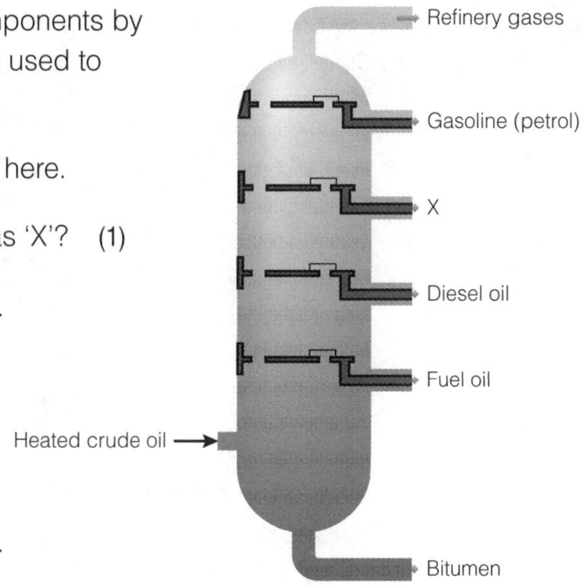
Refinery gases
Gasoline (petrol)
X
Diesel oil
Fuel oil
Heated crude oil
Bitumen

(a) What is the name of the fraction labelled as 'X'? (1)

....

(b) As you go down the fractionating column, what happens to the boiling point of the fractions? (1)

....

(c) Explain how crude oil is separated in a fractionating column. (3)

....

....

....

2 Most of the hydrocarbons found in crude oil are alkanes.

(a) What is the general formula of alkanes? (1)

....

(b) In the space below, draw the displayed formula for propane. (1)

(c) Write a balanced symbol equation for the complete combustion of propane. (2)

....

....

For more help on this topic, see Letts GCSE Chemistry Revision Guide pages 62–63

1 This question is about the alkene propene (C_3H_6).

(a) What is the general formula of alkenes? (1)

....

(b) In the space below, draw the displayed formula of propene. (2)

(c) With reference to your diagram in part **b**, explain why alkenes are unsaturated. (2)

....

....

(d) Write a balanced symbol equation for the complete combustion of propene. (2)

....

(e) Draw the displayed formula of the molecule formed when propene reacts with hydrogen. (1)

2 Cracking is a method of converting long-chain hydrocarbons into shorter, more useful hydrocarbons.

(a) Name a catalyst used to crack hydrocarbons. (1)

....

(b) The equation for a reaction that occurs during this process is:

$$C_{12}H_{26} \longrightarrow C_2H_4 + C_6H_{12} + X$$

In the balanced equation, what is the molecular formula of X? (1)

....

For more help on this topic, see Letts GCSE Chemistry Revision Guide pages 64–65

1 The alcohol ethanol and ethanoic acid, which is a carboxylic acid, react together to form an ester.

The displayed formula of ethanol is shown here.

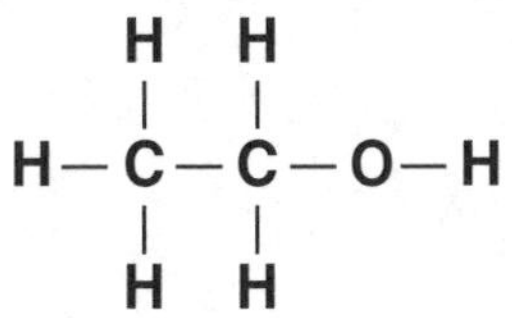

(a) What functional group is present in alcohols? .... (1)

(b) What is the structural formula of ethanol? (1)

....

(c) State two properties of alcohols. (2)

....

....

(d) Other than making esters, state two uses of alcohols. (2)

....

....

(e) In the space below, draw the displayed formula of ethanoic acid. (1)

(f) State two chemical properties of carboxylic acids, such as ethanoic acid. (2)

....

....

(g) How can ethanol be converted into ethanoic acid? (1)

....

(h) Name the ester formed when ethanol reacts with ethanoic acid. (1)

....

For more help on this topic, see Letts GCSE Chemistry Revision Guide pages 66–67

1 Poly(ethene) is a man-made polymer that has many uses in everyday life.

(a) Name the monomer used to make poly(ethene). (1)

....

(b) In the space below, draw the displayed formula for this monomer. (1)

(c) What type of polymer is poly(ethene)? (1)

....

(d) What feature of the monomer means that it is able to undergo this type of polymerisation? (1)

....

(e) State two uses of poly(ethene) and state what properties of poly(ethene) make it suitable for these uses. (3)

....

.... (2)

2 Many naturally occurring materials, e.g. proteins and starch, are formed by condensation polymerisation.

HT **(a)** What is meant by the term 'condensation polymerisation'? (2)

....

....

HT **(b)** Proteins are made from amino acids. What two functional groups are present in amino acids? (2)

....

....

(c) What is the monomer used to make starch? (1)

....

For more help on this topic, see Letts GCSE Chemistry Revision Guide pages 68–69

1 Paint and household cleaning chemicals are typical examples of everyday chemical formulations.

(a) What is a formulation? (1)

....

(b) Are formulations chemically pure? Explain your answer. (2)

....

....

(c) Give one other example of a type of formulation. (1)

....

2 Pen ink is typically a mixture of dyes. The individual dyes in pen ink can be separated by paper chromatography. The chromatogram below is for an unknown ink 'X' and the standard colours blue, red and green.

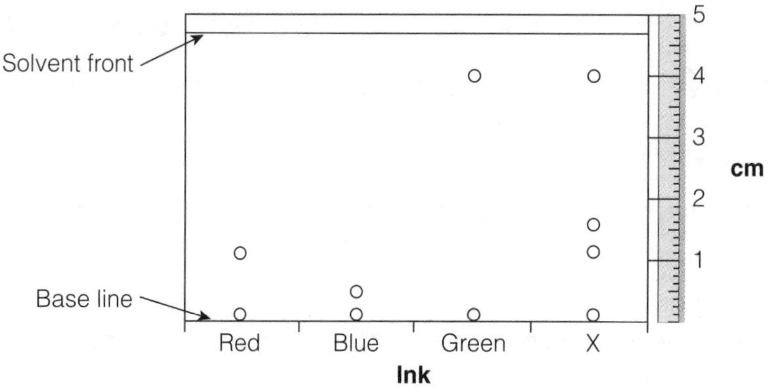

(a) What is the mobile phase in paper chromatography? (1)

....

(b) Which colours are present in ink X? Explain your answer. (2)

....

....

(c) Calculate the R_f for the blue ink. (2)

....

....

For more help on this topic, see Letts GCSE Chemistry Revision Guide pages 72–73

1 When carbon dioxide gas is bubbled through limewater the following reaction occurs:

$Ca(OH)_{2(aq)} + CO_{2(g)} \longrightarrow CaCO_{3(s)} + H_2O_{(l)}$

(a) What is the chemical name for limewater? (1)

....

(b) With reference to the above equation, explain why limewater turns cloudy when carbon dioxide is bubbled through it. (2)

....

....

2 **(a)** Describe what would be observed when moist blue litmus paper is added to a gas jar containing chlorine gas. (2)

....

....

(b) Is chlorine an acidic or alkaline gas?

What evidence is there to support your answer? (2)

....

....

3 Hydrogen and oxygen gases are both colourless, odourless gases.

(a) What is the chemical test and observation for hydrogen gas? (2)

....

....

(b) What is the chemical test and observation for oxygen gas? (2)

....

....

(c) When hydrogen gas burns in air it reacts with oxygen to form water. Write a balanced symbol equation for the reaction taking place. (2)

....

....

For more help on this topic, see Letts GCSE Chemistry Revision Guide pages 74–75

1 Draw lines to match the different flame test colours produced by some metal ions. The first one has been done for you. (4)

Metal ion	Flame test colour
K^+	Orange-red
Cu^{2+}	Crimson-red
Li^+	Lilac
Ca^{2+}	Yellow
Na^+	Green

2 Sodium hydroxide can be used to confirm the presence of some metal cations by precipitation reactions.

(a) What is a precipitation reaction? (2)

....

....

(b) What will be observed when sodium hydroxide solution is added to a solution containing Cu^{2+} ions? (1)

....

(c) Write an ionic equation (including state symbols) for the reaction occurring in part **b**. (2)

....

(d) Both Mg^{2+} ions and Al^{3+} ions give a white precipitate upon the addition of sodium hydroxide solution.
Explain how sodium hydroxide solution can be used to distinguish between Mg^{2+} ions and Al^{3+} ions. (2)

....

....

(e) Explain how sodium hydroxide can be used to distinguish between Fe^{2+} and Fe^{3+} ions. (2)

....

....

For more help on this topic, see Letts GCSE Chemistry Revision Guide pages 76–77

1 This question is about testing for sulfate and carbonate ions. The sulfate ion (SO_4^{2-}) can be identified by adding dilute hydrochloric acid followed by barium chloride solution.

(a) What colour precipitate is formed in a positive test for the sulfate ion? (1)

....

(b) Give the name and formula for this precipitate. (2)

....

(c) What is the formula for the carbonate ion? (2)

....

(d) Describe how to test for the presence of the carbonate ion in a solid such as calcium carbonate. (3)

....

....

....

2 The halide ions Cl^-, Br^- and I^- can be identified from their solutions by adding nitric acid followed by silver nitrate solution.

(a) Explain how this test can be used to distinguish between the Cl^-, Br^- and I^- ions. (2)

....

....

(b) Write an ionic equation for the reaction that occurs when silver nitrate solution reacts with chloride ions. Include state symbols in your equation. (2)

....

3 Instrumental methods can be used instead of chemical tests to analyse the composition of substances.

(a) Name the instrumental method used to identify metal ions. (1)

....

(b) Give two advantages of using an instrumental method of analysis when compared with a chemical test. (2)

....

....

For more help on this topic, see Letts GCSE Chemistry Revision Guide pages 78–79

1 Many scientists think that the Earth's early atmosphere may have been similar in composition to the gases typically released by volcanoes today.

The pie charts below show the composition of the atmosphere today and the composition of gases released by a volcano.

Composition of Earth's atmosphere today

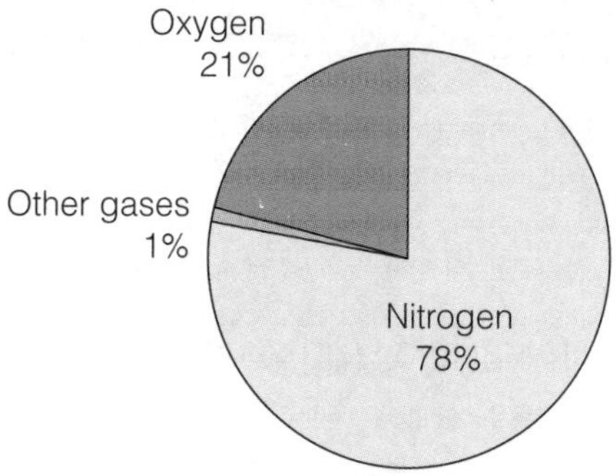
Oxygen
21%
Other gases
1%
Nitrogen
78%

Composition of gases from volcanoes

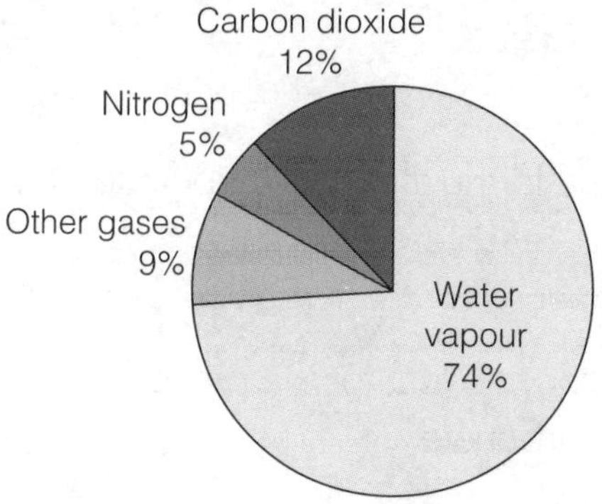
Carbon dioxide
12%
Nitrogen
5%
Other gases
9%
Water
vapour
74%

(a) Name a gas that is more abundant in the Earth's atmosphere today than in the early atmosphere. (1)

....

(b) Why is the amount of water vapour in the atmosphere significantly less now than in the early atmosphere? (2)

....

....

(c) Describe the process that caused the percentage of oxygen in the atmosphere to increase. (2)

....

....

(d) Outline two ways in which the amount of carbon dioxide in the early atmosphere decreased. (2)

....

....

For more help on this topic, see Letts GCSE Chemistry Revision Guide pages 82–83

1 When fossil fuels are burnt, carbon dioxide gas is produced and released into the atmosphere. Some people believe carbon dioxide to be a greenhouse gas.

(a) Explain how greenhouse gases maintain the temperature on Earth. (2)

....

....

(b) Name one other greenhouse gas. (1)

....

(c) Outline two ways in which human activity increases the amounts of greenhouse gases in the atmosphere. (2)

....

....

(d) Why is it not easy to predict the impact of changes on global climate change? (2)

....

....

(e) Describe two potential effects of increasing average global temperature. (2)

....

....

(f) Describe two forms of global action that can be taken to reduce the carbon footprint. (2)

....

....

(g) Outline two potential problems that governments might face when trying to reduce the carbon footprint. (2)

....

....

For more help on this topic, see Letts GCSE Chemistry Revision Guide pages 84–85

1 The combustion of fossil fuels, e.g. from cars, is a major source of atmospheric pollution.

(a) What is meant by a fossil fuel? (1)

....

(b) How are carbon and carbon monoxide formed from the combustion of fossil fuels? (1)

....

(c) State one harmful effect caused by the release of oxides of nitrogen into the atmosphere. (1)

....

(d) Give two detrimental consequences of releasing particulates into the air. (2)

....

....

(e) Explain why carbon monoxide is a toxic gas. (2)

....

....

(f) Fuels can contain sulfur as an impurity. Explain how burning this impurity can cause problems in the environment. (3)

....

....

....

For more help on this topic, see Letts GCSE Chemistry Revision Guide pages 86–87

1 We use the Earth's resources to provide us with warmth, shelter, food and transport. As the Earth is a finite source of resources, we need to ensure that we use them sustainably.

(a) What is sustainable development? (1)

....

(b) What is meant by the term 'potable water'? (1)

....

(c) After identification of an appropriate source of fresh water, what two stages then need to occur to turn this into potable water? (2)

....

....

(d) Outline the processes that are used to treat sewage. (3)

....

....

....

2 Salty water, e.g. seawater, can be desalinated (i.e. treated to reduce its salt content). One such method is distillation.

(a) In the space below, draw a labelled diagram to show how seawater can be distilled. Describe how distillation produces desalinated water. (5)

....

....

(b) What method of desalination involves the use of membranes? (1)

....

For more help on this topic, see Letts GCSE Chemistry Revision Guide pages 88–89

Module 37

HT Alternative methods of extracting metals

HT **1** As we mine more and more of the Earth's natural resources, we need to develop alternative methods of extracting metals such as copper. One such recently developed method is phytomining.

(a) What is an ore? (2)

....

....

(b) Aside from environmental reasons, why are methods of extracting metals such as phytomining being developed? (2)

....

....

(c) State two uses of copper and describe the properties that make it suitable for each purpose. (4)

....

....

(d) Describe the process of phytomining. (3)

....

....

....

(e) How can bacteria be used to extract metals such as copper? (1)

....

(f) Scrap metals, such as iron, can be used to obtain copper from solutions. Write a word equation for the reaction that occurs when iron reacts with copper sulfate solution. (2)

....

(g) Why would platinum not be a suitable metal for extracting copper from copper sulfate solution? (1)

....

(h) What is the name of the process involving electricity that can be used to extract a metal from a solution of its ions? (1)

....

For more help on this topic, see Letts GCSE Chemistry Revision Guide pages 90–91

1 Life-cycle assessments (LCAs) are carried out to evaluate the environmental impact of products at different stages of the life of a product.

(a) Other than transport and distribution, state two other stages of a product life cycle that will be considered when carrying out an LCA. (2)

....

....

(b) State two quantities that are considered when conducting an LCA. (2)

....

....

(c) Explain why the pollution value in a life-cycle value may result in the LCA not being totally objective. (2)

....

....

(d) Why might selective or abbreviated LCAs be misused? (1)

....

2 The table below shows an example of an LCA for the use of plastic (polythene) and paper shopping bags.

	Amounts per 1000 bags over the whole LCA	
	Paper	Plastic (polythene)
Energy use (mJ)	2590	713
Fossil fuel use (kg)	28	12.8
Solid waste (kg)	34	6
Greenhouse gas emissions (kg CO_2)	72	36
Fresh water use (litres)	3387	198

Based on the above figures, why might some people think that plastic (polythene) bags should be used instead of paper bags? Use information from the table in your answer. (3)

....

....

....

For more help on this topic, see Letts GCSE Chemistry Revision Guide pages 92–93

1 A student was investigating the corrosion/rusting of iron. He placed iron nails in test tubes as shown in the diagram below.

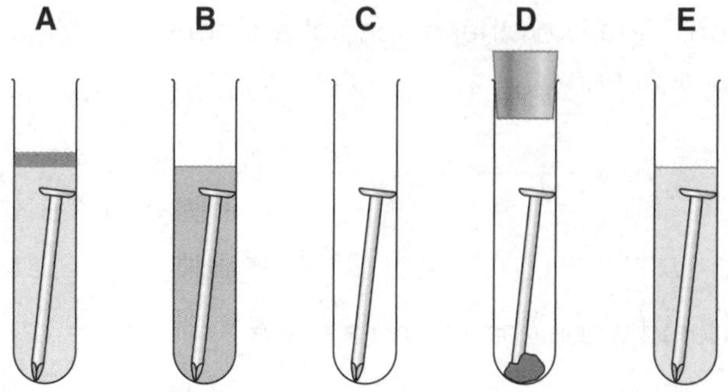
A
B
C
D
E
Boiled water and oil layer
Salt water
Air
Air and calcium chloride
Water and air

Oil acts as a barrier preventing air and water from entering the tubes. Calcium chloride is a drying agent – absorbing any water vapour present in the air. After two weeks, the nail in tube E exhibited some rust, the nail in tube C had a tiny amount of rust and the one in tube B was very rusty.

(a) Which two chemicals are necessary for rusting to occur? (2)

....

....

(b) Explain why metals located closer to the coast often experience a greater amount of rusting/corrosion than metals located inland. (2)

....

....

(c) Explain why the nail in tube A did not rust. (1)

....

(d) State two materials that metals such as iron can be coated with in order to prevent them from rusting. (2)

....

....

(e) Name a metal that is mixed with iron to make stainless steel. (1)

....

(f) What type of material is stainless steel? (1)

....

For more help on this topic, see Letts GCSE Chemistry Revision Guide pages 94–95

1 The Haber process is an important industrial process used to manufacture ammonia (NH_3) from nitrogen and hydrogen in the presence of a catalyst. The formation of ammonia is an exothermic process.

This is the equation for the formation of ammonia from its raw materials:

$$N_{2(g)} + 3H_{2(g)} \rightleftharpoons 2NH_{3(g)}$$

(a) How are the raw materials obtained? (2)

....

....

(b) Name the catalyst used in the manufacture of ammonia. .... (1)

(c) Consider the graph below, which shows the effect on the yield of ammonia at different operating temperatures and pressures.

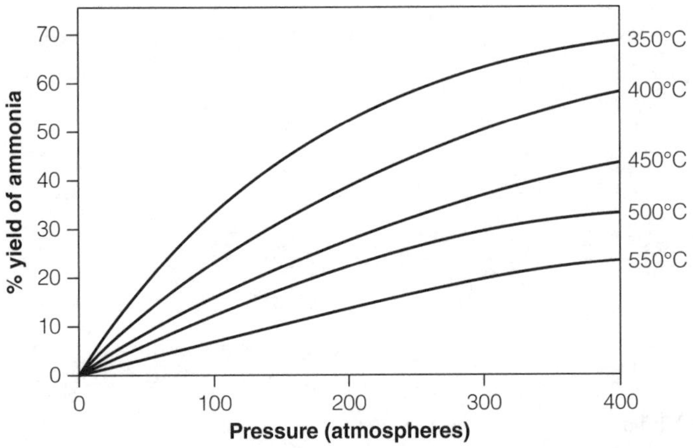

(i) Calculate the yield of ammonia in a plant operating at 200 atmospheres pressure and 500°C. .... (1)

(ii) With reference to the graph, deduce the effect on the yield of ammonia of increasing temperature. (1)

....

(d) State the normal temperature and pressure used in the production of ammonia. (2)

....

HT **(e)** Explain why a lower temperature is not used, even though it will give a higher yield and cost less. (2)

....

....

For more help on this topic, see Letts GCSE Chemistry Revision Guide pages 96–97

Letts

GCSE

CHEMISTRY

Higher Tier Chemistry 1H

H

Time allowed: 1 hour 45 minutes

You may use:

- a ruler
- a calculator
- a periodic table.

Instructions

- Answer all questions in the spaces provided.
- Do all rough work in this book. Cross through any work you do not want to be marked.

Information

- There are 100 marks available on this paper.
- The marks for questions are shown in brackets.
- You are expected to use a calculator where appropriate.
- You are reminded of the need for good English and clear presentation in your answers.
- When answering questions 06.6 and 08.3 you need to make sure that your answer:
  - is clear, logical, sensibly structured
  - fully meets the requirements of the question
  - shows that each separate point or step supports the overall answer.

Advice

- In all calculations, show clearly how you work out your answer.

Name: ______________________________

0 1 The periodic table lists all known elements.

0 1 . 1 Which statement about the periodic table is correct?
Tick (✓) **one** box. **[1 mark]**

Each row begins with elements with one outer electron. ☐

The columns are called periods. ☐

The elements are arranged in mass number order. ☐

The metallic elements are on the right. ☐

0 1 . 2 Which of these statements about the elements in Group 0 is correct?
Tick (✓) **one** box. **[1 mark]**

They are all liquids at room temperature. ☐

Their boiling points increase as you go down the group. ☐

They have very high melting points. ☐

Their molecules are made from pairs of atoms. ☐

0 1 . 3 Element X is a solid with a low melting point. When it reacts it forms covalent bonds with other elements or it forms negative ions.

Put an X where you would expect to find element X on the periodic table. **[1 mark]**

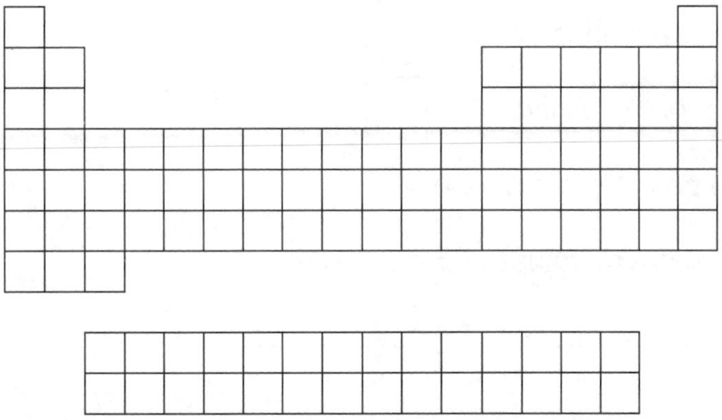

0 1 . 4 Which statement explains why group 1 elements are known as the alkali metals?
Tick (✓) **one** box. **[1 mark]**

They are tested with an alkali to show they are reactive. ☐

They are in the first column in the periodic table. ☐

They all react strongly with alkalis. ☐

They make an alkali when reacted with water. ☐

0 1 . 5 Sodium is below lithium in group 1 of the periodic table.

Explain why sodium reacts more vigorously with water than lithium. **[2 marks]**

____

____

0 2 This question is about metals.

0 2 . 1 Which list of metals correctly shows the order of reactivity, starting with the most reactive and ending with the least reactive?
Tick (✓) **one** box. **[1 mark]**

lithium, calcium, zinc, iron ☐

calcium, lithium, iron, copper ☐

potassium, iron, zinc, copper ☐

magnesium, copper, lithium, zinc ☐

0 2 . 2 Which of these properties applies only to transition metals?
Tick (✓) **one** box. **[1 mark]**

Easily hammered into shape ☐

Conduct heat ☐

Form coloured compounds ☐

Good conductor of electricity ☐

0 2 . 3 Steel is an alloy composed mainly of iron.

Explain why steel is a more useful metal than iron. **[2 marks]**

____

____

0 2 . 4 **Figure 1** shows the arrangement of particles in a metal.

Figure 1

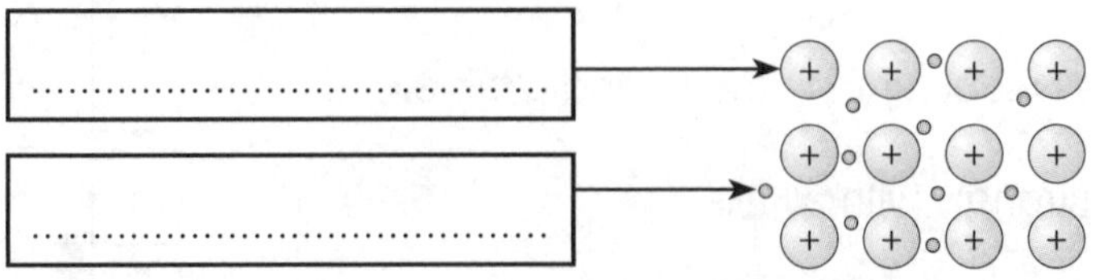

Add labels to **Figure 1** and use them to explain how metals conduct electricity. **[4 marks]**

____

____

0 3 This question is about carbon.

0 3 . 1 Graphite is commonly used as a lubricant in machines that operate at high temperatures.

Which properties of graphite explain why it is suitable for this use?
Tick (✓) **one** box. **[1 mark]**

Electrical conductor and high melting point ☐

Good heat and electrical conductor ☐

Good heat conductor and slippery ☐

High melting point and slippery ☐

0 3 . 2 Graphene is a form of carbon. It is formed of a sheet of carbon atoms, one atom thick.

A graphene sheet has a thickness of 3.4×10^{-8} cm. Calculate the area covered by 1 cm^3 of graphene.
Tick (✓) **one** box. **[1 mark]**

3.4×10^{8} cm^2 ☐

2.9×10^{7} cm^2 ☐

2.9×10^{-7} cm^2 ☐

3.4×10^{-8} cm^2 ☐

0 3 . 3 Carbon nanotubes are cylindrical fullerenes.

State two important physical properties of nanotubes. **[2 marks]**

____

____

0 3 . 4 Diamond has a tetrahedral structure, as shown in **Figure 2**.

Figure 2

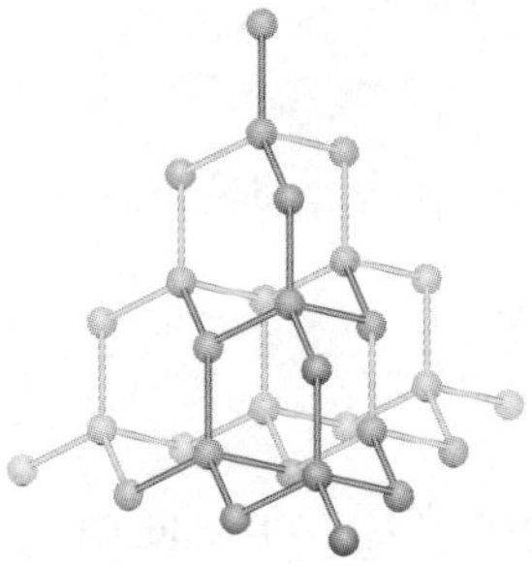

Explain why diamond has a very high melting point and why, unlike graphite, it does not conduct electricity. **[3 marks]**

____

____

____

0 4 Carbon dioxide is made by the thermal decomposition of copper(II) carbonate (see **Figure 3**). Copper(II) oxide is also made.

Figure 3

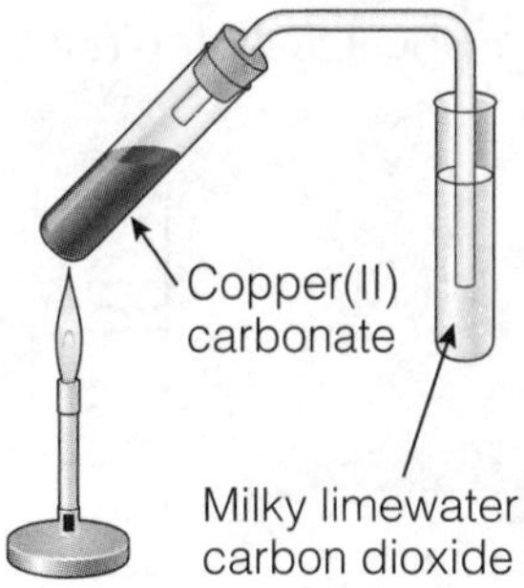
Copper(II) carbonate
Milky limewater shows carbon dioxide is present

0 4 . 1 Write the word equation for the decomposition reaction. **[1 mark]**

____

0 4 . 2 Calculate the mass of carbon dioxide made when 12.35 g of copper(II) carbonate is heated to make 7.95 g of copper(II) oxide. Show your working. **[2 marks]**

____

____

0 5 This is a question about magnesium.

0 5 . 1 Draw a diagram to show the arrangement of electrons in a magnesium atom. **[1 mark]**

0 5 . 2 Magnesium (Mg) burns in oxygen (O_2) to make magnesium oxide (MgO).
Balance the formula equation for this reaction. **[1 mark]**

$$[\quad\quad]Mg + [\quad\quad]O_2 \rightarrow [\quad\quad]MgO$$

0 5 . 3 The reaction to make magnesium oxide has a 100% atom economy. How can you tell from the equation? **[1 mark]**

____

0 5 . 4 Draw a dot-and-cross diagram to show the bonding in magnesium oxide. **[2 marks]**

0 5 . 5 Ria made 9.6 g of magnesium chloride by reacting magnesium oxide with hydrochloric acid:

$$MgO + 2HCl \rightarrow MgCl_2 + H_2O$$

She calculated that from the amounts she used, she should have made 12.8 g.

Calculate the percentage yield of magnesium chloride. Show your working. **[2 marks]**

____

____

____________________ %

0 6 This question is about atoms, ions and isotopes.

0 6 . 1 Which of these statements about a neutral atom is always correct?
Tick (✓) **one** box. **[1 mark]**

It has the same number of electrons and neutrons. ☐

It has the same number of protons and neutrons. ☐

It has the same number of protons, neutrons and electrons. ☐

It has the same number of electrons and protons. ☐

0 6 . 2 Fe^{2+} ions are formed during some chemical reactions. Look at the information given below and then complete **Table 1**. **[1 mark]**

$$^{56}_{26}Fe$$

Table 1

Number of protons in the ion	
Number of neutrons in the ion	
Number of electrons in the ion	

0 6 . 3 Explain how you worked out each of the three numbers in **Table 1**. **[3 marks]**

Number of protons:

____

____

Number of neutrons:

____

____

Number of electrons:

0 6 . 4 The element chlorine has two naturally occurring isotopes.

What are the similarities and differences in the atomic structure of the two isotopes? **[3 marks]**

0 6 . 5 Gold metal can be rolled into very thin sheets called gold leaf.

The radius of a gold atom is 1.5×10^{-10} m.

Gold leaf has a typical thickness of 1.2×10^{-6} m.

Calculate how many gold atoms are packed on top of each other to achieve this thickness. **[2 marks]**

0 6 . 6 Our understanding of the model of the atom has developed from the work of a number of scientists, starting from Dalton's theory that an atom was a solid sphere.

Outline how our understanding of the atom has changed. Link the key scientists with the improvements they made to our understanding. **[6 marks]**

0 7 Acids react with bases to form salts and water.

0 7 . 1 Which pair of reactants can be used to prepare copper sulfate?
Tick (✓) **one** box. **[1 mark]**

Copper and sulfuric acid ☐

Copper hydroxide and nitric acid ☐

Copper oxide and sulfuric acid ☐

Copper oxide and hydrochloric acid ☐

0 7 . 2 Josh put a sample of potassium hydroxide solution into a beaker. He measured the pH. Then he slowly added dilute nitric acid until no further reaction took place.

How would the pH of the solution in the beaker change?
Tick (✓) **one** box. **[1 mark]**

The pH would start high and decrease to below 7. ☐

The solution would change to a pH of 7. ☐

The pH would stay the same. ☐

The pH would start low and increase to above 7. ☐

0 7 . 3 Which of the following 0.1 mol/dm^3 acid solutions has the lowest pH?
Tick (✓) **one** box. **[1 mark]**

Carbonic acid ☐

Citric acid ☐

Ethanoic acid ☐

Nitric acid ☐

0 7 . 4 An acid–base reaction was completed between hydrochloric acid (HCl) and calcium oxide (CaO) to make calcium chloride ($CaCl_2$).

This is the equation for the reaction: $2HCl + CaO \rightarrow CaCl_2 + H_2O$

An excess of solid calcium oxide was added to the acid.

Calculate the minimum mass of calcium oxide needed to make 5.55 g of calcium chloride. Show your working. (The relative atomic masses are found on the periodic table at the end of the paper.) **[4 marks]**

____

____

____

____

07.5 Lithium nitrate can be made using a similar method to that described in question 07.4, by reacting solid lithium carbonate with nitric acid.

This is the equation for the reaction: $Li_2CO_3 + 2HNO_3 \rightarrow 2LiNO_3 + CO_2 + H_2O$

Use the equation to calculate the percentage atom economy for making lithium nitrate from lithium carbonate. **[3 marks]**

$$\frac{\text{relative formula mass of desired product from equation}}{\text{sum of relative formula masses of all reactants from equation}} \times 100$$

____

____

____

08 Copper(II) sulfate solution can undergo electrolysis using the apparatus shown in **Figure 4**.

Figure 4

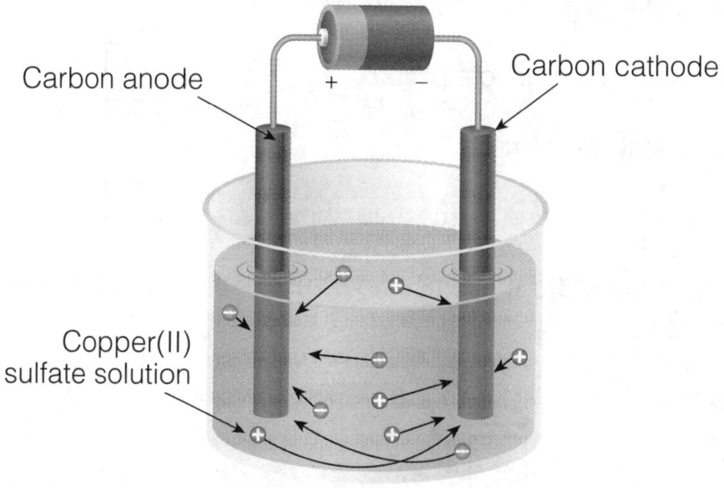
Carbon anode
+
–
Carbon cathode
Copper(II)
sulfate solution

08.1 Describe the meaning of the term electrolysis. **[2 marks]**

____

____

08.2 These are the reactions at the electrodes during the electrolysis of copper(II) sulfate solution:

Cathode $Cu^{2+} + 2e^- \rightarrow Cu$

Anode $4OH^- \rightarrow O_2 + 2H_2O + 4e^-$

Which reaction is reduction and which reaction is oxidation? Explain your answer. **[2 marks]**

____

____

____

0 8 . 3 Iron (III) oxide is roasted with carbon (coke) in a blast furnace to produce iron.

Aluminium is extracted by the electrolysis of molten aluminium oxide (Al_2O_3).

Compare the two methods of extraction explaining why not all metals can be extracted by heating the metal oxide with carbon. **[6 marks]**

____

____

____

____

____

____

____

____

____

____

0 9 This question is about hydrogen fuel cells.

0 9 . 1 Hydrogen fuel cells can be used to make electricity: $2H_2 + O_2 \rightarrow 2H_2O$

Give two advantages of using hydrogen fuel cells rather than using batteries. **[2 marks]**

____

____

0 9 . 2 Hydrogen gas is converted into hydrogen ions at the anode in the fuel cell.

Write an ionic half equation to show how hydrogen ions are made at the anode. **[1 mark]**

____

0 9 . 3 Oxygen gas is converted into oxide ions at the cathode in the fuel cell.

Write an ionic half equation to show how oxide ions are made at the cathode. **[1 mark]**

____

0 9 . 4 Look at **Figure 5**. Complete the energy level diagram for the hydrogen fuel cell. **[2 marks]**

Figure 5

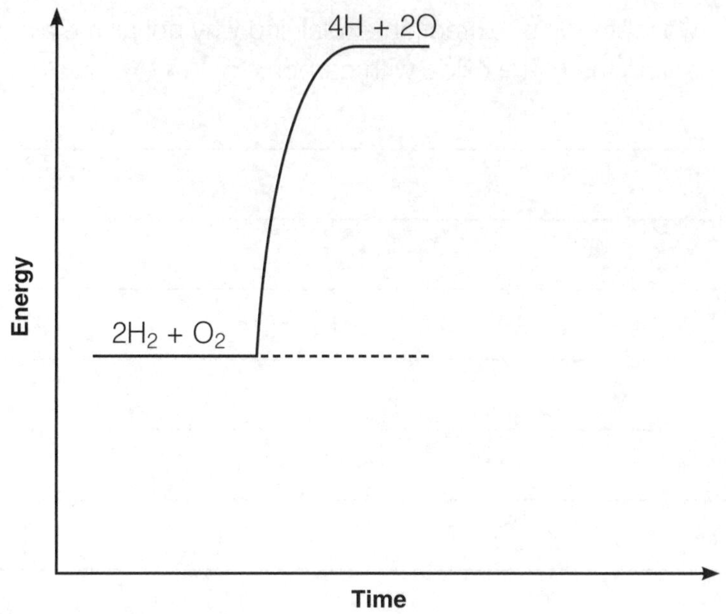

4H + 2O
Energy
2H2 + O2
Time

0 9 . 5 Label the activation energy for the reaction on **Figure 5**. **[1 mark]**

1 0 Ella measured 15 cm³ of water into a test tube, as shown in **Figure 6**.

Figure 6

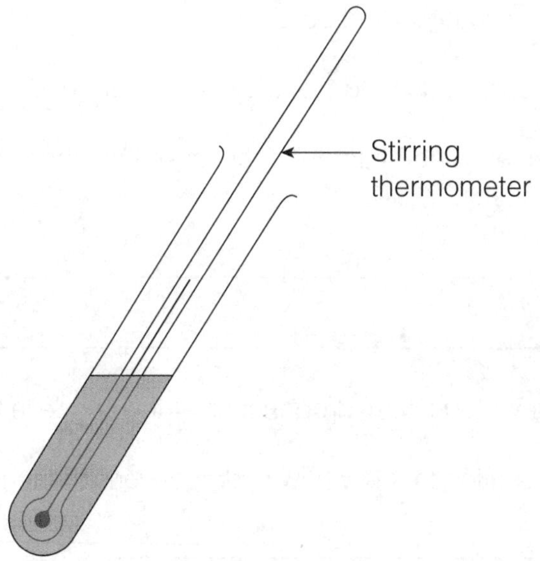

Stirring thermometer

She measured the temperature of the water and added 2 g of a solid. She stirred until there was no further temperature change. She repeated the experiment with other solids.

10.1 Complete the results table (**Table 2**). **[2 marks]**

Table 2

Solid	Start temperature (°C)	End temperature (°C)	Temperature change (°C)
Ammonium chloride	15	9	–6
Potassium hydroxide	16	29	+13
Ammonium nitrate	18	4	....
Sodium hydroxide	17	35	....

10.2 Which of the solids had the largest endothermic energy change? Explain your answer. **[3 marks]**

____

____

____

11 Oxygen has a boiling point of –183°C and a melting point of –219°C.

11.1 Describe what happens to the arrangement and movement of oxygen molecules as the temperature is changed from –190°C to –170°C. **[2 marks]**

____

____

____

11.2 A small, portable oxygen cylinder for medical use (like **Figure 7**) contains 15 000 g of liquid oxygen.

Figure 7

The M_r of oxygen (O_2) is 32. One mole of any gas at room temperature and pressure has a volume of 24 dm^3.

What volume of oxygen gas in dm^3 will this cylinder provide at room temperature and pressure? Show your working. **[2 marks]**

____

____

1 2 This question is about group 7 elements.

1 2 . 1 Finlay added an aqueous solution of sodium iodide to a solution of bromine. The colour changed from orange to deep brown.

Finlay then added an aqueous solution of sodium chloride to the bromine solution. The orange colour did not change.

Explain these observations. **[4 marks]**

1 2 . 2 Chlorine is composed of diatomic molecules, Cl_2.

Draw a dot-and-cross diagram to show the bonding in a chlorine molecule. You should only show the outer shell electrons in your diagram. **[2 marks]**

1 2 . 3 Chlorine and iodine are both in group 7 of the periodic table.

Explain why chlorine is a gas and iodine is a solid at room temperature. **[2 marks]**

1 2 . 4 Explain why solid iodine does not conduct electricity. **[1 mark]**

1 3 When 1 mole of carbon burns completely, 393 kJ of energy is released.

$$C_{(s)} + O_{2(g)} \rightarrow CO_{2(g)}$$

The relative atomic mass (A_r) of carbon = 12.

1 3 . 1 Calculate the energy released when 14.4 g of carbon is burned. Show your working. **[2 marks]**

13.2 Energy is released when carbon burns. Use ideas about bond making and bond breaking to explain why. **[3 marks]**

____

____

____

____

13.3 Amy measured the energy released by reacting hydrochloric acid with sodium hydroxide solution. Both solutions had the same concentration.

This was the method used.

1. Measure 25 cm^3 sodium hydroxide solution using a 100 cm^3 measuring cylinder.
2. Pour the sodium hydroxide solution into a 250 cm^3 beaker.
3. Use the 100 cm^3 measuring cylinder to measure 25 cm^3 hydrochloric acid.
4. Pour the acid into the sodium hydroxide in the beaker.
5. Measure the start temperature with a thermometer.
6. After one minute, measure the final temperature.

This method gave a poor result. Suggest three improvements to the method. **[3 marks]**

1: ____

____

2: ____

____

3: ____

____

END OF QUESTIONS

GCSE

CHEMISTRY

Higher Tier Chemistry 2H

H

Time allowed: 1 hour 45 minutes

You may use:

- a ruler
- a calculator
- a periodic table.

Instructions

- Answer all questions in the spaces provided.
- Do all rough work in this book. Cross through any work you do not want to be marked.

Information

- There are 100 marks available on this paper.
- The marks for questions are shown in brackets.
- You are expected to use a calculator where appropriate.
- You are reminded of the need for good English and clear presentation in your answers.
- When answering questions 07.1 and 11.2 you need to make sure that your answer:
  - is clear, logical, sensibly structured
  - fully meets the requirements of the question
  - shows that each separate point or step supports the overall answer.

Advice

- In all calculations, show clearly how you work out your answer.

Name: ____

0 1 This question is about chemical analysis.

0 1 . 1 Which one of the following gases will bleach damp litmus paper?

Tick (✓) **one** box. **[1 mark]**

Carbon dioxide ☐

Chlorine ☐

Hydrogen ☐

Methane ☐

0 1 . 2 Sodium hydroxide is added to a solution of Cu(II) ions. State the colour of the precipitate formed.

Tick (✓) **one** box. **[1 mark]**

Brown ☐

White ☐

Blue ☐

Green ☐

0 1 . 3 **Figure 1** shows the result of a chromatography experiment on an unknown black ink.

Figure 1

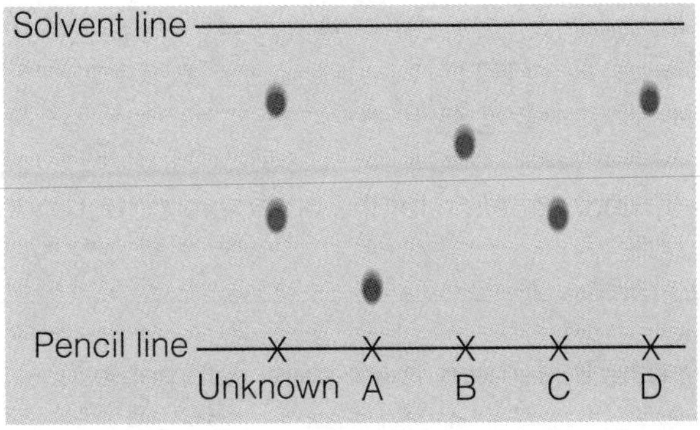

Which inks does the unknown ink in **Figure 1** contain?

Tick (✓) **one** box. **[1 mark]**

A and B ☐

A and C ☐

B and D ☐

C and D ☐

0 1 . 4 The R_f value of ink B is 0.86. The solvent line moved 7.91 cm from the pencil line.

Calculate how far ink B moved up the paper. Show your working. Give your answer to an appropriate number of significant figures. **[2 marks]**

____

____

0 1 . 5 The experiment was repeated using a different solvent.

Describe and explain how this could affect the R_f value. **[3 marks]**

____

____

0 2 This question is about hydrocarbons.

0 2 . 1 Which of the following molecules has the formula C_4H_{10}? Tick (✓) **one** box. **[1 mark]**

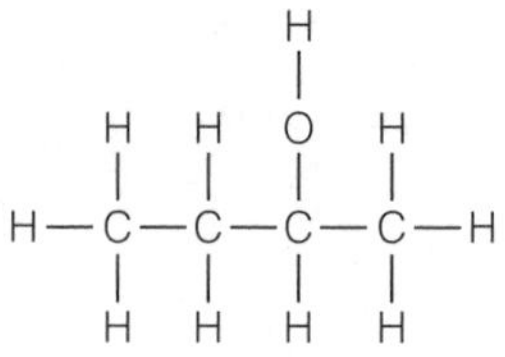 ☐

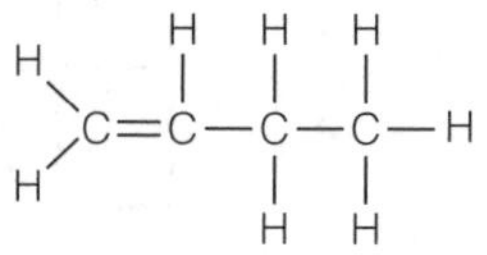 ☐

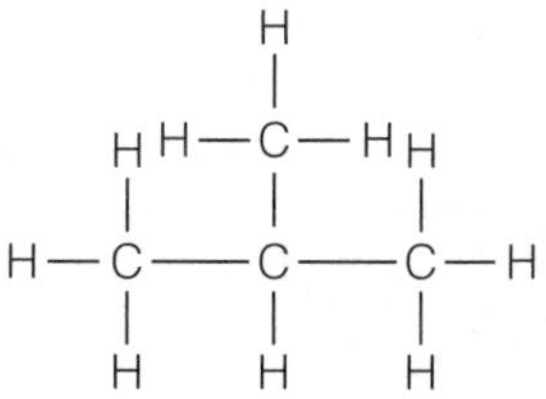 ☐

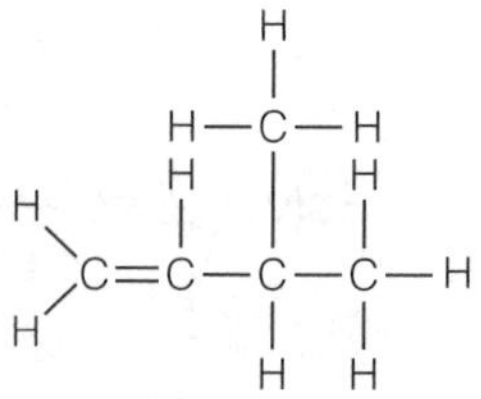 ☐

0 2 . 2 Write the balanced symbol equation for the complete combustion of C_4H_{10}. **[2 marks]**

____

0 2 . 3 Which of the following hydrocarbons is the most flammable?
Tick (✓) **one** box. **[1 mark]**

C_8H_{18} ☐

$C_{11}H_{24}$ ☐

C_5H_{12} ☐

$C_{14}H_{30}$ ☐

0 2 . 4 Explain how the difference in strength of intermolecular forces between hydrocarbons allows them to be separated by fractional distillation. **[3 marks]**

____

____

____

0 2 . 5 Cracking is used to meet the supply and demand of hydrocarbons. The apparatus used in the laboratory for cracking long-chain hydrocarbons is shown in **Figure 2**.

Figure 2

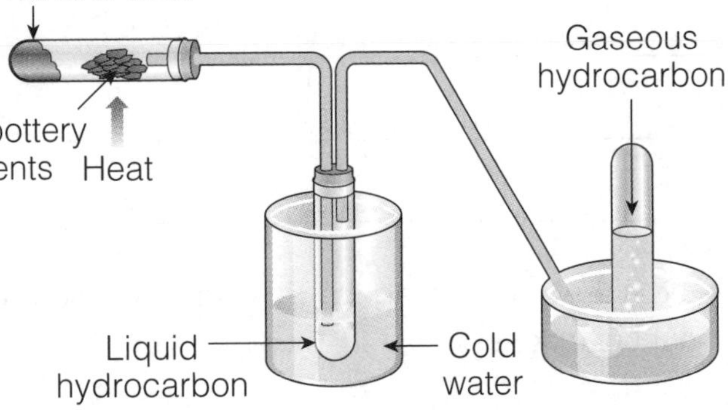
Paraffin (hydrocarbon) on mineral wool
Gaseous hydrocarbon
Broken pottery fragments
Heat
Liquid hydrocarbon
Cold water

Explain what is meant by **cracking** long-chain hydrocarbons. **[2 marks]**

____

____

0 2 . 6 What is the purpose of the broken pottery fragments in **Figure 2**? **[1 mark]**

____

0 2 . 7 The paraffin on the mineral wool in **Figure 2** has the formula $C_{16}H_{34}$. The gaseous product is ethene (C_2H_4) and the liquid hydrocarbon is decane ($C_{10}H_{22}$).

Construct a balanced symbol equation for the reaction. **[2 marks]**

____

0 3 Five students each have a test tube containing 10 cm³ of hydrochloric acid of the same concentration. They each have a different-sized strip of magnesium ribbon.

They drop the magnesium into the acid and time how long it takes for the fizzing to stop.

Table 1 shows the results of the experiment.

Table 1

Student	Iram	Alex	Dylan	Georgie	Noah
Time (s)	246	258	204	300	272

0 3 . 1 Which student had the fastest reaction? **[1 mark]**

____

0 3 . 2 Georgie noticed that there was some magnesium left in the test tube when the fizzing stopped. In all the other test tubes, there was no magnesium left. Explain these two observations. **[2 marks]**

____

____

____

03.3 Georgie repeated her experiment.

This time she measured the volume of gas made with a gas syringe. She measured 94.5 cm^3 of gas made in 225 seconds.

Calculate the mean rate of reaction. Show your working and include the unit in your answer. **[3 marks]**

____

____

____

03.4 Georgie repeated her experiment again. This time she used double the volume of acid and double the amount of magnesium.

Predict what happened to the amount of gas made in the reaction. Explain your answer. **[2 marks]**

____

____

____

04 Ethanol (C_2H_5OH) is an alcohol made by the fermentation of glucose ($C_6H_{12}O_6$):

$$C_6H_{12}O_6 \rightarrow 2C_2H_5OH + 2CO_2$$

04.1 The optimum temperature for this reaction is 35°C. Describe two other conditions for the reaction. **[2 marks]**

____

____

04.2 Explain why the yield of ethanol reduces if the temperature is above 35°C. **[2 marks]**

____

____

04.3 In some parts of the world, ethanol is mixed with petrol to make a fuel for cars. Describe one advantage and one disadvantage of using ethanol from fermentation as a fuel. **[2 marks]**

____

____

04.4 Name the ester made when ethanol reacts with ethanoic acid in the presence of concentrated sulfuric acid. **[1 mark]**

____

0 5 This question is about different formulations.

0 5 . 1 Which of the following formulations could be used as an NPK fertiliser?

Tick (✓) **one** box. **[1 mark]**

Ammonium nitrate and sodium chloride ☐

Ammonium phosphate and potassium chloride ☐

Potassium chloride and potassium nitrate ☐

Potassium sulfate and sodium nitrate ☐

0 5 . 2 A nine carat wedding ring weighs 4.5 g. What is the weight of pure gold in the ring?

Pure gold is 24 carats.

Tick (✓) **one** box. **[1 mark]**

0.50 g ☐

0.90 g ☐

1.69 g ☐

4.05 g ☐

0 5 . 3 **Table 2** shows some metals and their alloys.

Table 2

	Order of hardness	Density (g/cm^3)	Melting point (°C)	Order of strength
Copper	5	8.9	1083	5
Brass (alloy of copper)	3	8.6	920	3
Iron	2	7.9	1538	2
Steel (alloy of iron)	1	7.8	1420	1
Lead	6	11.3	327	6
Solder (alloy of lead)	5	9.6	170	4

Use the data in the table to outline what alloying does to the properties of pure metals. **[4 marks]**

____

____

____

____

0 6 This question is about the Earth's atmosphere.

0 6 . 1 These statements describe the process by which the Earth's atmosphere has changed.

A Oceans formed as the temperature at the surface fell below 100°C.

B Photosynthesis released oxygen into the atmosphere and used up carbon dioxide.

C Nitrifying bacteria used up ammonia and released nitrogen.

D Hot volcanic earth released carbon dioxide and ammonia into the atmosphere.

Put each letter in the correct box to show the order that scientists now believe the atmosphere developed. **[2 marks]**

☐ → ☐ → ☐ → ☐

0 6 . 2 How the Earth's atmosphere evolved is a theory. What is a theory? **[2 marks]**

____

____

0 6 . 3 Explain why the way that the Earth's atmosphere evolved can only be a theory. **[1 mark]**

____

____

0 7 The local water authority tested some river water.

The river was near a copper mine and it was suspected that the water was contaminated with copper(II) ions, Cu^{2+}, and sulfate ions, SO_4^{2-}.

Table 3 shows the results of the tests on the river water.

Table 3

Test	Result
Flame test	Crimson flame
Acidified silver nitrate solution	Colourless to cream precipitate
Acidified barium chloride solution	Colourless to white precipitate
Sodium hydroxide solution	Colourless to brown precipitate

0 7 . 1 Describe how to carry out a flame test. Explain what the results of the four tests in **Table 3** mean and decide whether they support the idea that the river water contains copper(II) and sulfate ions. **[6 marks]**

____

____

____

0 7 . 2 The water sample was then analysed using flame emission spectroscopy. What extra information would this provide? **[2 marks]**

0 8 Meg carried out a rate of reaction experiment by reacting hydrochloric acid with sodium thiosulfate solution. A yellow precipitate of sulfur formed.

As shown in **Figure 3**, the reaction was followed by timing how long it took a cross drawn under a flask to disappear.

Figure 3

All reactions were carried out at 25°C. **Table 4** shows the results.

Table 4

Concentration of acid (mol/dm^3)	Time taken for cross to disappear (s)
0.1	60
0.2	40
0.4	24
0.6	13
0.8	8
1.0	4

0 8 . 1 Plot the results on the graph paper in **Figure 4**. **[3 marks]**

Figure 4

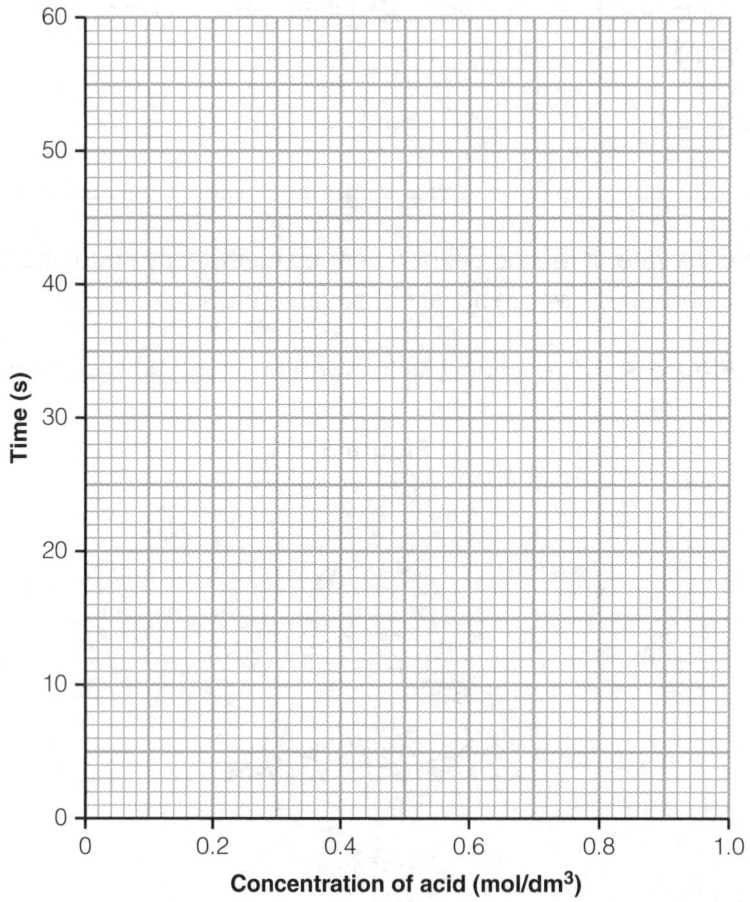

0 8 . 2 Describe and explain how the rate of reaction changes as the concentration of acid changes.

[3 marks]

____

____

____

0 8 . 3 The experiment was repeated at 35°C. Predict how the reaction times would change. Give a reason for your answer. **[2 marks]**

____

____

0 9 **Figure 5** shows how the yield of the Haber process changes with different conditions.

Figure 5

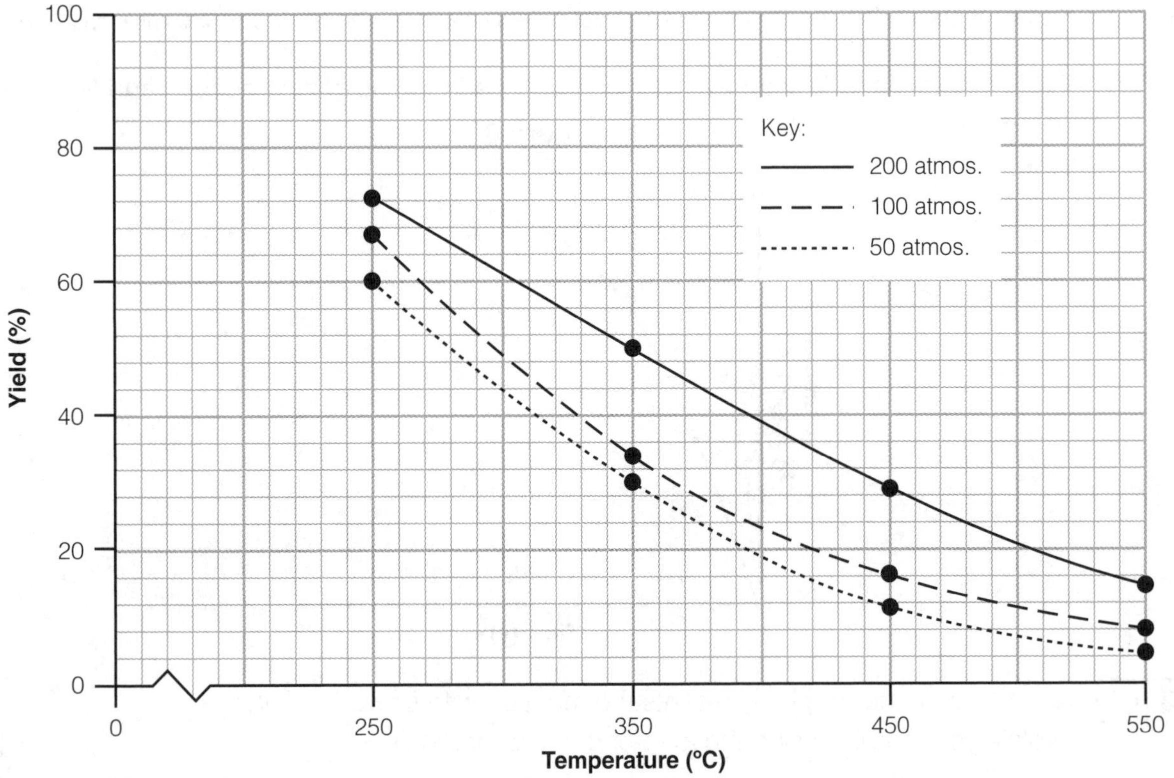

0 9 . 1 Write down the yield at 200 atmospheres and at a temperature of 350°C. **[1 mark]**

____

0 9 . 2 Describe what happens to the yield as the temperature is increased. **[1 mark]**

____

0 9 . 3 This is the equation for the reaction: $N_{2(g)} + 3H_{2(g)} \rightleftharpoons 2NH_{3(g)}$

Use the equation to explain why the yield increases with increased pressure. **[2 marks]**

____

____

____

0 9 . 4 Very high yields of ammonia can be achieved at a pressure of 500 atmospheres.

Explain why the normal operating pressure for the Haber process is much lower. **[2 marks]**

____

____

____

1 0 **Figure 6** shows the results of an investigation into the reaction of zinc metal with hydrochloric acid.

Experiments A and B used 2 g of zinc: one experiment used zinc powder and the other used zinc granules.

Figure 6

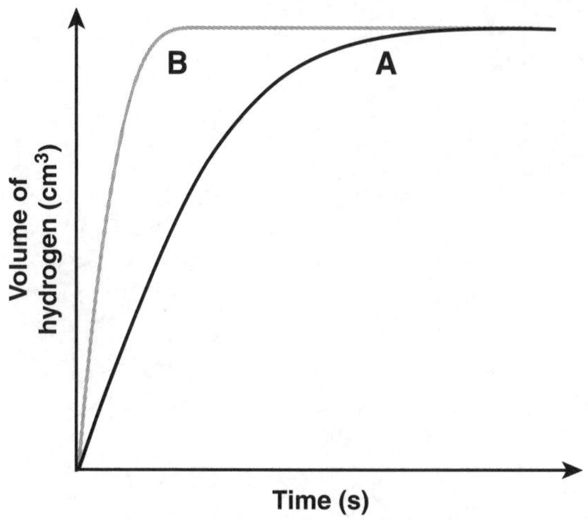

1 0 . 1 Which line on the graph represents the reaction with powdered zinc?
Explain your answer using the idea of reacting particles. **[4 marks]**

____

____

____

____

10.2 Copper ions (Cu^{2+}) act as a catalyst for the reaction.

Figure 7 shows the reaction profile without a catalyst.

Figure 7

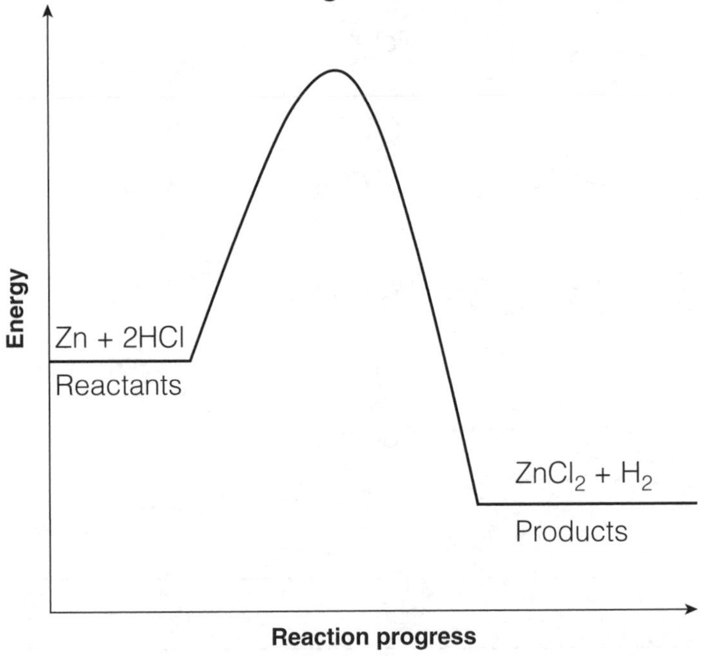

Draw on the graph the reaction profile with the catalyst. **[1 mark]**

11 This question is about polymers.

11.1 Look at the displayed formula of propene in **Figure 8**.

Figure 8

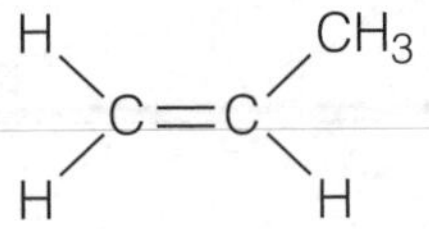

Propene molecules can join together to form the addition polymer, poly(propene).

Draw a diagram to show the structure of the polymer. **[3 marks]**

1 1 . 2 **Figure 9** shows the packing of some polymer molecules. Use the information given in the diagram to compare and explain the properties of polymers A–D. **[6 marks]**

Figure 9

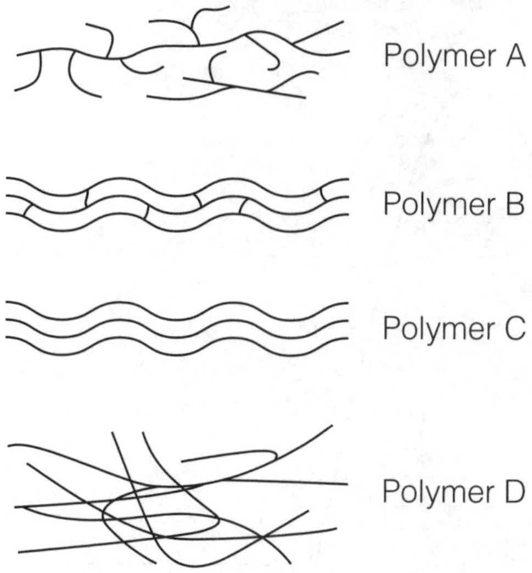
Polymer A
Polymer B
Polymer C
Polymer D

1 2 Sulfuric acid is manufactured in the contact process.

In one of the reactions in the process, sulfur dioxide is converted to sulfur trioxide:

$$2SO_{2(g)} + O_{2(g)} \rightleftharpoons 2SO_{3(g)}$$

This is a reversible reaction and it will reach a position of equilibrium.

1 2 . 1 Describe how the reaction reaches equilibrium from the start. Use ideas about rate of reaction. **[2 marks]**

1 2 . 2 Predict and explain the effect of reducing the pressure on the position of equilibrium for this reaction. **[2 marks]**

____

____

____

1 2 . 3 What is the effect of using a catalyst on the position of equilibrium in this reaction? **[1 mark]**

____

1 2 . 4 Outline the extra information you need to determine the effect on the equilibrium position of increasing the temperature of the reaction mixture. **[1 mark]**

____

1 3 PET is a polymer that is used to manufacture water bottles (see **Figure 10**). PET is a polyester. The monomers that make PET contain two functional groups.

Figure 10

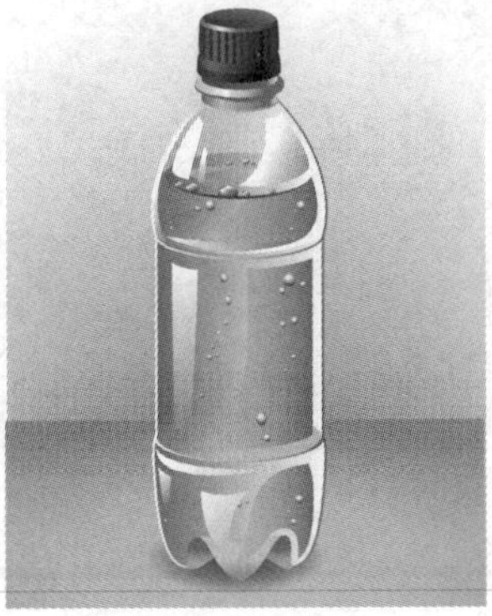

1 3 . 1 Which two functional groups are needed to form a polyester? **[2 marks]**

____

____

1 3 . 2 Explain why the reaction that forms PET is called a condensation reaction. **[1 mark]**

____

1 3 . 3 In a recent life-cycle assessment, the energy use for 1 kg of PET was 120 000 kJ. The assessment included an estimate for the energy use in transport of 14 000 kJ.

Explain why the transport energy use is an estimate. **[1 mark]**

____

1 4 Petrol and diesel are both used to fuel vehicles.

1 4 . 1 Compare the properties of the two fuels and explain why petrol is a more dangerous fuel than diesel. **[3 marks]**

____

____

____

____

1 4 . 2 Catalytic converters are fitted to modern cars to reduce carbon monoxide and nitrogen dioxide emissions formed during the combustion of fuel (see **Figure 11**).

Figure 11

Describe how nitrogen dioxide gas is formed by the car. **[3 marks]**

____

____

____

1 4 . 3 Sulfur dioxide can also be formed from burning fuels such as petrol or diesel. Catalytic converters cannot reduce sulfur dioxide emissions.

Give one reason why sulfur dioxide is an atmospheric pollutant. **[1 mark]**

____

1 4 . 4 Suggest how emissions of sulfur dioxide can be reduced from cars that use diesel and petrol. **[1 mark]**

____

END OF QUESTIONS

Answers

Page 4

1. **(a)** Na **(1)** Cl **(1)**
   (b) Sodium + chlorine ⟶ sodium chloride **(reactants 1, products 1)**
   (c) A compound **(1)** as the elements are chemically combined/joined **(1)**
   (d) A mixture **(1)** as the salt and water are together but not chemically combined **(1)**
   (e) Crystallisation **(1)**; simple distillation **(1)**

Page 5

1. **(a)** The plum pudding model proposed that an atom was a ball of positive charge/today's model has the positive charge contained in the nucleus/protons **(1)** The plum pudding model proposed that electrons were embedded/spread throughout the positive charge/today's model has the electrons in different energy levels/shells surrounding the positive charge **(1)**
   (b) Some of the positively charged particles/alpha particles (when fired at gold foil) were deflected **(1)**
   (c) Niels Bohr suggested that electrons orbit the nucleus at specific distances/are present in energy levels/shells **(1)** His calculations were backed up by experimental results **(1)**
   (d)

Particle	Relative charge	Relative mass
Proton	+1	1
Neutron	0	1
Electron	–1	Very small/ approx. 1/2000

(4)

   (e) **(i)** 11 **(1)**
   (ii) 23 **(1)**

Page 6

1. **(a)** 3 **(1)**
   (b) 2,7 **(1)**
   (c) 7 **(1)** As an atom of fluorine has 7 electrons in its outer shell **(1)**
2. **(a)** By increasing atomic number **(1)**
   (b) Because they both have similar chemical properties **(1)**
   (c) **Accept two from:** have high melting/boiling points; conduct heat and electricity; react with oxygen to form alkalis; malleable/ductile **(2)**

Page 7

1. **(a)** The atoms have full outer shells/energy levels **(1)** so they do not bond **(1)**
   (b) It increases **(1)**
2. **(a)** $2Na_{(s)} + 2H_2O_{(l)} \longrightarrow 2NaOH_{(aq)} + H_{2(g)}$ **(1 for correct formula; 1 for correct balancing in equation. Ignore state symbols, even if wrong)**
   (b) Blue **(1)** as an alkali solution/the hydroxide ion is formed **(1)**
   (c) A potassium atom is larger (than a sodium atom), so the outer electron is further away from the nucleus **(1)** so there is less attraction/the electron is more easily lost **(1)**
3. **(a)** $2Na_{(s)} + Cl_{(g)} \longrightarrow 2NaCl_{(s)}$ **(1 for each side; any correctly balanced equation scores both marks, e.g. $4Na + 2Br_2 \longrightarrow 4NaBr$)**
   (b) Ionic **(1)**
   (c) chlorine + sodium bromide ⟶ sodium chloride **(1)** + bromine **(1)**
   (d) Displacement **(1)** A more reactive element (chlorine) takes the place of a less reactive element (bromine) in a compound **(1)**

Page 8

1. **(a)** Metal M **(1)** as it is denser and has a higher melting point than metal L **(1)**
   (b) less **(1)**
   (c) Mercury **(1)**
2. **(a)** They form coloured compounds **(1)**
   (b) The iron is a catalyst **(1)** It speeds up the reaction/reduces the time taken for equilibrium to be reached **(1)**

Page 9

1. sodium – metallic **(1)**; chlorine – simple molecular **(1)**; sodium chloride – ionic **(1)**
2. **(a)**

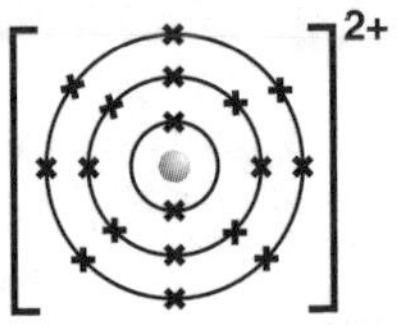

Ca^{2+} ion [2,8,8]

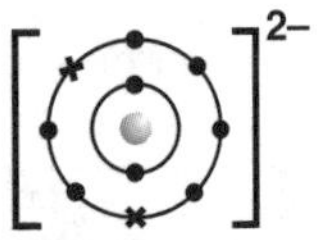

O^{2-} ion [2,8] **(2)**

   (b) Calcium: 2+, oxygen: 2– **(2)**
3. **(a)**

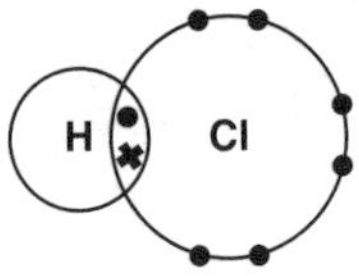

(1)

   (b) 2 **(1)**

Page 10

1. **(a)** Electrostatic forces **(1)** between the anions and cations
   (b) CaO **(1)** There are an equal number of calcium ions and oxygen ions and so the ratio of each is 1:1 **(1)**
2. **(a)** A polymer **(1)**
   (b) CH_2 **(1)** There are twice as many hydrogen atoms as carbon atoms, so ratio of carbon to hydrogen is 1:2 **(1)**
3. Giant covalent/macromolecular **(1)** it is a large molecule consisting of atoms that are covalently bonded together with a theoretically infinite structure **(1)**

Page 11

1. **(a)**

(1 for regular arrangement of particles, 1 for no gaps between the particles)

   (b) Intermolecular forces/forces between particles **(1)**
2. **(a)** It conducts electricity when liquid but not as a solid **(1)**
   (b) The ions **(1)** are not free to move **(1)**
   (c) Giant covalent/macromolecular **(1)** It has a high melting point <u>and</u> does not conduct electricity **(1)**
   (d) There are no free **(1)** charged particles/electrons/ions **(1)**

Page 12

1. **(a)** The layers **(1)** (of ions) are able to slide over each other **(1)**
   (b) There is a strong attraction **(1)** between the metal cations and the delocalised electrons **(1)**
   (c) The electrons **(1)** are free to move/flow through the structure **(1)**
2. **(a)** A mixture of metals/a metal mixed with another element **(1)**
   (b) The layers are not able to slide over each other **(1)** because the other atoms are larger and prevent movement **(1)**
3. **(a)** **Accept two from:** for drug delivery into the body/as lubricants/reinforcing materials, e.g. in tennis rackets **(2)**
   (b) **Accept two from**: tensile strength; electrical conductivity; thermal conductivity **(2)**
   (c) A carbon nanotube is a cylindrical fullerene **(1)**

Page 13

1. Coarse particles/dust (PM_{10}) – Between 1×10^{-5} and 2.5×10^{-6} m **(1)**; Fine particles ($PM_{2.5}$) – Between 1×10^{-7} and 2.5×10^{-6} m **(1)** Nanoparticles – Less than 1×10^{-7} m (100 nm) **(1)**
2. **(a)** Owing to their higher/different surface area to volume ratio **(1)**
   (b) That smaller quantities may be needed to be effective compared with materials with normal-sized particles **(1)**

3. (a) Decreasing particle size increases **(1)** the surface area to volume ratio (or converse argument: increasing particle size decreases **(1)** the surface area to volume ratio)
(b) **Accept two from:** synthetic skin; controlled drug delivery; electronics; development of new catalysts for fuel-cell materials; in deodorants and fabrics to prevent the growth of bacteria **(2)**
(c) Advantages: better skin coverage **(1)**; more effective protection from the Sun's ultraviolet rays **(1)**; Potential disadvantages: cell damage in the body **(1)**/harmful effects on the environment **(1)**

Page 14

1. (a) Total mass of reactants = total mass of the products, i.e. there is no net mass loss or gain during a chemical reaction **(1)**
(b)

Substance	A_r / M_r
Al	27
Fe_2O_3	160
Al_2O_3	102
Fe	56

(4)

2. (a) Oxygen **(1)** is added **(1)** to the magnesium
(b) $2Mg_{(s)} + O_{2(g)} \longrightarrow 2MgO_{(s)}$ **(1 for reactants and products, 1 for correct balancing)**
(c) The magnesium carbonate loses/gives off **(1)** carbon dioxide **(1)**
(d) $MgCO_{3(s)} \longrightarrow MgO_{(s)} + CO_{2(g)}$ **(1 for correct formulae products; 1 for balanced equation; ignore state symbols, even if wrong)**

Page 15

1. (a) 2.408×10^{24} ($4 \times 6.02 \times 10^{23}$) **(1)**
(b) 92 g (4 × 23 g) **(1)**
(c) 0.5 (11.5 ÷ 23) **(1)**
(d) 4 moles of Na form 2 moles of Na_2O (2:1 ratio), therefore 0.5 mole of Na forms 0.25 mole of Na_2O mass = 0.5 × 62 **(1 for correct M_r of Na_2O)** = 31 g **(1)**
2. (a) +/– 0.005 g (i.e. half of the uncertainty) **(1)**
(b) 24.5 cm^3 and 25.5 cm^3. **(1)** The uncertainty is half the scale division (i.e. half of 1 cm^3 or +/– 0.5 cm^3). Therefore, the volume lies between 25 cm^3 – 0.5 cm^3 = 24.5 cm^3 and 25 cm^3 + 0.5 cm^3 = 25.5 cm^3 **(1)**
3 (a) 0.48 ÷ 24 **(1)** = 0.02 **(1)**
(b) Magnesium **(1)** as magnesium and sulfuric acid react in a 1:1 ratio and the number of moles of sulfuric acid present is greater than the number of moles of magnesium. **(1)**
(c) 0.02 **(1)**. One mole of hydrogen is formed for every one mole of magnesium reacting. Therefore, if 0.02 moles of magnesium react 0.02 moles of hydrogen will be formed. **(1)**

Page 16

1. (a) (11.5 ÷ 15) × 100 **(1)** = 76.7% (3 sig. fig.) **(1)**
(b) (i) 7 ÷ 28 **(1)** = 0.25 **(1)**
(ii) 0.25 **(1)** due to the 1:1 ratio of moles of ethene to moles of ethanol **(1)**
(iii) 0.5 × 46 **(1)** = 23 g **(1)**
(iv) (11÷ 23) × 100 **(1)** = 47.8% **(1)**
(c) Fermentation method: (92 ÷ 180) × 100 = 51.1% **(1)** ethene with steam method: [(46 ÷ (28 + 18)] × 100 = 100% **(1)**

Page 17

1. (a) Pipette **(1)**
(b) Burette **(1)**
(c) The indicator will change colour **(1)**
2. (a) (23.80 × 0.2) ÷1000 **(1)** = 0.00476 **(1)**
(b) 0.00476 **(1)** due to the 1:1 mole ratio of LiOH to HCl **(1)**
(c) (0.00476 × 1000) ÷ 25 **(1)** = 0.19 mol/dm^3 **(1)**
(d) 0.19 × 36.5 **(1)** = 6.94 g/dm^3 **or** 6.95 g/dm^3 **(1)**
(e) (6.94 ÷ 1000) × 25 **(1)** = 0.17 g **(1)**

Page 18

1. (a) 120 ÷ 24 000 (also accept 0.12 ÷ 24) = 0.005 **(1)**
(b) Moles of magnesium reacting = 6 ÷ 24 = 0.25 **(1)**
moles of oxygen reacting = 0.5 × 0.25 = 0.125 **(1)**
volume of oxygen = 0.125 × 24 = 3 dm^3 (or 0.125 × 24 000 = 3000 cm^3) **(1)**

2.

Chemical	Pb	O_2	PbO
Mass from question/g	41.4	3.2	44.6
A_r or M_r	207	32	223
Moles = $\frac{\text{mass}}{M_r}$	$\frac{41.4}{207}$ = 0.2	$\frac{3.2}{32}$ = 0.1	$\frac{44.6}{223}$ = 0.2
÷ smallest	$\frac{0.2}{0.1}$ = 2	$\frac{0.1}{0.1}$ = 1	$\frac{0.2}{0.1}$ = 2

Balanced equation: $2Pb + O_2 \longrightarrow 2PbO$ **(1 for each row in table, 1 for correct balanced equation)**

Page 19

1. (a) calcium + oxygen ⟶ calcium oxide **(1 for reactants, 1 for product)**
(b) Calcium gains **(1)** oxygen **(1)** (**Also accept** Oxygen **(1)** is added **(1)** **or** Calcium loses **(1)** electrons **(1)**)
(c) Potassium, sodium or lithium (or any other metal in group 1 or strontium, barium or radium) **(1)** the metal is more reactive than calcium/is above calcium in the reactivity series **(1)**
(d) Metal + calcium oxide ⟶ metal oxide + calcium, e.g. potassium + calcium oxide ⟶ potassium oxide + calcium **(1 for reactants, 1 for products)**
(e) Calcium oxide **(1)**
2. (a) Electrolysis **(1)**
(b) $2Fe_2O_3 + 3C \longrightarrow 4Fe + 3CO_2$ **(1 for correct formulae, 1 for balanced equation; allow any correct balanced equation, e.g. $4Fe_2O_3 + 6C \longrightarrow 8Fe + 6CO_2$ ignore state symbols)**
(c) Reduction **(1)** as electrons are gained **(1)** by the Al^{3+} **(1)**
(d) K **(1)** as it loses electrons **(1)** $K \longrightarrow K^+ + e$

Page 20

1. (a) Zinc sulfate **(1)**
(b) Zinc oxide + hydrochloric acid ⟶ zinc chloride **(1)** + water **(1)**
(c) Carbon dioxide **(1)** CO_2 **(1)**
(d) (i) calcium (as it loses electrons) **(1)**
(ii) H^+ **(1; allow $2H^+$ not hydrogen)**
(e) When a substance loses **(1)** electrons **(1)**
2. (a) **Accept three from:** measure out some sulfuric acid (e.g. 25 cm^3 in a measuring cylinder); transfer to a beaker and warm the acid; add copper oxide, stir and repeat until no more copper oxide dissolves; filter the mixture; leave the filtrate somewhere warm/heat the filtrate **(3)**
(b) Nitric acid **(1)**

Page 21

1. (a) 1–6 **(1)**
(b) Hydrogen ion **(1)** H^+ **(1)**
(c) Hydrochloric acid **(1)**
(d) $H^+_{(aq)} + OH^-_{(aq)} \longrightarrow H_2O_{(l)}$ **(1 for correct formulae, 1 for correct state symbols)**
2. (a) A strong acid completely ionises/fully dissociates in water **(1)** a weak acid partially ionises/dissociates in water **(1)**
(b) $CH_3COOH_{(aq)} \rightleftharpoons CH_3COO^-_{(aq)} + H^+_{(aq)}$ **or** $CH_3COOH_{(aq)} + aq \rightleftharpoons CH_3COO^-_{(aq)} + H^+_{(aq)}$/$CH_3COOH_{(aq)} + H_2O_{(l)} \rightleftharpoons CH_3COO^-_{(aq)} + H_3O^+_{(aq)}$ **(1 for reactants, 1 for products; ignore state symbols)**
(c) Lower **(1)** Nitric acid is a stronger acid and so there will be more H^+ ions than in a weak acid and therefore will be more acidic **(1)**
(d) It increases **(1)** by 1 **(1)**

Page 22

1. (a) Cations **(1)**
(b) Anions **(1)**
(c) So that the ions **(1)** are free to move **(1)**
(d) Oxidation **(1)** as electrons are lost **(1)**

(a)

Solution	Product at anode	Product at cathode
NaCl	H_2	Cl_2
KNO_3	H_2	O_2
$CuSO_4$	Cu	O_2
Water diluted with sulfuric acid	H_2	O_2

(6)

(b) Hydrogen is produced because hydrogen ions are present in the solution **(1)** and hydrogen is less reactive than sodium **(1)**

(c) $4OH^- \longrightarrow O_2 + 2H_2O + 4e^-$ (or $4OH^- - 4e^- \longrightarrow O_2 + 2H_2O$) **(1 for reactants and products, 1 for balanced equation; ignore state symbols)**

Page 23

(a)

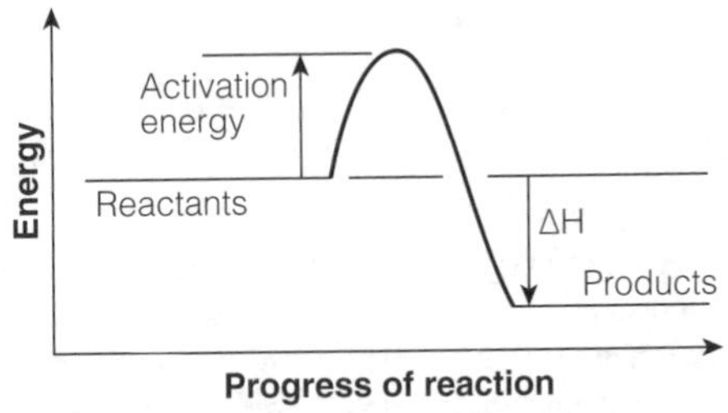

(1 for products lower in energy than the reactants, each correct label scores 1)

(b) More energy is released when the bonds in the product molecules are made **(1)** than is used to break the bonds in the reactant molecules **(1)**

(c) **Accept one from**: any thermal decomposition reaction (e.g. metal carbonate ⟶ metal oxide + carbon dioxide); The reaction between citric acid and sodium hydrogencarbonate **(1)**

(a) ΔH = Bonds broken – bonds formed = 2144 **(1)** – 2348 **(1)** = –204 kJ/mol **(1)**

(b) Exothermic **(1)** the value of ΔH is negative/more energy is released when the bonds in the product molecules are made than is used to break the bonds in the reactant molecules **(1)**

Page 24

1. Two different metals **(1)** in contact with an electrolyte **(1)**
2. The metals are of different reactivity **(1)** and electrons flow from the more reactive metal to the less reactive metal **(1)**
3. Changing one or both of the metals **(1)** changing the electrolyte **(1)**
4. One of the reactants gets used up **(1)**
5. A fuel cell has a constant supply of fuel/in a chemical cell, all of the fuels are contained within the cell **(1)**
6. $2H_{2(g)} + O_{2(g)} \longrightarrow 2H_2O_{(l)}$ **(1 for reactants and products, 1 for balanced equation; ignore state symbols)**

Page 25

1. **(a)** 70°C **(1)**
   (b) Increased temperature increases the rate of reaction **(1)** the higher the temperature, the more kinetic energy the particles have and so the frequency of collisions/successful collisions increases **(1)**
2. **(a)** 1st experiment: 69 ÷ 46 = 1.5 **(1)** cm^3/s; 2nd experiment: 18 ÷ 10 = 1.8 **(1)** cm^3/s **(1 for correct units)**
   (b) The second experiment **(1)** as the rate is greater **(1)**

Page 26

1. **(a)** The particles must collide with enough energy/the activation energy **(1)**
   (b) **(i)** At a higher concentration, there are more particles per unit volume/in the same volume of solution **(1)** meaning that there will be more collisions **(1)**
   (ii) At a higher pressure there are more gas molecules per unit volume **(1)**, which means that there is an increased likelihood of a collision **(1)**

(c)

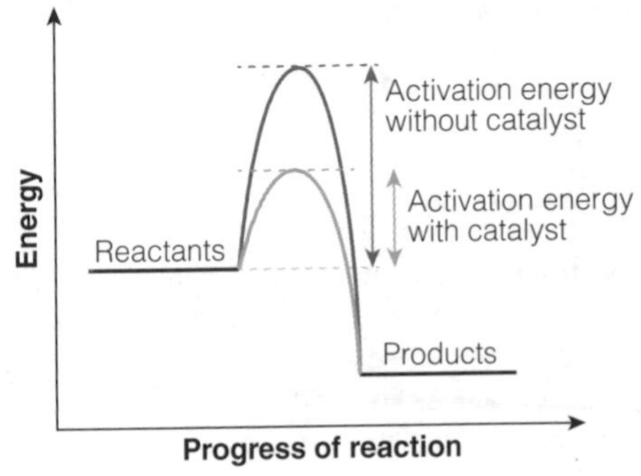

(1)

(d) Catalysts provide an alternative reaction pathway **(1)** of lower activation energy **(1)**

Page 27

1. **(a)** The blue crystals will turn white **(1)**
   (b) hydrated copper(II) sulfate ⇌ anhydrous copper(II) sulfate + water **(allow arrow ⟶ instead of ⇌) (1 for formulae, 1 for balanced equation)**
   (c) The white powder will turn blue **(1)**
   (d) Exothermic reaction **(1)**
2. **(a)** A reversible reaction **(1)**
   (b) The yield of SO_3 would increase **(1)** higher pressure favours the reaction/shifts the equilibrium **(1)** to the side that produces fewer molecules of gas **(1)**
   (c) The yield of SO_3 would decrease **(1)** increasing temperature favours the endothermic reaction **(1)**, which in this case is the reverse reaction **(1)**

Page 28

1. **(a)** Kerosene **(1)**
   (b) It increases **(1)**
   (c) 1. Crude oil is heated/boiled **(1)** 2. In the fractionating column there is a temperature gradient (hotter at bottom/cooler at top) **(1)** 3. The hydrocarbons travel up the fractionating column and condense at their boiling point **(1)**
2. **(a)** C_nH_{2n+2} **(1)**
   (b)

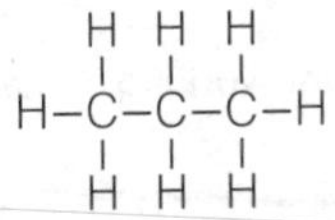

(1)

   (c) $C_3H_{8(g)} + 5O_{2(g)} \longrightarrow 3CO_{2(g)} + 4H_2O_{(l)}$ **(1 for correct formulae, 1 for correct balancing; ignore state symbols)**

Page 29

1. **(a)** C_nH_{2n} **(1)**
   (b)

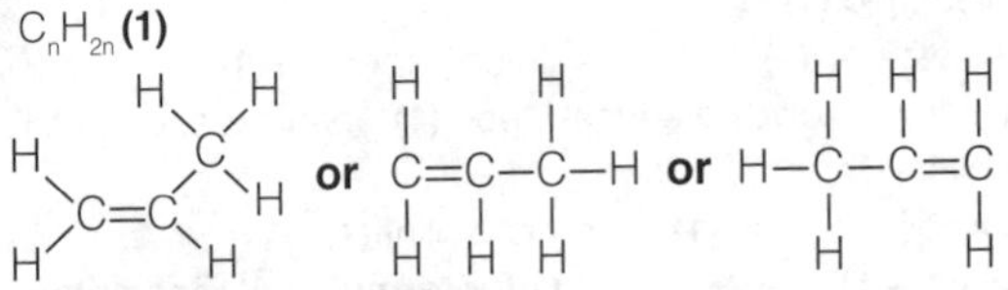

(2)

   (c) Alkenes are unsaturated because there is a carbon-carbon **(1)** double bond **(1)**
   (d) $2C_3H_{6(g)} + 9O_{2(g)} \longrightarrow 6CO_{2(g)} + 6H_2O_{(l)}$ **or** $C_3H_{6(g)} + 4\frac{1}{2}O_{2(g)} \longrightarrow 3CO_{2(g)} + 3H_2O_{(l)}$ **(1 for formula of reactants and products, 1 for correctly balanced equation; ignore state symbols)**
   (e)

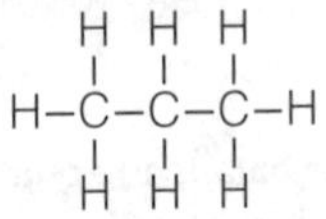

(2)

2. **(a)** **Accept one from:** silica, alumina, porcelain **(1)**
   (b) C_4H_{10} **(1)**

Page 30

1. **(a)** R–OH **(allow –OH or OH) (1)**
   (b) CH_3CH_2OH **(1)**
   (c) **Accept two from:** dissolve in water to form neutral solutions; react with sodium to produce hydrogen; burn in air to produce carbon dioxide and water **(2)**

(d) **Accept two from:** as fuels; as solvents; ethanol is the alcohol in alcoholic drinks **(2)**

(e) 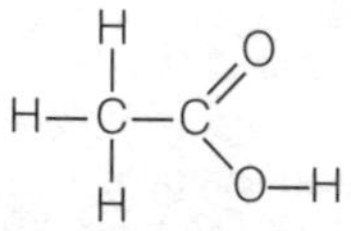 **(1)**

(f) **Accept two from:** dissolve in water to form acidic solutions; react with carbonates to form carbon dioxide; are weak acids i.e. they do not completely ionise when dissolved in water; react with alcohols in the presence of an acid catalyst to produce esters **(2)**

(g) It can be oxidised by heating with acidified potassium manganate(VII)/permanganate **(1)**

(h) Ethyl ethanoate **(1)**

Page 31

1. (a) Ethene **(1)**

(b) 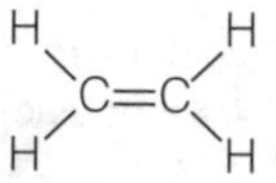 **(1)**

(c) Addition polymer **(1)**

(d) The carbon–carbon double bond **(1)**

(e) Plastic shopping bags/carrier bags **(1)** water bottles **(1)** strong and light/easily moulded into shape **(1)**

2. (a) A polymer formed when molecule containing two functional groups react/join together **(1)** while eliminating a small molecule such as water **(1)**

(b) A carboxylic acid group **(1)** and an amine group **(allow –COOH and –NH_2/COOH and NH_2) (1)**

(c) Glucose **(1)**

Page 32

1. (a) A mixture that has been designed as a useful product **(1)**

(b) No **(1)** something that is chemically pure contains a single element or compound **(1)**

(c) **Accept one from:** fuels; medicines; foods; fertilisers **(1)**

2. (a) The liquid solvent **(1 allow water)**

(b) red and green **(1)** The spots of these colours are at the same height as spots in ink X **(1)**

(c) $\frac{0.5}{4.65} = 0.11$ **(allow 0.10–0.12; 1 mark for working, 1 mark for correct answer)**

Page 33

1. (a) Calcium hydroxide **(1)**

(b) A precipitate **(1)** of $CaCO_3$ **(1)** is formed

2. (a) The litmus paper turns red **(1)** before turning white/being bleached **(1)**

(b) Acidic gas **(1)** as it turns litmus paper red **(1)**

3. (a) Hydrogen gives a squeaky pop **(1)** when exposed to a lit splint **(1)**

(b) Oxygen relights **(1)** a glowing splint **(1)**

(c) $2H_{2(g)} + O_{2(g)} \longrightarrow 2H_2O_{(l)}$ **(1 for formulae of reactants/products, 1 for correctly balanced equation; ignore state symbols)**

Page 34

1. Cu^{2+} – green **(1)** Li^+ – crimson-red **(1)** Ca^{2+} – orange-red **(1)** Na^+ – yellow **(1)**

2. (a) A reaction in which a solid is produced **(1)** when two solutions react **(1)**

(b) A blue precipitate **(1)**

(c) $Cu^{2+}_{(aq)} + 2OH^-_{(aq)} \longrightarrow Cu(OH)_{2(s)}$ **(1 for balanced equation/correct formulae, 1 for correct state symbols)**

(d) Upon adding excess sodium hydroxide solution **(1)** the aluminium hydroxide precipitate will dissolve while the magnesium hydroxide precipitate remains **(1)**

(e) Fe^{2+} gives a green precipitate with sodium hydroxide solution **(1)** Fe^{3+} gives a brown precipitate with sodium hydroxide solution **(1)**

Page 35

1. (a) White **(1)**

(b) Barium sulfate **(1)** $BaSO_4$ **(1)**

(c) CO_3^{2-} **(2)**

(d) Add dilute (hydrochloric) acid **(1)** test the gas evolved by bubbling it through limewater **(1)**, which will turn milky/cloudy **(1)** in the presence of carbon dioxide gas

2. (a) Each halide ion forms a different coloured **(1)** precipitate **(1)** e.g. chloride ions form a white precipitate, bromide ions form a cream/off-white precipitate and iodide ions form a yellow precipitate

(b) $Ag^+_{(aq)} + Cl^-_{(aq)} \longrightarrow AgCl_{(s)}$ **(1 for balanced equation, 1 for correct state symbols)**

3. (a) Flame emission spectrometer/flame photometer **(1)**

(b) **Accept two from:** rapid; more accurate; more sensitive; can be used with very small sample sizes **(2)**

Page 36

1. (a) Nitrogen or oxygen **(1)**

(b) The water vapour originally in the atmosphere cooled **(1)** and condensed **(1)** forming the oceans

(c) Green plants/algae **(1)** form oxygen as a waste product of photosynthesis **(1)**

(d) **Accept two from:** green plants; algae use carbon dioxide for photosynthesis; carbon dioxide is used to form sedimentary rocks; carbon dioxide is captured in oil; coal **(2)**

Page 37

1. (a) Greenhouse gases allow short wavelength radiation from the Sun to pass through the atmosphere **(1)** but absorb long wavelength radiation reflected back from the earth trapping heat **(1)**

(b) **Accept one from:** methane; water vapour **(1)**

(c) **Accept two from:** combustion of fossil fuels; deforestation; increased animal farming; decomposing rubbish in landfill sites **(2)**

(d) There are many different factors contributing to climate change **(1)** and it is not easy to predict the impact of each one **(1)**

(e) **Accept two from:** rising sea levels, which may cause flooding and coastal erosion; more frequent and/or severe storms; changes to the amount, timing and distribution of rainfall; temperature and water stress for humans and wildlife; changes to the food-producing capacity of some regions/changes to the distribution of wildlife species **(2)**

(f) **Accept two from:** use of alternative energy supplies; increased use of renewable energy; energy conservation; carbon capture and storage techniques; carbon taxes and licences; carbon offsetting/carbon neutrality **(2)**

(g) **Accept two from:** disagreement over the causes and consequences of global climate change; lack of public information and education; lifestyle changes, e.g. greater use of cars and aeroplanes; economic considerations, i.e. the financial costs of reducing the carbon footprint; incomplete international co-operation **(2)**

Page 38

1. (a) Fuel formed in the ground over millions of years from the remains of dead plants and animals **(1)**

(b) Due to incomplete combustion/burning of fuels in a poor supply of oxygen **(1)**

(c) **Accept one from:** forms acid rain; can cause respiratory problems **(1)**

(d) Global dimming **(1)** health problems due to lung damage **(1)**

(e) It combines with haemoglobin/red blood cells **(1)** preventing the transport of oxygen **(1)**

(f) When sulfur burns it react with oxygen to form sulfur dioxide **(1)** Sulfur dioxide dissolves in rain water **(1)** The rain water is now acidic/acid rain which can damage buildings and destroy wildlife **(1)**

age 39

(a) The needs of the current generation are met without compromising the potential of future generations to meet their own needs **(1)** Improving agricultural practices/using chemical processes to make new materials **(1)**

(b) Water that is safe to drink **(1)**

(c) Filtration/passed through filter beds to remove solid impurities **(1)** sterilised to kill microbes **(1)**

(d) **Accept three from:** screening and grit removal; sedimentation to produce sewage sludge and effluent; anaerobic digestion of sewage sludge; aerobic biological treatment of effluent **(3)**

(a)

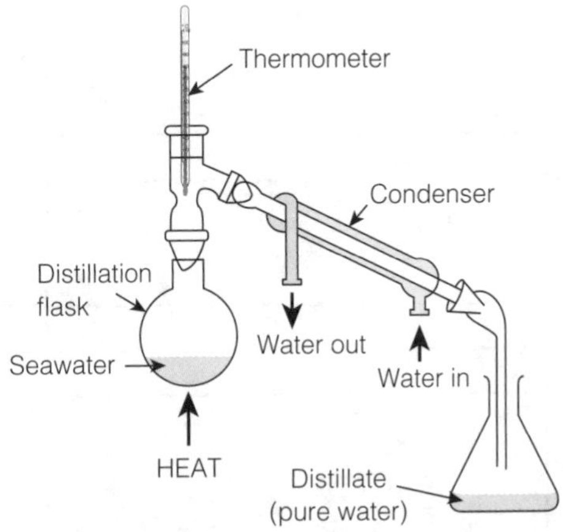

(3 for labelled diagram: seawater in flask, condenser, pure water being collected)

The water from the seawater boils/evaporates at 100°C and is condensed back into water in the condenser **(1)** the salt remains behind in the original flask **(1)**

(b) Reverse osmosis **(1)**

age 40

(a) A naturally occurring mineral **(1)** from which it is economically viable to extract a metal **(1)**

(b) We still require the raw materials **(1)** but it is becoming increasingly difficult/uneconomic to mine them in traditional ways **(1)**

(c) Electrical wiring **(1)** as it is a good conductor of electricity **(1)** water pipes **(1)** as it does not react with water/corrode **(1)**

(d) Plants grow in a medium that enables them to absorb metal compounds **(1)** the plants are then harvested/burned leaving ash that is rich in the metal compounds **(1)** the ash is then further treated to extract the metal **(1)**

(e) Bacteria extract metals from low-grade ores producing a solution rich in metal compounds **(1)**

(f) iron + copper sulfate ⟶ iron sulfate + copper **(1 for reactants, 1 for products)**

(g) Platinum is less reactive than copper/too low in reactivity/in the reactivity series **(1)** and so is unable to displace copper from copper compounds

(h) Electrolysis **(1)**

age 41

(a) **Accept two from:** extracting and processing raw materials; manufacturing and packaging; disposal at end of useful life **(2)**

(b) **Accept two from:** how much energy is needed; how much water is used; what resources are required; how much waste is produced; how much pollution is produced **(2)**

(c) Allocating numerical values to pollutant effects is not always easy or straightforward **(1)** so value judgments have to be made which may not always be objective **(1)**

(d) To support claims for advertising purposes **(1)**

2. Over the life of the product, plastic bags when compared with paper bags (**accept two from the following**): use less energy; use less fossil fuel; produce fewer CO_2 emissions; produce less waste; use less freshwater **(2)** meaning that plastic/polythene bags are less damaging to the environment/have less of an environmental impact **(1)** than paper bags **(Allow reverse argument)**

Page 42

1. **(a)** Oxygen **(1)** and water **(1)**

(b) Salt from the sea **(1)** speeds up/increases the rate **(1)** of rusting

(c) The water was boiled to remove air/oxygen **(1)**; the oil prevented oxygen from entering **(1)**

(d) **Accept two from:** greasing; painting; galvanising **(2)**

(e) Nickel/chromium **(1)**

(f) An alloy **(1)**

Page 43

1. **(a)** Nitrogen from (fractional distillation of liquid) air **(1)** hydrogen from natural gas **(1)**

(b) Iron/Fe **(1)**

(c) **(i)** Answer between 15% and 25% **(1)**

(ii) As temperature increases, the yield of ammonia decreases **(1)**

(d) 450°C **(1)**, 200 atms pressure **(1)**

(e) Rate is too slow **(1)**, so ammonia will not be produced economically **(1)**

PAPER 1

Question number	Answer	Notes	Marks
01.1	Each row begins with elements with one outer electron.		1
01.2	Their boiling points increase as you go down the group.		1
01.3	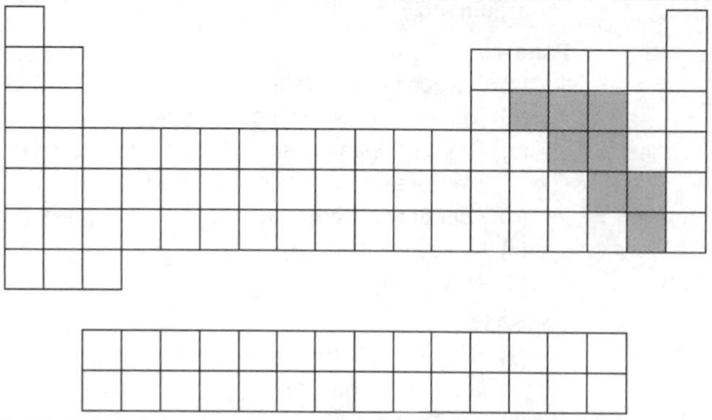	Give 1 mark for an X anywhere in the grey area.	1
01.4	They make an alkali when reacted with water.		1
01.5	The outer electron in sodium is further from the nucleus. Less energy needed to remove the outer electron / the outer electron is less tightly held / less attractive force from nucleus to outer electron.		1 1
02.1	lithium, calcium, zinc, iron		1
02.2	Form coloured compounds		1
02.3	Any two from: Steel is harder than iron. Steel is stronger than iron. Steel is less likely to corrode / rust than iron.	The answer must be a comparison.	2
02.4	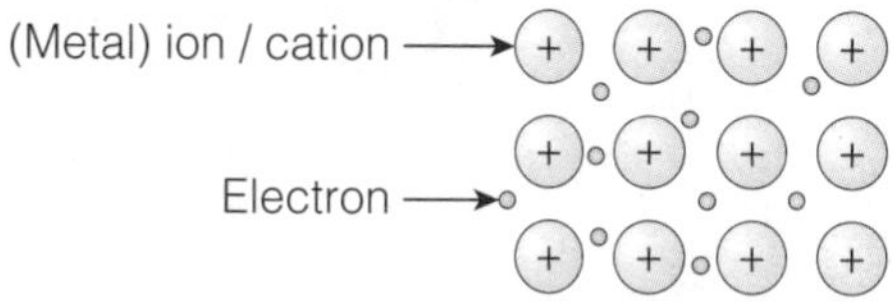 Electrons are delocalised / 'sea of electrons' Free to move	Give 1 mark for the (metal) ion / cation label and 1 mark for the electron label.	1 1 1 1
03.1	High melting point and slippery		1
03.2	2.9×10^7 cm^2	This is how the answer is calculated: volume = area × height (thickness) $1 = \text{area} \times 3.4 \times 10^{-8}$ $\text{area} = \dfrac{1}{3.4 \times 10^{-8}}$ $= 2.9 \times 10^7$ cm^2	1
03.3	Any two from: high (tensile) strength high electrical conductivity high thermal conductivity.		2
03.4	High melting point because of: giant structure / lots of bonds / macromolecule strong bonds / lots of energy to break bonds. Does not conduct electricity because: there are no free / mobile electrons **or** all its electrons are used in bonding.		1 1 1
04.1	copper(II) carbonate ⟶ copper(II) oxide + carbon dioxide	Accept copper carbonate and copper oxide without (II)	1
04.2	12.35 – 7.95 = 4.40 (g)	Accept 4.4 (g)	1 1
05.1	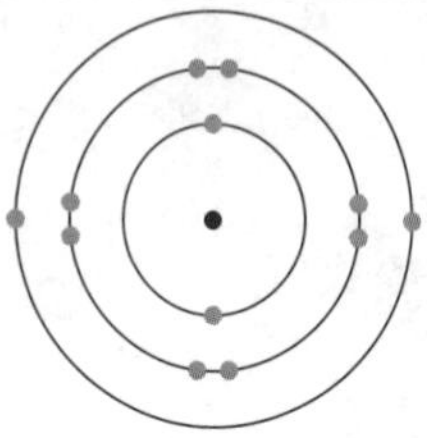	Accept – / e / x as electrons.	1

Question number	Answer	Notes	Marks
05.2	[2]Mg + O_2 → [2]MgO		1
05.3	There is only one product / all atoms end up in the product.		1
05.4	Accept either of the diagrams below: 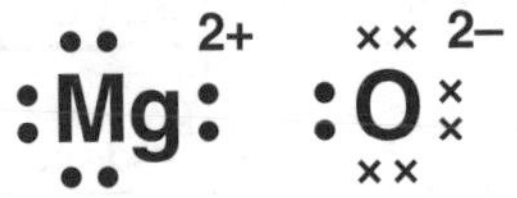 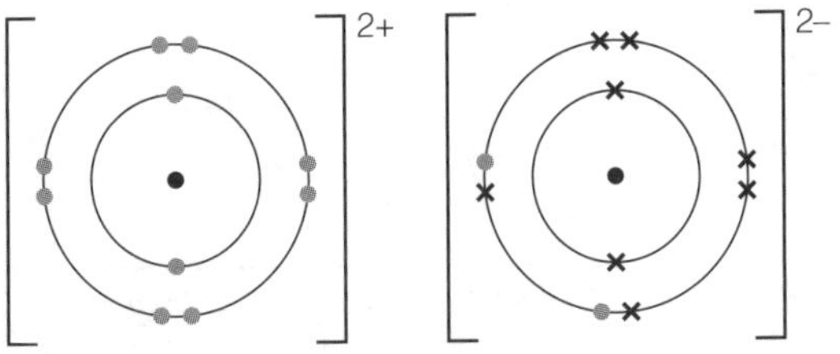 	Allow either dots for magnesium's electrons and crosses for oxygen's electrons **or** crosses for magnesium's electrons and dots for oxygen's electrons. Give 1 mark for both correct structures. Give 1 mark for both charges correct.	1 1
05.5	% yield = $\frac{\text{mass product actually made}}{\text{maximum theoretical mass of product}} \times 100$ **or** $\frac{9.6}{12.8} \times 100$ = 75%		1 1
06.1	It has the same number of electrons and protons.		1
06.2	Number of protons in the ion: **26** Number of neutrons in the ion: **30** Number of electrons in the ion: **24**	Only award 1 mark if all three numbers are correct.	1
06.3	**Protons:** the atomic number / number on the bottom left of symbol **Neutrons:** 56 – 26 = 30 / mass number – atomic number **Electrons:** 26 – 2 = 24 / atomic number but 2 electrons have been removed to make 2+		1 1 1
06.4	**Similarities:** They have the same number of protons / atomic number. They have the same number of electrons. **Difference:** Different number of neutrons / mass number.		1 1 1
06.5	$\frac{1.2 \times 10^{-6}}{1.5 \times 10^{-10}} =$ 8000 or 8.0×10^3	Allow 1 mark for working, even if the answer is not correct.	1 1
06.6	**Indicative content** 'Plum pudding' model of the atom / existence of electrons – J.J. Thomson Nuclear model / 'solar system' atom – Marsden and Rutherford Electron orbits – Niels Bohr Existence of neutrons – James Chadwick	**Level 3:** Correct descriptions of the development of at least three atomic models and the linking of two scientists. **Level 2:** Correct descriptions of the development of at least two atomic models and the linking of one scientist. **Level 1:** One correct description of the development of any atomic model. **Level 0:** No relevant content	5–6 3–4 1–2 0
07.1	Copper oxide and sulfuric acid		1
07.2	The pH would start high and decrease to below 7.		1
07.3	Nitric acid		1
07.4	M_r CaO = 56 **and** M_r $CaCl_2$ = 111 5.55 g = $\frac{1}{20}$ mole or 0.05 mole $CaCl_2$ Reaction ratio: 1:1 $\frac{1}{20} \times 56$ or $0.05 \times 56 = 2.8$ g		1 1 1 1

<table>
<tr><th>Question number</th><th>Answer</th><th>Notes</th><th>Marks</th></tr>
<tr><td>07.5</td><td>69%

$\frac{138}{200} \times 100$</td><td>Allow 2 marks for working, even if the answer is not correct:

Total product = 138
Total reactant = 200</td><td>1

1
1</td></tr>
<tr><td>08.1</td><td>The breakdown / decomposition of a substance
using an electric current.</td><td>
Also accept: using electricity.</td><td>1
1</td></tr>
<tr><td>08.2</td><td>Cathode reaction is reduction because of
gain of electrons or
decrease in oxidation number.
Anode reaction is oxidation because of
loss of electrons or
increase in oxidation number.</td><td></td><td>1

1</td></tr>
<tr><td>08.3</td><td>Indicative Content
Method of extraction depends on position in the reactivity series.
Aluminium is above carbon so is extracted by electrolysis.
Iron is below carbon so is extracted by reduction with carbon.
Both metals take part in a reduction process.
In the blast furnace the carbon reacts with oxygen to produce carbon monoxide.
Iron oxide is reduced iron by carbon monoxide.
The equation is $Fe_2O_3 + 3CO \rightarrow 2Fe + 3CO_2$
In electrolysis aluminium ions are reduced at the cathode to produce aluminium:
$Al^{3+} + 3e^- \rightarrow Al$
Oxide ions are oxidised at the cathode to produce oxygen gas:
$2O^{2-} \rightarrow 2O_2 + 4e^-$</td><td>Level 3: Correct description and explanation of each method of extraction including equations
Level 2: Correct description and explanation of each method of extraction
Level 1: Correct description and explanation of one method
Level 0: No relevant content</td><td>5–6
3–4
1–2
0</td></tr>
<tr><td>09.1</td><td>Any two from:
They don't run out (provided there is a supply of fuel).
They do not have to be recharged.
The only product is water / there is no pollution.</td><td></td><td>2</td></tr>
<tr><td>09.2</td><td>$H_2 \rightarrow 2H^+ + 2e^-$</td><td>Accept 2e.</td><td>1</td></tr>
<tr><td>09.3</td><td>$O_2 + 4e^- \rightarrow 2O^{2-}$</td><td>Accept 4e.</td><td>1</td></tr>
<tr><td>09.4</td><td>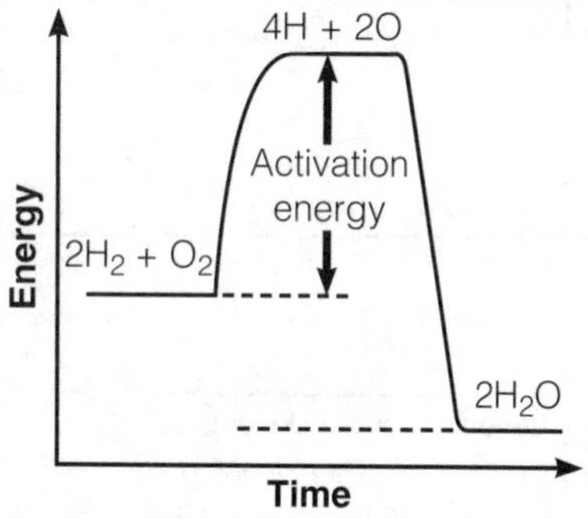

The product line ($2H_2O$) needs to be below the reactant line.
$2H_2O$ should be on the product line.</td><td></td><td>1
1</td></tr>
<tr><td>09.5</td><td>Activation energy should be labelled correctly (the arrows must touch or almost touch the lines) – see diagram in 09.4 above.</td><td></td><td>1</td></tr>
<tr><td>10.1</td><td><table>
<tr><th>Solid</th><th>Start temperature (°C)</th><th>End temperature (°C)</th><th>Temperature change (°C)</th></tr>
<tr><td>Ammonium chloride</td><td>15</td><td>9</td><td>–6</td></tr>
<tr><td>Potassium hydroxide</td><td>16</td><td>29</td><td>+13</td></tr>
<tr><td>Ammonium nitrate</td><td>18</td><td>4</td><td>–14</td></tr>
<tr><td>Sodium hydroxide</td><td>17</td><td>35</td><td>+18</td></tr>
</table></td><td>Award 1 mark for two correct numbers and 1 mark for two correct signs.</td><td>2</td></tr>
</table>

Question number	Answer	Notes	Marks
10.2	Ammonium nitrate Endothermic reactions cause the temperature to decrease. Ammonium nitrate had the biggest drop in temperature.		1 1 1
11.1	**Arrangement** – any one from: Molecules move further apart. Molecules are less ordered / more random. **Movement** – any one from: Molecules gain kinetic energy. Molecules move faster. Molecules move more randomly.		1 1
11.2	15 000 g of oxygen = $\frac{15\,000}{32}$ = 468.75 moles Volume = 468.75 moles × 24 = 11 250 dm^3		1 1
12.1	First test – the iodide converted (oxidised) to iodine. Bromine is more reactive than iodine. No reaction in second test because bromine is less reactive than chlorine.		1 1 1 1
12.2	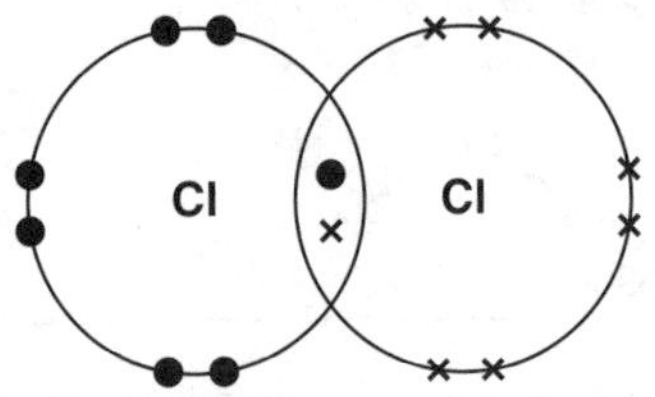 **or** 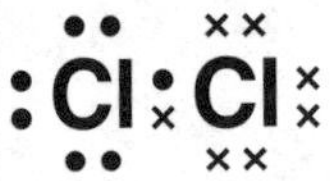 	Give 1 mark for the shared pair of electrons. Give 1 mark if the rest of the diagram is correct.	1 1
12.3	Chlorine has weaker forces between molecules / weaker intermolecular forces than iodine. Less energy is needed to separate molecules in chlorine than iodine.	Allow 'stronger' forces for iodine. Allow 'more energy' for iodine.	1 1
12.4	It has no free electrons / the electrons cannot move / all outer electrons are involved in bonding.		1
13.1	$\frac{14.4}{12}$ = 1.2 mole 1.2 × 393 = 472 kJ	Accept 471.6 kJ	1 1
13.2	Energy is taken in to break (oxygen) bonds. Energy is given out, making (C=O) bonds. More energy is given out than taken in.		1 1 1
13.3	Any three from: Use a more accurate method of measuring the volumes, e.g. a 25 cm^3 pipette or a 25 cm^3 measuring cylinder. Use an insulated beaker / polystyrene cup. Use separate apparatus to measure the acid. Measure the start temperature before adding the acid. Wait until there is no further temperature change before measuring the final temperature. Repeat the method at least two more times.		3

PAPER 2

Question number	Answer	Notes	Marks
01.1	Chlorine		1
01.2	Blue		1
01.3	C and D		1
01.4	$0.86 = \frac{\text{distance moved by B}}{7.91} = 0.86 \times 7.91$ $= 6.8$	 6.80 / 6.802 / 6.8026 is worth 1 mark.	1 1
01.5	The solubility of different solutes is different in different solvents So the distance travelled up the paper will vary Therefore, R_f values may be bigger or smaller		1 1 1
02.1	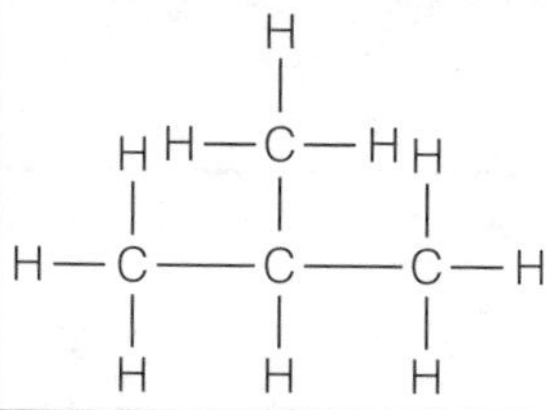		1
02.2	$2C_4H_{10} + 13O_2 \rightarrow 8CO_2 + 10H_2O$	If balancing is not correct, allow 1 mark for: $C_4H_{10} + O_2 \rightarrow CO_2 + H_2O$ If all the numbers are correct, allow multiples for balancing.	2
02.3	C_5H_{12}		1
02.4	Any three from: Small molecules have weaker (intermolecular) forces / large molecules have stronger forces. Small molecules have lower boiling point / large molecules have higher boiling point. Stronger forces lead to a higher boiling point / weaker forces lead to a lower boiling point. Fractions are separated by different boiling points.		3
02.5	Breaking up / decomposing (large molecules) into smaller / more useful substances / molecules.		1 1
02.6	Any one from: They act as a catalyst. They speed up the reaction. They provide a surface on which the reaction happens.		1
02.7	$C_{16}H_{34} \rightarrow C_{10}H_{22} + 3C_2H_4$	If balancing is not correct, allow 1 mark for: $C_{16}H_{34} \rightarrow C_{10}H_{22} + C_2H_4$	2
03.1	Dylan		1
03.2	The acid was the limiting reagent in her experiment / all of the acid had been used up in her experiment. Magnesium was the limiting reagent in the other experiments / all of the magnesium was used up in the other experiments.	Allow: magnesium in excess. Allow: acid in excess.	1 1
03.3	mean rate $= \frac{\text{quantity of product formed}}{\text{time taken}} = \frac{94.5}{225} =$ 0.42 Unit = cm^3/s		1 1 1
03.4	The volume of gas will double because the volume of gas is dependent on the amount of magnesium.		1 1
04.1	Any two from: yeast absence of air in aqueous solution / dissolved in water.		2

Question number	Answer	Notes	Marks
04.2	The reaction stops because yeast is killed / enzymes in yeast are denatured.	Do not accept: the enzymes are killed.	1 1
04.3	**Advantage** – any one from: it is renewable flammable burns with a clean flame / no incomplete combustion fermentation does not need high temperatures. **Disadvantage** – any one from: it has to be purified / purification is expensive reaction has low yield carbon dioxide is made by the reaction; it is a greenhouse gas land used to grow sugar crops rather than food crops.		1 1
04.4	Ethyl ethanoate		1
05.1	Ammonium phosphate and potassium chloride		1
05.2	1.69 g	Pure gold = 24 carats, 9 carats = $\frac{9}{20th}$ gold $\frac{9}{24} \times 4.5 = 1.69$ (rounded up)	1
05.3	Alloys are harder. Alloys have a lower density. Alloys have a lower melting point. Alloys are stronger.	Allow the reverse argument, e.g. pure metals are softer.	1 1 1 1
06.1	D, A, C, B	Allow 1 mark if D and A are in the correct order.	2
06.2	It is a simple or complex testable explanation put forward by scientists to try and explain observations/facts		1 1
06.3	It cannot be proved because it was so long ago / there is insufficient evidence to confirm the theory.		1
07.1	**Indicative content** **Flame test** Use a flame test wire / spray sample through the flame. Dip wire into solution. Put wire or substance into a (blue) Bunsen flame. Observe the colour of the flame. **Tests** The flame test indicates lithium ions in the water. Acidified silver nitrate indicates bromide ions in the water. Acidified barium chloride indicates sulfate ions in the water. Sodium hydroxide indicates iron(III) ions in the water. The results support the idea that the river water contains sulfate ions but not copper(II) ions.	**Level 3:** Correct explanation of each of the four tests and a full description of a flame test. Confirms the presence of sulfate but not copper(II) ions. **Level 2:** Correct explanation of two of the four tests **and** a full description of a flame test. **Level 1:** Correct explanation of two of the four tests **or** a full description of a flame test. **Level 0:** No relevant content A full description includes at least three of these points.	5–6 3–4 1–2 0
07.2	It would show if other metal ions are present. It would measure the concentration of the metal ions.		1 1

Question number	Answer	Notes	Marks
08.1	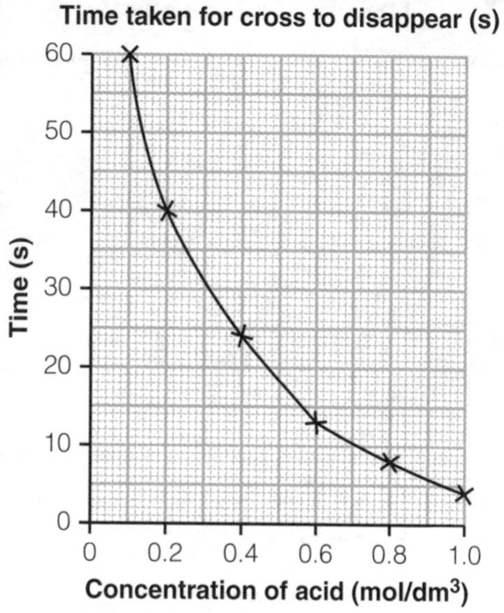 All six points correctly plotted Smooth curve	Allow 1 mark for four or five points correctly plotted; 1 mark deducted if the graph is plotted dot to dot rather than as a smooth curve.	2 1
08.2	Rate increases as concentration increases. Increased concentration means more crowded particles / more particles in same space / volume. More chance of collision / more frequent collisions.		1 1 1
08.3	The reaction times would be smaller / shorter / less. There will be more successful collisions as the particles move quicker at higher temperatures.		1 1
09.1	50%		1
09.2	The yield decreases.		1
09.3	If pressure increases, the reaction goes in the direction that reduces the number of moles of gas / the volume of gases, i.e. the direction with the fewest number of moles of gas. The equilibrium moves to the right / forward direction / to the product side.		1 1
09.4	High pressures need energy / equipment that can tolerate high pressures, and this is expensive. The costs outweigh the benefits of a higher yield.		1 1
10.1	B Powder reacts faster / line steeper on graph because powder has a larger surface area. More chance of successful collisions / more frequent successful collisions.		1 1 1 1
10.2	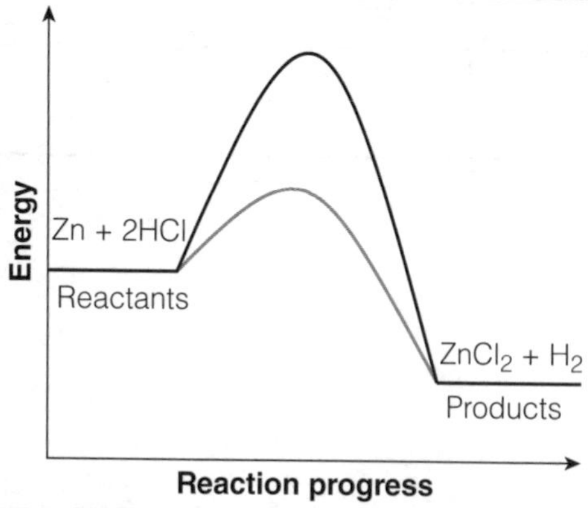	The curve must start at reactants, be lower than the original curve and end at products.	1
11.1	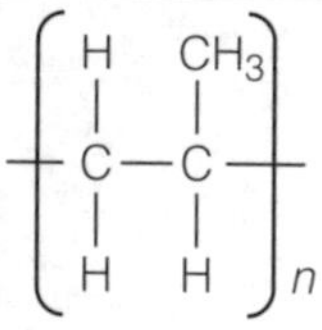 Accept curved or square brackets.	Award 1 mark for side links; 1 mark for *n*; I mark for the rest of the molecule (must have only one CH_3 group).	3

Question number	Answer	Notes	Marks
11.2	**Indicative content** Polymers A,C,D are thermosoftening polymers. Polymers A,C,D are flexible, feel softer and can be reshaped when heated. The polymer chains A,C,D have weak forces between them so it is easy for them to slide over each other Polymer B is a thermosetting polymer Polymer B has cross links between the polymer chains which means the forces between the chains are strong. This makes polymer B rigid and hard. It cannot be reshaped when heated	**Level 3:** Correct explanation of the properties of all the polymers **Level 2:** Correct explanation of the properties of some of the polymers **Level 1:** Correct explanation of the properties of one of the polymers **Level 0:** No relevant content	5–6 3–4 1–2 0
12.1	As the reaction progresses, the rate of the backward reaction increases until the rates of the forward and backward reactions are the same.		1 1
12.2	Favours the reverse reaction / equilibrium position moves to the left / moves to the reactant side. Reaction goes in the direction to increase the number of moles / reactants have a larger volume / reaction works to increase pressure on the side with higher moles of gas.		1 1
12.3	No effect on the equilibrium position.		1
12.4	Which reaction direction is exothermic / which reaction direction is endothermic.		1
13.1	Alcohol / –OH Carboxylic acid / –COOH	Allow acyl chloride.	1 1
13.2	Water is also made / a small molecule is also made.		1
13.3	Difficult to know how far a product or waste will travel.		1
14.1	Petrol and diesel are both liquid fuels with similar number of carbons, boiling points, viscosity and flammability. Petrol has shorter carbon chains, flows more easily/is less viscous and has a low boiling point so it vaporises and ignites more easily than diesel. Petrol can vaporise and ignite too easily when it gets warm and so can be more dangerous a fuel than diesel.		1 1 1
14.2	Nitrogen **and** oxygen from the air react in the high temperatures in the engine.		1 1 1
14.3	One from: causes acid rain / causes respiratory problems.		1
14.4	Remove sulfur from the fuel before use.		1

Notes

Notes

Key

Metals

Non-metals

Relative atomic mass	1
Atomic symbol	**H**
Name	hydrogen
Atomic number	1

1	2											3	4	5	6	7	0 or 8
																	4 **He** helium 2
7 **Li** lithium 3	9 **Be** beryllium 4											11 **B** boron 5	12 **C** carbon 6	14 **N** nitrogen 7	16 **O** oxygen 8	19 **F** fluorine 9	20 **Ne** neon 10
23 **Na** sodium 11	24 **Mg** magnesium 12											27 **Al** aluminium 13	28 **Si** silicon 14	31 **P** phosphorus 15	32 **S** sulfur 16	35.5 **Cl** chlorine 17	40 **Ar** argon 18
39 **K** potassium 19	40 **Ca** calcium 20	45 **Sc** scandium 21	48 **Ti** titanium 22	51 **V** vanadium 23	52 **Cr** chromium 24	55 **Mn** manganese 25	56 **Fe** iron 26	59 **Co** cobalt 27	59 **Ni** nickel 28	63.5 **Cu** copper 29	65 **Zn** zinc 30	70 **Ga** gallium 31	73 **Ge** germanium 32	75 **As** arsenic 33	79 **Se** selenium 34	80 **Br** bromine 35	84 **Kr** krypton 36
85 **Rb** rubidium 37	88 **Sr** strontium 38	89 **Y** yttrium 39	91 **Zr** zirconium 40	93 **Nb** niobium 41	96 **Mo** molybdenum 42	[98] **Tc** technetium 43	101 **Ru** ruthenium 44	103 **Rh** rhodium 45	106 **Pd** palladium 46	108 **Ag** silver 47	112 **Cd** cadmium 48	115 **In** indium 49	119 **Sn** tin 50	122 **Sb** antimony 51	128 **Te** tellurium 52	127 **I** iodine 53	131 **Xe** xenon 54
133 **Cs** caesium 55	137 **Ba** barium 56	139 **La*** lanthanum 57	178 **Hf** hafnium 72	181 **Ta** tantalum 73	184 **W** tungsten 74	186 **Re** rhenium 75	190 **Os** osmium 76	192 **Ir** iridium 77	195 **Pt** platinum 78	197 **Au** gold 79	201 **Hg** mercury 80	204 **Tl** thallium 81	207 **Pb** lead 82	209 **Bi** bismuth 83	[209] **Po** polonium 84	[210] **At** astatine 85	[222] **Rn** radon 86
[223] **Fr** francium 87	[226] **Ra** radium 88	[227] **Ac*** actinium 89	[261] **Rf** rutherfordium 104	[262] **Db** dubnium 105	[266] **Sg** seaborgium 106	[264] **Bh** bohrium 107	[277] **Hs** hassium 108	[268] **Mt** meitnerium 109	[271] **Ds** darmstadtium 110	[272] **Rg** roentgenium 111							